Stanton's American Steam Vessels

The Classic Illustrations

Samuel Ward Stanton

DOVER PUBLICATIONS, INC.
Mineola, New York

Copyright

Introduction copyright © 2002 by Dover Publications, Inc.
All rights reserved under Pan American and International Copyright Conventions.

Bibliographical Note

This Dover edition, first published in 2002, is an unabridged republication (in black and white, and reduced in scale) of the work published as *American Steam Vessels* by Smith & Stanton, New York, in 1895. The Introduction was prepared especially for this edition by George King III of the Steamship Historical Society of America.

Library of Congress Cataloging-in-Publication Data

Stanton, Samuel Ward.
    Stanton's American steam vessels : the classic illustrations / Samuel Ward Stanton.
        p. cm.
    Originally published: American steam vessels. New York : Smith & Stanton, 1895.
    ISBN 0-486-42330-1 (pbk.)
     1. Steamboats—United States—Pictorial works. I. Stanton, Samuel Ward. American steam vessels. II. Title.

VM307 .S73 2002
623.8'204—dc21

2002067446

Manufactured in the United States of America
Dover Publications, Inc., 31 East 2nd Street, Mineola, N.Y. 11501

INTRODUCTION

Samuel Ward Stanton was born at Newburgh, New York on January 8, 1870. He was raised on the banks of the Hudson River and was keenly influenced by his surroundings. As a child of a shipbuilder in the age of steam, he witnessed from close up the realization of industrial innovations from the designs of fertile technological minds.

Nowhere were the lessons so vivid as in his father's shipyard. Ward, Stanton and Company was formed in 1872 to build marine and stationary engines and other types of machinery. Each of the three partners, including Stanton's father, Samuel, was a skilled artisan in one of the metal trades.

The company introduced iron shipbuilding to the Hudson River around 1876. Ward, Stanton built complete steamboats. The hulls, boilers, and engines were all constructed at its yard in Newburgh. The company earned a reputation both for constructing high-quality vessels of innovative design, and for ethical business practices. It lasted only twelve years—eight as a shipbuilder—but it made an indelible impression on the young Samuel Ward Stanton, providing him with both an ethical standard by which he would always conduct himself, and a store of historical and technological interests from which he drew throughout his life. Indeed, the scrapbooks filled with steamboat stories and articles that Stanton delighted in maintaining as a boy were the basis of a series of 126 articles that appeared in *The Nautical Gazette* between August 15, 1907 and May 10, 1910.

The elder Samuel Stanton was a visionary designer who dreamed of fast passenger steamers to rival the railroads, fast steam yachts with thin steel hulls, and a versatile workboat featuring "a hoisting engine and a powerful rotary pump for pumping out vessels in distress, and, possibly, with a portable sawmill."[1] Ward, Stanton developed unique construction techniques to meet the special needs of its customers. The iron-hulled steamer *Montclair*, for instance, was "erected in the shipyard using bolts instead of rivets, knocked down for shipment, and re-erected" at its owner's site.[2]

Another interesting vessel built by Ward, Stanton was the passenger steamer *Manatee* (you can see it on page 155). This 108-foot iron-hulled, two-deck sidewheel steamer was designed by Samuel Stanton for himself. During a visit to Florida in 1882, Mr. Stanton had seen a need for steamboat service between Tampa and the Manatee River and decided that he would meet it. He purchased land facing the river in Braidentown (now Bradenton) and later added gardens and orchards on Terra Ceia Bay, a few miles downriver.[3]

On August 7, 1884, the *Manatee* departed Newburgh with the Stanton family on board, along with their household goods and personal effects and machinery to build a sawmill, and proceeded south to Tampa Bay. The enterprising Stantons erected their sawmill and produced sufficient lumber to build several homes for Samuel and his extended family.

Ward, Stanton & Co. closed in December 1884, as a result of an uninsured loss of $50,000 in a disastrous fire in 1882. The Stantons remained in Florida. In 1888, however, Samuel Ward Stanton returned to New York to accept a position on the staff of the nautical weekly *Seaboard*.

It is fortunate for the maritime historian that Samuel Ward Stanton was immersed in steamboat history from his youth and thought it important to document it. He was in a position to do research in primary sources, and produced from them accurate descriptions and illustrations. His environment, his education, and his personal experience and interest combined with his artistic abilities to enable him to produce a record that would be impossible to create today.

Before the 1890s photographs were not used to illustrate magazines and newspapers. Visual images were the painstaking work of illustrators working in pen and ink or engraving. Stanton's art evolved from pen-and-ink drawings and watercolors in his teenage years to monochrome oils, and finally to color. He displayed exceptional skill as a draftsman and always sought to depict his subject with documented accuracy. (For his achievement he received a medal at the World's Columbian Exposition in 1893.[4])

Stanton's portfolio of steamboat illustrations grew to more than 800 by 1895. This collection is the basis for *American Steam Vessels*, which was published that year. This now rare and valuable volume was completed when its creator was but 25 years old.

Stanton's illustrations are the most accurate depictions of these vessels that exist. Their accuracy is due to Stanton's insistence on doing things right. In his Preface to *American Steam Vessels*, he explains his documentation of the earliest steamers, citing the prints, lithographs, drawings, and paintings he sought out to ensure correctness of detail. He cites, for example, a drawing of the *Clermont* (later the *North River*) credited to Robert Fulton as the basis for his illustration of that famous vessel. "In no case," he says, "have I made use of a picture that did not bear the stamp of authenticity."

The accuracy of depictions of steam vessels built nearly two hundred years ago is of paramount importance to students of our maritime heritage. Far too often we must rely on newspaper descriptions, eyewitness accounts, or patent papers, and cannot really know how close our image is to the real thing. Stanton's insistence on good documentation assures us that his illustrations are trustworthy and provide us with an excellent foundation from which to trace the evolution of steam power on America's waterways.

Another reason Stanton's work is so valuable is that he did not focus on one geographic area or type of vessel. "It should be borne in mind," Stanton writes in his Preface, "that the steam vessels of the United States vary greatly in appearance and construction, according to locality." A shallow-draft sternwheeler from a western river would have been impractical on the choppy waters of Long Island Sound; likewise, a deep-draft Sound steamer would not have got far in the shallow waters of the Mississippi. Stanton traveled the entire country documenting the variety of steam craft of the oceans, coasts, lakes, and rivers. Examples of all appear in this book.

Stanton's illustrations are also noteworthy as art. "With only a few strokes of his pencil or pen," writes historian William duBarry Thomas, "Samuel Ward Stanton was able to distill the essence of the vessel he was depicting." Not just "boat pictures," the illustrations in *American Steam Vessels* capture the scope of steamboat travel. Fine points of background, ancillary small craft, and details of sea and weather conditions give the viewer of Stanton's scenes a deep sense of the maritime experience. Stanton also embellished the pages of his book with ornamentation framing the main illustration and text.

The success of this volume resulted in an increased demand for Stanton's illustrative talents. In 1898 he and his brother William became the publishers of *Seaboard*, promptly restoring its original title, *The Nautical Gazette*, and his work continued to appear there. Stanton was engaged to illustrate several other books including Beer's *History of the Great Lakes* in 1899, Morrison's *History of American Steam Navigation* in 1903, and Buckman's *Old Steamboat Days on the Hudson River* in 1907.[5]

Finally, Stanton was commissioned to decorate several of his beloved steamboats themselves. He was hired to do the Catskill Evening Line's *Clermont* in 1911 and the Nantasket Beach Steamboat Company's *Rose Standish* the same year.[6] He was also commissioned to decorate the Hudson River Day Line's new steamer *Washington Irving*. As was typical of him, he went to great lengths to achieve accuracy and authenticity in his work. To this end he visited the sites in Spain that were prominent in Irving's works, studying them and preparing sketches for his planned murals. He then went to Paris to study briefly under the history painter Jean-Paul Lorens and visit his old friend, the noted American muralist Francis Davis Millet. Forgoing a visit to London, Stanton decided to return to the United States from France with Millet.[7] On April 10, 1912, the two artists departed Cherbourg on the new White Star Liner *Titanic*. They were not among the survivors.

GEORGE KING III
Steamship Historical Society of America

[1] William duBarry Thomas, "History of Ward, Stanton and Company," 1998, unpublished manuscript.

[2] Ibid.

[3] William duBarry Thomas, "A Steamboat for Samuel Stanton," 1998, unpublished manuscript.

[4] William A. Fox, "Samuel Ward Stanton 1870–1912," *Steamboat Bill*, winter 1990, pp. 261–274.

[5] Ibid.

[6] Ibid.

[7] Ibid.

THIS VOLUME IS RESPECTFULLY DEDICATED TO

ALEXANDER R. SMITH

AS A SLIGHT TOKEN OF MY ESTEEM

THE AUTHOR

PREFACE

THE purpose of the author in compiling this volume was to bring together in compact form, for the first time, correct illustrations and descriptions of all of the various types of American steam vessels from the beginning of their successful construction up to the present day.

It should be borne in mind that the steam vessels of the United States vary greatly in appearance and construction, according to locality. Thus, the steamships of the coast, the steamboats on the rivers emptying into the oceans, the steamers of the Great Lakes and the steamboats of our Western Rivers, are all distinctive and different. It has been my aim to use, wherever possible, the most famous and historical of American steamers, as illustrative of the various types in all parts of the country. The pictures of the numerous early time steamers that appear in the following pages have all been secured and have been drawn from reliable scources — from early prints, lithographs, drawings and paintings, mostly in the possession of private parties or steamboat companies — and those of later days from photographs, plans, sketches, etc. Of the early steamers that of the Clermont has been drawn from the accepted illustration of this boat, similar to the drawing which is credited to Robert Fulton. All available descriptions of her were carefully consulted, and the illustration I have given was first drawn to a scale from the known dimensions of this boat. The Paragon is taken from one of Mr. Fulton's drawings, and the Hope, 1811, from a wood cut of the period. The Delaware River steamboat Philadelphia is from a painting in the possession of the Stevens estate, at Hoboken, and the Chancellor Livingston is from an old print. The Walk-in-the-Water has been drawn from the accepted picture of this boat, and the type of vessel in use on the Great Lakes in those days; the Savannah from a lithograph; the United States from a wood cut that appeared in the New York *Evening Post*, of June 23, 1821; the Constitution from a wood cut on a hand-bill of 1826, and the Albany, 1839, is likewise from a wood cut.

And so the whole list might be gone through, the Commerce, DeWitt Clinton, Champlain, Highlander, Rochester and Utica being drawn from the pictures of Mr. James Bard, a gentleman who began this class of work before 1830. To him the maritime world owes gratitude for his contributions to it of correct likenesses of many of the noted steamboats of early days. The Burlington is from a picture in the possession of the Lake Champlain Steamboat Company; the Troy, Empire, etc., from lithographs. The Arctic, transatlantic steamship, 1849, from a daguerreotype; etc., etc. In no case have I made use of a picture that did not bear the stamp of authenticity.

Much of the data given with each vessel I have obtained from Custom-house records, Steamboat Inspector's reports, newspapers and other documents, and the facts and figures given are believed to be absolutely correct in each case.

Samuel Ward Stanton

CONTENTS

ACME, ... 207
ALABAMA, ... 233
ALBANY (1827), ... 23
ALBANY (1880), ... 135
AL. FOSTER, ... 226
ALGONQUIN, ... 202
ALIDA, ... 51
ALPHA, ... 212
ALVA, ... 161
ANDREW FLETCHER, ... 100
ANDREW J. WHITE, ... 234
ANTHONY GROVES, JR., ... 240
ARAGO, ... 77
ARASAPHA, ... 132
ARCTIC, ... 58
ARMENIA, ... 50
ARMERIA, ... 190
ATALANTA, ... 150
ATLANTIC (LAKES), ... 52
ATLANTIC (SOUND), ... 47
B. S. FORD, ... 172
BADGER STATE, ... 91
BAILEY GATZERT, ... 198
BALLYMENA, ... 174
BALTIMORE, ... 180
BANGOR, ... 41
BAY STATE, ... 56
BELLE MEMPHIS, ... 137
BERKSHIRE, ... 97
BLACK WARRIOR, ... 65
BRANDYWINE, ... 159
BREMEN, ... 211
BRISTOL, ... 102
BURLINGTON, ... 36
C. H. NORTHAM, ... 114
CAMBRIDGE, ... 108
CAMBRIDGE (BALTIMORE), ... 172
CARACAS, ... 185
CARONDELET, ... 89
CHAMPLAIN, ... 25
CHANCELLOR LIVINGSTON, ... 17
CHARLES MACALESTER, ... 186
CHARLES P. CHOUTEAU, ... 122
CHATEAUGAY, ... 175
CHATTAHOOCHEE, ... 164

CHICAGO, ... 116
CHICORA, ... 224
CHRISTOPHER COLUMBUS, ... 241
CIENFUEGOS, ... 151
CINCINNATI, ... 218
CITY OF ALPENA, ... 136
CITY OF AUGUSTA, ... 138
CITY OF CHESTER, ... 168
CITY OF CHICAGO, ... 191
CITY OF CLEVELAND, ... 136
CITY OF DETROIT, ... 183
CITY OF JACKSONVILLE, ... 164
CITY OF KINGSTON, ... 156
CITY OF LOWELL, ... 248
CITY OF NEW YORK, ... 88
CITY OF PEKING, ... 118
CITY OF TOLEDO, ... 213
CITY OF WORCESTER, ... 140
CLEOPATRA, ... 33
CLERMONT (1807), ... 12
CLERMONT, ... 228
CODORUS, ... 231
COLUMBIA (BALTIMORE), ... 123
COLUMBIA (PHILADELPHIA), . . . 121
COLUMBIA (STEAMSHIP), ... 139
COMMANDER, ... 242
COMMERCE, ... 22
COMMONWEALTH, ... 74
CONNECTICUT, ... 184
CONSTITUTION, ... 21
COTTAGE CITY, ... 204
CYGNUS, ... 141
DANIEL WEBSTER, ... 73
DANVILLE, ... 144
DAUNTLESS, ... 132
DEAN RICHMOND, ... 99
DELAWARE, ... 132
DEMOLOGOS, ... 16
DE WITT CLINTON, ... 24
DOROTHY, ... 209
DOUGLAS H. THOMAS, ... 220
EASTERN CITY, ... 64
EDGAR F. LUCKENBACH, ... 214
ED. RICHARDSON, ... 127
EDWIN FORREST, ... 84

EDWIN H. MEAD, ... 180
EL DORADO, ... 60
ELEANOR, ... 252
ELECTRA, ... 153
EL RIO, ... 222
EMMA GILES, ... 163
EMPIRE, ... 43
EMPIRE STATE, ... 112
ERICSSON, ... 247
ETHEL, ... 212
EXCELSIOR (FERRY), ... 120
EXCELSIOR (STEAMSHIP), ... 146
FALMOUTH, ... 110
FAVORITE, ... 244
FLORENCE, ... 84
FRANCIS SKIDDY, ... 61
FRANK E. KIRBY, ... 203
FRANK JONES, ... 223
FULTON (STEAMSHIP), ... 78
FULTON THE FIRST, ... 16
FULTON THE SECOND, ... 37
GENL. J. S. SCHULTZE, ... 119
GENERAL SLOCUM, ... 208
GEORGE M. WINSLOW, ... 180
GOLDEN CITY, ... 96
GOLIAH, ... 57
GRAND REPUBLIC, ... 133
GREAT REPUBLIC, ... 105
GREYHOUND (PUGET SOUND), . . 205
GREYHOUND (LAKES), ... 107
GUIDING STAR, ... 129
HENRY E. BISHOP, ... 84
HIGHLANDER, ... 28
HOMER RAMSDELL, ... 166
HONEY BROOK, ... 227
HOPE, ... 14
HUDSON (OHIO RIVER), ... 160
HUDSON (STEAMSHIP), ... 117
ILLINOIS, ... 63
INDIA, ... 236
INDIANA (1841), ... 40
INDIANA (1890), ... 193
INDIANA (U. S.), ... 253
IRON QUEEN, ... 221
IRONSIDES, ... 98

CONTENTS
(*Concluded*)

ISAAC NEWTON, ... 48
J. M. WHITE, ... 131
JACOB STRADER, ... 68
JAMES W. BALDWIN, ... 86
JAMESTOWN, ... 246
JATHNIEL, ... 189
JOHN STEVENS, ... 42
JOHN SYLVESTER, ... 103
JOHN A. WARNER, ... 84
JOHN G. McCULLOUGH, ... 196
JOHN H. CORDTS, ... 152
JOHN I. BRADY, ... 216
JOHN K. SPEED, ... 230
JOHN W. CANNON, ... 134
JOHN W. RICHMOND, ... 38
JOPPA, ... 172
JOSEPHINE, ... 84
KAATERSKILL, ... 145
KATAHDIN, ... 251
KEARSARGE, ... 87
KEWEENAW, ... 219
LIVINGSTONE, ... 187
LOUISIANA, ... 72
LOUISE, ... 94
LURLINE, ... 128
MADELEINE, ... 220
MAINE, ... 229
MAJOR REYBOLD, ... 66
MANATEE, ... 155
MANITOU, ... 239
MARION, ... 62
MARYLAND, ... 195
MARY POWELL, ... 90
MASSACHUSETTS, ... 35
MATOA, ... 200
MAY FLOWER (1845), ... 44
MAYFLOWER, ... 217
MERCHANT, ... 93
MERIDA, ... 236
METROPOLIS, ... 76
MICHIGAN, ... 26
MILWAUKEE, ... 82
MINNEAPOLIS, ... 249
MISSISSIPPI, ... 69
MONITOR, ... 92
MONMOUTH, ... 176
NELLIE HUDSON No. 2, ... 188

NEWBURGH, ... 147
NEW MARY HOUSTON, ... 124
NEWPORT, ... 101
NEW ORLEANS, ... 115
NEW YORK (1836), ... 29
NEW YORK, ... 167
NEW WORLD, ... 53
NORTHFIELD, ... 180
NORTH STAR, ... 70
NORTH WEST, ... 250
NORTHWEST, ... 107
NORWICH, ... 34
NOTTINGHAM, ... 245
NOURMAHAL, ... 157
OLIVETTE, ... 165
OLYMPIA, ... 232
ONTARIO, ... 22
OSWEGO, ... 54
OUACHITA, ... 201
OWEGO, ... 179
PACIFIC, ... 81
PARAGON, ... 13
PARTHIAN, ... 171
PEERLESS, ... 113
PENOBSCOT, ... 148
PETOSKEY, ... 169
PEYTONA, ... 85
PHILADELPHIA, ... 15
PILGRIM, ... 149
PLEASURE, ... 243
PLYMOUTH ROCK, ... 71
POCAHONTAS, ... 158
PORTLAND, ... 199
POWHATAN, ... 67
PREMIER, ... 170
PRINCETON, ... 46
PRISCILLA, ... 254
PURITAN, ... 182
QUEEN OF ST. JOHNS, ... 164
REPUBLIC, ... 130
RICHARD PECK, ... 235
RICHARD STOCKTON, ... 59
RIP VAN WINKLE, ... 45
ROBERT E. LEE, ... 104
ROBERT GARRETT, ... 173
ROCHESTER, ... 30
ROSA, ... 164
RHODE ISLAND, ... 31
S. R. SPAULDING, ... 83

SAGUENAY, ... 73
SAN FRANCISCO, ... 197
SAN MARCOS, ... 142
SAN SALVADOR, ... 83
SANTA LUCIA, ... 187
SANTA ROSA, ... 154
SARANAC, ... 194
SARATOGA, ... 125
SASSAFRAS, ... 172
SAUSALITO, ... 225
SAVANNAH, ... 19
SAXON, ... 236
SCRANTON, ... 238
SEAWANHAKA, ... 106
SEGURANCA, ... 192
SHEBOYGAN, ... 109
SILVER STAR, ... 84
SOO CITY, ... 177
STATE OF MAINE, ... 55
STATE OF OHIO, ... 136
ST. IGNACE, ... 181
ST. JOHN, ... 95
ST. LAWRENCE, ... 64
ST. LOUIS, ... 255
SUSQUEHANNA, ... 162
SYLVAN DELL, ... 111
SYLVAN GLEN, ... 112
SYLVAN GROVE, ... 112
SYLVAN SHORE, ... 112
SYLVAN STREAM, ... 112
T. J. POTTER, ... 178
TAURUS, ... 143
THOMAS CLYDE, ... 126
THOMAS CRANAGE, ... 236
THOMAS JEFFERSON, ... 27
THOMAS PICKLES, ... 237
THOMAS POWELL, ... 49
TROY, ... 39
UNITED STATES, ... 20
UTICA, ... 32
VANDERBILT, ... 79
VAMOOSE, ... 210
VIRGINIA, ... 215
W. H. GILCHER, ... 206
WALK-IN-THE-WATER, ... 18
WENONAH, ... 132
WESTERN METROPOLIS, ... 80
WESTERN WORLD, ... 75
WINFIELD S. CAHILL, ... 225

WORLD'S FAIR AWARD.

The majority of the full page drawings of American Steam Vessels were exhibited at the World's Columbian Exhibition in Chicago, 1893, and their delineator, Samuel Ward Stanton, was awarded a medal and diploma.

The diploma reads :

" A very finely executed and interesting collection of drawings which show with great skill and cleverness various types of war ships, mercantile ocean steamers, lake and river steamers and yachts. They are of general interest and show artistic merit and historical technical value."

S.W.Stanton

ROBERT FULTON'S CLERMONT, THE WORLD'S FIRST SUCCESSFUL STEAMBOAT.

Clermont.

Designed by Robert Fulton.

BUILT 1807, at NEW YORK.

HULL, OF WOOD, constructed by CHARLES BROWN   Length 133 feet; breadth of beam 18 feet; depth of hold 7 feet

ENGINE, built by BOULTON & WATT, in England. Diameter of cylinder 24 inches; by 4 feet length of piston stroke.

BOILER, OF COPPER, low pressure Length 20 feet, height 7 feet; width 8 feet.

WHEELS, 15 feet in diameter; 8 buckets to each wheel. 4 feet in length, dip 2 feet

THE CLERMONT was the World's first successful steamboat. She was built under the supervision of Robert Fulton and left New York for Albany on her first trip August 7, 1807 Her speed averaged nearly five miles an hour. During the winter of 1807-8 she was enlarged and her name changed to NORTH RIVER, and she continued to ply on the Hudson River in the FULTON & LIVINGSTON LINE as a passenger boat for a number of years; was finally broken up.

HUDSON RIVER STEAMBOAT PARAGON, 1811.

PARAGON.

Designed by Robert Fulton.

BUILT 1811, at NEW YORK.

HULL, OF WOOD, BUILT BY **Charles Brown.** Length 173 feet; breadth of beam 27 feet; depth of hold 9 feet

ENGINE, LOW PRESSURE; Diameter of cylinder 32 inches, stroke 4 feet.

BOILER, OF COPPER. Length 21 feet; breadth 9 feet; height 10 feet.

WHEELS, 16 feet in diameter. Length of bucket 4 feet 5 inches; dip 2 feet 7 inches.

·TONNAGE 331·

THE PARAGON was the third steamboat built for the navigation of the Hudson River in the Fulton and Livingston Line. She was an improvement on her predecessors. Her boiler was of copper, similar to that of the Clermont, but differing as to the interior arrangements. It was sought to improve upon the boiler and facilitate the generation of steam by the introduction of numerous pipes. Some injury resulting to the boiler on the first experiment from the application of the fire the pipes were taken out and abandoned. The fuel used was wood.

She ran a great many years between New York and Albany, earning a great deal of money for her owners. About the year 1820 while going up the river she ran on a rock, sunk and was abandoned.

HUDSON RIVER STEAMBOAT HOPE, 1811.

HOPE

The "Hope" and "Perseverance," sister boats, were built to ply as passenger steamers on the Hudson River, in opposition to the Fulton & Livingston line. The engine and the two boilers were constructed by Robert M°Queen, and were as successful as any of those of early days.

On the second trip of the Hope to Albany, through negligence on the part of the fireman, the boilers came near exploding, off Esopus, the water in same having entirely disappeared, and both were red-hot.

The new line did not remain in existence long, being compelled by law to stop running, the Fulton & Livingston Line having exclusive control of the right to navigate the waters of the State of New York by steam

DELAWARE RIVER STEAMBOAT PHILADELPHIA, 1813.

PHILADELPHIA:

BUILT 1813, at HOBOKEN, N.J

HULL, OF WOOD.

ENGINE, SQUARE, OR "CROSS-HEAD"

BOILER, OF COPPER

This boat, the second regular "steam packet" that ran on the Delaware River, was built by Robert L. Stevens, and ran under his direction. She was familiarly known during her time as the "Old Sal," on account of a grotesque female figure-head which she carried. She ran between Philadelphia and Trenton, stages there connecting for New York. She was finally dismantled; other boats taking her place.

15

DEMOLOGOS:
(FULTON THE FIRST)

Designed by Robert Fulton.

BUILT 1814, at NEW YORK.

HULL, OF WOOD, CONSTRUCTED BY ADAM & NOAH BROWN. Length 156 feet; breadth of beam 56 feet, depth of hold 20 feet.

ENGINE, WITH CYLINDER 48 inches in diameter by 5 feet stroke.

BOILER, OF COPPER Length 22 feet, height 8 feet, breadth 12 feet.

WHEEL, RADIAL, IN CENTER Diameter 16 feet, buckets 14 feet in length, dipping 4 feet.

This notable vessel was the first war steamer ever built. She was known as "Fulton the First" and was intended for use as a harbor defense boat for New York Bay. Her designer, Robert Fulton, superintended her construction, her keel being laid on June 14, 1814, and on October 29 (a little more than 4 months after) she was launched. Her hull consisted of two parts—the paddle wheel being placed between them,—the distance apart being 15 feet. They were joined at the ends, the canal being but 66 feet long. The boiler was situated on one side of the boat, the engine on the other. Her trial trip, made on June 1, 1815, practically demonstrated her efficiency as a steam vessel, and a month later she made a trip to sea. She was never put into actual war service, there being no occasion for her use. She was moored at the Navy Yard being used as a recruiting ship. On June 4, 1829, she was accidently blown up, by which occurrence over 25 people lost their lives.

TRANSVERSE SECTION OF THE DEMOLOGOS.
From a drawing by Robert Fulton.

A - her boiler. B - the Steam Engine. C - the water wheel. D - her gun deck. E - her wooden walls, 5 feet thick, diminishing to below water line as at FF.
DRAFT OF WATER 9 FEET.

LONG ISLAND SOUND STEAMBOAT CHANCELLOR LIVINGSTON, 1827.

CHANCELLOR LIVINGSTON.

Designed by Mr Steudinger

BUILT 1816, at NEW YORK.

HULL, OF WOOD, BUILT BY **Henry Eckford**. Length 157 feet; breadth of beam 33½ feet; depth of hold 10 feet; average draft of water 7 feet 3 inches.

ENGINE, SQUARE, or "CROSS-HEAD," CONSTRUCTED BY **James P. Allaire**, New York. Diameter of cylinder 44 inches, by 5 feet stroke Horse power 65 New Engine, 1828, with a 56-inch cylinder by 6 feet stroke; 120 horse power

BOILER, OF COPPER, BUILT BY JAMES P ALLAIRE. Length 28 feet; width 12 feet; weight, about 44,000 pounds, with a large cylindrical flue and two small return flues, with false front; 2 smoke stacks New Boilers for Sound route, three in number, with 3 smoke stacks.

WHEELS, 17 feet in diameter, with buckets 5 feet 10 inches long.

JOINER WORK, by DAVID COOK, New York.

~TONNAGE 496~

AFTER the building of the CLERMONT the most important steamboat that appeared on the Hudson River was the CHANCELLOR LIVINGSTON. She was constructed for the North River Steam-boat Company, and was built of oak, locust and cedar timber. She was elegantly fitted up, her entire cost being $110,000. She was placed on the route from New York to Albany in 1817, and was the favorite boat for many years. On December 5, 1817, she went to Albany from New York in 18 hours, the quickest passage that had yet been made She continued to run on the river until 1826, when she was transferred to Long Island Sound, and ran between Newark and Providence for some years. In 1832 she was placed on the Boston and Portland route and ran for two years when she was dismantled, her engine being placed in the new steamboat PORTLAND.

17

GREAT LAKES STEAMBOAT WALK-IN-THE-WATER, 1818.

THE SAVANNAH, PIONEER TRANSATLANTIC STEAMSHIP, 1819.

SAVANNAH.
PIONEER TRANSATLANTIC STEAMSHIP

BUILT 1818, at NEW YORK

HULL, OF WOOD, BUILT BY CROCKER & FICKETT.

ENGINE, LOW PRESSURE, SQUARE, CONSTRUCTED BY JAMES P. ALLAIRE, NEW YORK.

BOILER, OF COPPER, BUILT BY DANIEL DODGE, at Elizabethtown Point, N.J.

— TONNAGE 380 —

One of the most famous of the World's steam vessels. The SAVANNAH was built at Corlaer's Hook, on the East River New York City and was launched August 22 1818. She was intended to be used as a sailing packet between New York and Liverpool, but was purchased before being finished by William Scarborough & Co. of Savannah Ga, and fitted with machinery. The paddle wheels were so constructed as to fold up, and could be placed on deck in stormy weather; the wheel was enclosed in canvas held in place by iron rims. Her model was considered very fine and her passenger accommodations elegant.

She went to Savannah in 1819, and left that port for Liverpool England, May 26, 1819, being the first steam vessel that ever crossed the Atlantic. She arrived at Liverpool in 22 days, having used her engine 14 days. She then went to St Petersburg, Russia, returning to Savannah in November, 1819. She afterwards had her machinery taken out and was converted into a sailing packet. She ran some time between New York and Savannah, finally running ashore on Long Island, and was broken up.

LONG ISLAND SOUND STEAMBOAT UNITED STATES, 1821.

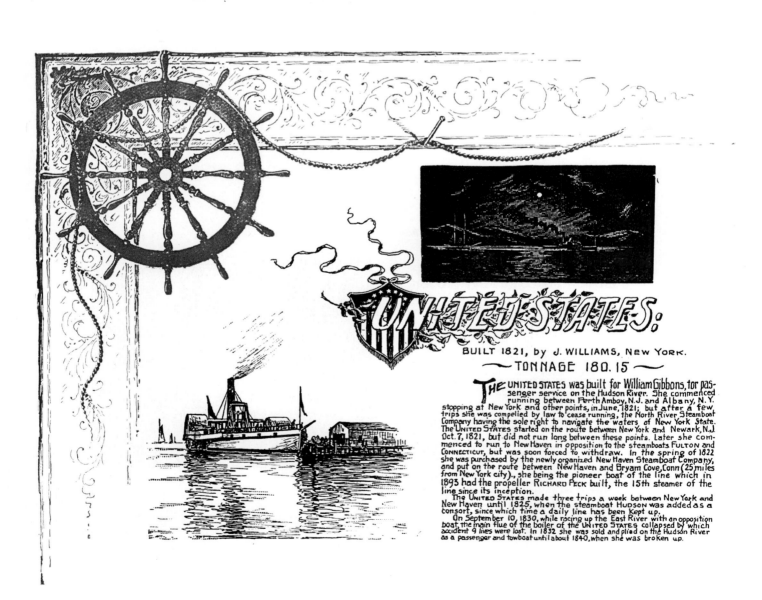

UNITED STATES.

BUILT 1821, by J. WILLIAMS, NEW YORK.
~ TONNAGE 180.15 ~

THE UNITED STATES was built for William Gibbons, for passenger service on the Hudson River. She commenced running between Perth Amboy, N.J. and Albany, N.Y. stopping at New York and other points, in June, 1821; but after a few trips she was compelled by law to cease running, the North River Steamboat Company having the sole right to navigate the waters of New York State. The UNITED STATES started on the route between New York and Newark, N.J. Oct. 7, 1821, but did not run long between these points. Later she commenced to run to New Haven in opposition to the steamboats FULTON and CONNECTICUT, but was soon forced to withdraw. In the spring of 1822 she was purchased by the newly organized New Haven Steamboat Company, and put on the route between New Haven and Bryam Cove, Conn (25 miles from New York city)., she being the pioneer boat of the line which in 1893 had the propeller RICHARD PECK built, the 15th steamer of the line since its inception.

The UNITED STATES made three trips a week between New York and New Haven until 1825, when the steamboat HUDSON was added as a consort, since which time a daily line has been kept up.

On September 10, 1830, while racing up the East River with an opposition boat, the main flue of the boiler of the UNITED STATES collapsed by which accident 9 lives were lost. In 1832 she was sold and plied on the Hudson River as a passenger and towboat until about 1840, when she was broken up.

S W Stanton

Constitution:

BUILT 1825, at NEW YORK.

HULL, OF WOOD, CONSTRUCTED BY BROWN & BELL.
Length 145 feet; beam 27 feet.

ENGINE, "SQUARE," BUILT BY J. BIRBECK, New York.
Diameter of cylinder 42 inches; stroke 9 feet.

TONNAGE 267½

The CONSTITUTION and her mate, the CONSTELLATION, were built for the Hudson River route between New York and Albany, the CONSTITUTION being launched on March 30, 1825. Their construction was on an improved model and in all particulars were considered superior to any of the other boats on the river, their passenger accommodations being more extensive and their cabins more elegantly fitted up.

Landings were made at all principal points on the river, and their running time between the two cities averaged 13 hours. The CONSTITUTION exploded one of her boilers when near Poughkeepsie, June 21, 1825, and two people were killed. She was repaired and continued running in the passenger trade a number of years. She was afterwards converted into a towboat and called INDIANA.

HUDSON RIVER STEAMBOAT COMMERCE, 1825.

ONTARIO:
FORMERLY COMMERCE.

BUILT 1825, by C. BERGH, New York
Length, 130 feet, breadth 24 feet 4 inches, and 8 feet 7 inches depth
of hold 371 67 tons, old measurement
Engine, cross head, Wolff double cylinder, built by JAMES P ALLAIRE,
New York Diameter of cylinders 16 and 50 inches, by 4 feet stroke

The steamboat COMMERCE had a consort in the
SWIFTSURE They were built to ply between New
York and Albany, on the Hudson River as passenger
vessels and to tow passenger barges They were afterwards used as tow boats
  In 1856 the COMMERCE was rebuilt, in Brook-
lyn, the hull being enlarged and remodeled, and when she was
launched again she had been changed end for end She
was renamed ONTARIO, and was 216 feet in length, 27 feet
beam, 9 feet depth of hold, measuring 395 93 gross and
283 52 net tons The engine, also enlarged, was now 48
inches diameter of cylinder by 12 feet stroke The ONTARIO
was used as a towboat on the Hudson River up to the year
1893 when she was dismantled at Perth Amboy, N J

22

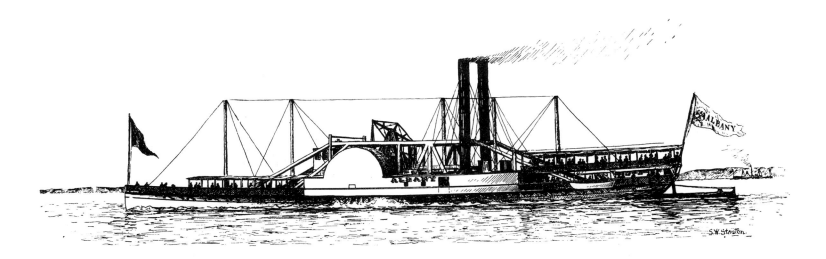

HUDSON RIVER STEAMBOAT ALBANY, AS REBUILT, 1839.

ALBANY

BUILT 1826, by J. VAUGHN, at PHILADELPHIA, PA.

HULL: Length of keel 207 feet; over all 212 feet; width of hull 26 feet; depth of hold 9 feet.

ENGINE: Vertical beam, 65 inches diameter of cylinder by 10 feet stroke.

WHEELS: 24 feet in diameter, 14 feet in width, and 30 inches dip of buckets.

— TONNAGE 398 $\frac{88}{95}$ —

The ALBANY arrived at New York from Philadelphia April 8, 1827. She was built to ply on the Hudson River, between New York and Albany, and was one of the most successful boats of her time. She was one of the fleet belonging to the Messrs. Stevens, of Hoboken, and was splendidly fitted up, her cabins being finely furnished, and decorated with a number of paintings by noted artists of the day.

During the winter of 1839 she was lengthened to 289 feet and her breadth increased 2 feet, and the bow now being sharp and with a false stern, gave her finer lines and enabled her to make better speed. On September 25, 1840, she ran from New York to Albany in 8 hours and 33 minutes.

— The Albany in 1827. —

23

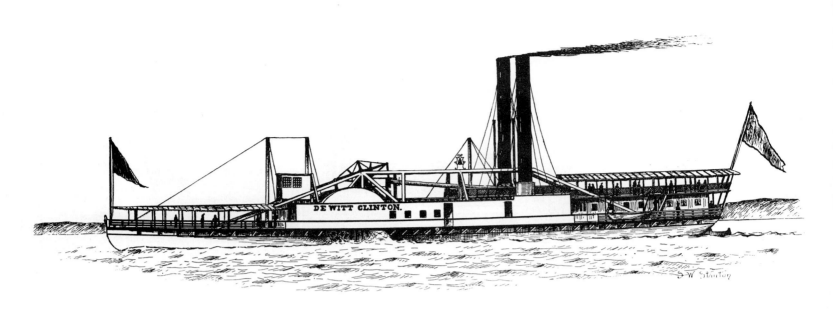

HUDSON RIVER STEAMBOAT DE WITT CLINTON, AS REBUILT, 1832.

DeWitt Clinton.

Built 1828, at ALBANY, N.Y.

HULL, OF WOOD, CONSTRUCTED BY M. KENYON. HULL TWICE ENLARGED UP TO 1833, THE DIMENSIONS THAT YEAR BEING AS FOLLOWS: ENTIRE LENGTH ON DECK 235 FEET, BREADTH HULL AT WATER LINE 28 FEET; BREADTH OVER GUARDS 64 FEET; DEPTH OF HOLD 10 FEET. HEIGHT OF UPPER DECK 11 FEET; LENGTH OF MAIN CABIN—IN HOLD—175 FEET. DRAFT OF WATER, FULLY LOADED, 4 FEET 6 INCHES.

ENGINE, VERTICAL BEAM. DIAMETER OF CYLINDER 66 INCHES, BY PISTON STROKE OF 10 FEET,—THE LARGEST ENGINE OF THE TIME.

BOILERS, TWO, OF IRON, PLACED ON THE GUARDS.

WHEELS, 22 FEET IN DIAMETER; LENGTH OF BUCKETS 14 FEET, DIPPING 28 INCHES.

TONNAGE 373⁹⁄₁₀

THE DE WITT CLINTON was one of the leading early Hudson River steamboats, being one of the first that was placed on the river soon after the old Fulton and Livingston line passed out of existence.

She had a mate in the steamboat VICTORY, and was at first managed by an independent company, but was soon purchased by the "North River Steam Boat Line" the principal company then operating steamers on the river. For many years she plied, as a night boat, on the New York and Albany route, finally being broken up and her engine placed in the new steamboat KNICKERBOCKER, in 1843

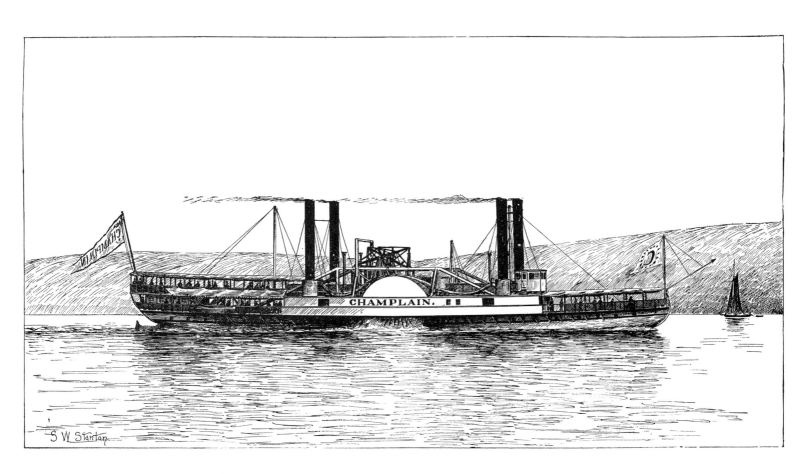

HUDSON RIVER STEAMBOAT CHAMPLAIN, 1832.

CHAMPLAIN:

BUILT 1832, by BROWN & BELL, NEW YORK.

Length 180 feet; Breadth 28 feet; Depth of hold 9 feet; Tonnage 471$\frac{35}{95}$

Two Engines, each 42 inch cylinder and 10 feet stroke, by West Pt. Foundry.

THE Champlain had a mate in the steamboat Erie, built at the same time. These boats ran as day steamers between New York and Albany and Troy. The Champlain began running regularly June 12, 1832, and continued on this route, during the season, until the summer of 1840, when she was laid by in favor of newer and finer steamers.

The Champlain's paddle wheels were 22 feet in diameter, and were driven at the rate of 26 to 28 revolutions per minute. Her speed was 15 miles an hour.

GREAT LAKES STEAMBOAT MICHIGAN, 1833.

MICHIGAN.

BUILT 1833, at DETROIT, MICH.

HULL, by F. CHURCH, 156 feet in length, from stem to stern; 29 feet beam, 11 feet 2 inches depth of hold. 472 43/95 tons.

TWO BEAM ENGINES, of 80 horse power each, built by SILAS BATTELL, of BUFFALO, N.Y.

The MICHIGAN was owned by the Lake Michigan Steamboat Company, and ran mainly between Buffalo & Detroit. She also made a number of trips each season from Buffalo to Chicago and Milwaukee. The two engines of the Michigan were afterward taken out and one was placed in the R.R. Elliot and the other in the City of Sandusky, both lake steamboats.

GREAT LAKES STEAMBOAT THOMAS JEFFERSON, 1834.

THOMAS JEFFERSON:

BUILT 1834, at ERIE, Pa.

HULL, of wood, built by S. JENKINS. Length from stem to stern 174 feet; breadth of beam 26 feet 8 inches; depth of hold 9 feet 8 inches.

ENGINE, cross-head, constructed by JAS. P. ALLAIRE. New York. 150 horse power.

TONNAGE 428 60/95

THE THOMAS JEFFERSON was built for C.M. REED and others, and she ran between Buffalo, Detroit and other lake ports. In 1846 the engine of the THOMAS JEFFERSON was put into the new lake steamboat LOUISIANA, and it was lost with her in 1858.

HUDSON RIVER STEAMBOAT HIGHLANDER, 1835.

HIGHLANDER.

BUILT 1835, at NEW YORK.

HULL, OF WOOD, BUILT BY **Lawrence & Sneden.**
Length of Keel 160 feet, over all 175 feet; breadth
of Beam 24 feet; depth of hold 8 feet

ENGINE, VERTICAL BEAM, CONSTRUCTED BY THE **West
Point Foundry,** COLD SPRING, N.Y. Diameter of
cylinder 41 inches, by 10 feet stroke

BOILERS, TWO, OF IRON, ON GUARDS

WHEELS, 24 feet in diameter; buckets 10 feet
in length, dip 29 inches

— TONNAGE 313 —

THE HIGHLANDER was built for
Powell, Johnson & Wardrop,
for the Hudson River. She
was one of the best boats
on the river when she first came out,
as well as one of the fastest. She
ran on the Newburgh and New York
line until the "Thomas Powell"
appeared, 1846. She was then
used as an excursion boat;
later she ran to Rondout as
a passenger boat. In 1852
she was taken to the Delaware
River, and was used as a towboat. In 1866 she was dismantled, and her engine
erected in the new towboat
"William H. Aspinwall."

LONG ISLAND SOUND STEAMBOAT NEW YORK, 1836.

NEW YORK:
BUILT 1835 AT NEW YORK.

HULL, OF WOOD, BUILT BY Lawrence & Sneden. Length between perpendiculars 230 feet; breadth of beam 23 feet; depth of hold 11 feet

ENGINE, SQUARE, CONSTRUCTED BY James P. Allaire, New York Diameter of cylinder 52 inches, by 10 feet stroke..

BOILER, ONE, OF IRON, IN HOLD

WHEELS, 24½ feet in diameter, buckets 12 feet in length; dip 30 inches

TONNAGE 524 ⅓

The New York was built for the New York and New Haven Line, and was one of the finest steamers on Long Island Sound when she appeared She commenced regular trips April 4, 1836, and continued to ply on this route for about 20 years. She was then converted into a towboat for the Hudson River.

HUDSON RIVER STEAMBOAT ROCHESTER, 1836.

LONG ISLAND SOUND STEAMBOAT RHODE ISLAND, 1836.

RHODE ISLAND.

BUILT 1836 at NEW YORK.

HULL, OF WOOD, BUILT BY BROWN & BELL.
Length 211 feet; beam 28 feet; hold 10 feet.

ENGINE, SQUARE.
Diameter of cylinder 50 inches; stroke 11 feet.
Horse power 350.

BOILERS, TWO, OF IRON

WHEELS. Diameter 24 feet; buckets 11 feet
in length, dipping 30 inches.

TONNAGE 588½

THE RHODE ISLAND was one of the finest of the Long Island steamboats in her day. She was built for Captain Seth Thayer for the line between New York and Providence and made her first trip in 12 hours and 24 minutes. Her lower, or main cabin was 165 feet in length, and contained 176 berths. She ran from New York to Providence [also to Stonington] for about 10 years. In 1849 she was placed on the route from New York to Philadelphia, and soon after started for California and foundered in a storm in the Atlantic.

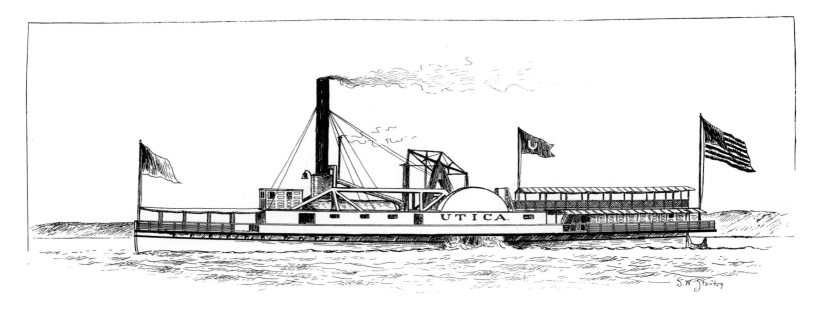

HUDSON RIVER STEAMBOAT UTICA, 1836.

UTICA:

BUILT 1836, at BROOKLYN.

HULL, OF WOOD, BUILT BY WM. CAPES. Length 180 feet; breadth of beam 21½ feet; depth of hold 8 feet 4 inches.

ENGINE, VERTICAL BEAM CONSTRUCTED by the WEST POINT FOUNDRY. Diameter of cylinder 39 inches, by 10 feet stroke.

BOILER, OF IRON, ON DECK. Length 18 feet; width 9 feet; height 8 feet.

WHEELS, RADIAL. Diameter 22 feet, length of buckets, 10 feet.

~ TONNAGE 340 69 ~

THE UTICA was built for the "People's Line," to run as a passenger boat on the Hudson River, between New York and Albany. She was one of the best of her time, and of good speed. She was used, at times, on the route between New York and Piermont, in connection with the N.Y. & Erie Railroad. Was finally converted into a towboat, and used as such on the Hudson River many years. Condemned Nov. 20, 1875, and broken up.

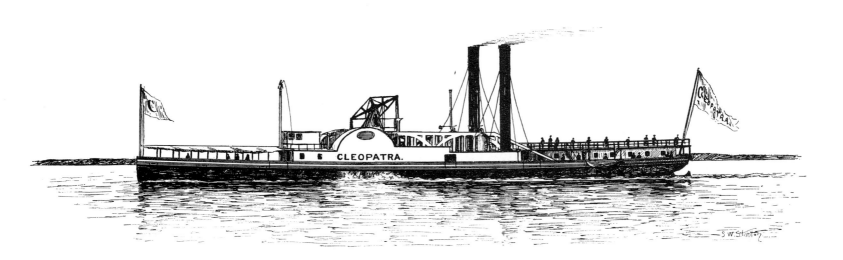

LONG ISLAND SOUND STEAMBOAT CLEOPATRA, 1836.

CLEOPATRA.
BUILT 1836, at NEW YORK.
HULL, by BISHOP & SIMONSON
Length from stem to stern 193 feet; breadth of beam, 23 feet; depth of hold, 8 feet 11 inches.
ENGINE, vertical beam, constructed by W. KEMBLE

BOILERS, two, of copper, on guards
TONNAGE 402 84/95

THE CLEOPATRA was built for the navigation of Long Island Sound and was owned by Commodore Vanderbilt. She ran between New York and Hartford and afterwards to Providence and Norwich. In 1846 she plied between Greenport, L.I. and Allyn's Point, Conn. She continued to be used on the Sound a great number of years; before going out of existence she ran as an excursion boat at New York.
Her engine was finally taken out and placed in the sidewheel tug Underwriter.

33

HUDSON RIVER TOWBOAT NORWICH.

NORWICH.

BUILT 1836, at NEW YORK.

HULL, OF WOOD, BUILT BY Lawrence & Sneden. Length from stem to stern 160 feet; breadth of beam 25 feet 3 inches; depth of hold 9 feet.
ENGINE, "SQUARE," CONSTRUCTED BY Cunningham & Hall, New York. Diameter of cylinder 40 inches by 10 feet stroke.
BOILER, ONE, OF IRON.
TONNAGE, Old Measurement 346 95/100; New Measurement 255 71/100 Gross, 127 31/100 Net Tons.

BUILT for the "New York and Norwich Steamboat Company," the NORWICH ran for a number of years as a Long Island Sound boat. She was afterwards placed on the New York and Rondout line, and from that time to the present day has remained on the Hudson River. Since about 1850 she has been used as a towboat, continually, and has long been known as the "Ice King," being used each Spring to break a passage through the ice. For half a century the NORWICH has been a familiar object to the residents along the banks of the Hudson

NORWICH, as Passenger Boat, 1836

The NORWICH, as a Towboat on Hudson River, 1894

34

LONG ISLAND SOUND STEAMBOAT MASSACHUSETTS, 1836.

BUILT 1836
at NEW YORK

HULL, OF WOOD, BUILT BY BROWN & BELL. Length 202 feet, on deck; breadth of beam 30 feet; depth of hold 12 feet.

ENGINES, TWO, VERTICAL BEAM, each 44 inches diameter of cylinder, by 9 feet stroke. 145 horse power each.

BOILERS, TWO, OF COPPER, on guards

WHEELS, 21½ feet in diameter.

— TONNAGE 626 71/95

The MASSACHUSETTS, when finished, was pronounced by experts to be the strongest and best boat of her class in the world. She was built of live oak, locust and ceder, and saw more years of constant service and lasted longer than the majority of the early steamboats. She was built for the navigation Long Island Sound, and on her first trip between New York and Providence, R.I., she made the run in 13 hours and 32 minutes. Her cabin (in the hold) was 170 feet in length and there were 142 berths. Her original cost was over $100,000. Soon after she was built a longer bow was added, which made her faster and increased her tonnage to 920 ½. Two new iron boilers were placed in her in 1849.

Her regular route was from New York to Providence, but often ran to Stonington. She was used as an excursion boat around New York in 1855.

LAKE CHAMPLAIN STEAMBOAT BURLINGTON, 1837.

BURLINGTON:
Designed by LAVATUS S WHITE
BUILT 1837, at SHELBURNE, Vermont

HULL, OF WOOD Length between perpendiculars 190 feet, over all 200 feet; breadth of beam 25 feet, depth of hold 9 feet; average draft of water 6 feet.

ENGINE, VERTICAL BEAM, CONSTRUCTED BY THE EAGLE FOUNDRY, MONTREAL, CANADA Diameter of cylinder 44 inches; stroke 10 feet

BOILERS, TWO, OF IRON, ON GUARDS, BUILT IN PHILADELPHIA

WHEELS, each 28 feet in diameter by 10 feet in width.

— TONNAGE 405 —

THE BURLINGTON was one of the finest of the early inland steamboats. She was built for the navigation of Lake Champlain, running between Whitehall, N.Y. and St. Johns, L.C., being owned by the Champlain Transportation Company. She cost $75,000, and had a speed of 14 miles an hour Charles Dickens, in his "American Notes," 1842, says. "The BURLINGTON is a perfectly exquisite achievement of neatness, elegance, and order The decks are drawing-rooms, the cabins are boudoirs, choicely furnished and adorned with prints, pictures and musical instruments; every nook and corner in the vessel is a perfect curiosity of graceful comfort and beautiful contrivance."

UNITED STATES WAR VESSEL FULTON 2D, 1837.

FULTON (2d):

BUILT 1837-8, at NEW YORK.

HULL, or wood Length between perpendiculars, 180 feet, breadth of beam (extreme) 34 feet 8 inches; depth of hold 12 feet 2 inches; weight of hull 470 tons, estimated tonnage 973 tons; average draft 10½ feet.

ENGINES, TWO, HORIZONTAL CONDENSING (on spar deck) CONSTRUCTED BY WEST POINT FOUNDRY. Diameter of cylinders 50 inches, by 9 feet length of stroke.

BOILERS, ORIGINALLY FOUR IN NUMBER, OF COPPER (RETURN FLUE), WITH FOUR SMOKE PIPES Length of each 16 feet; breadth 10½ feet; height 9 feet 3 inches

WHEELS, RADIAL (SHAFTS COULD BE DISCONNECTED FROM ENGINE), diameter at outside of paddles 22 feet 2 inches ; length of paddles 11½ feet ; breadth of paddles 3 feet.

The FULTON the SECOND was the second steam war vessel constructed for the United States Government, and was built to take the place of the destroyed DEMOLOGOS ("Fulton the First"). She was a speedy craft for her time, but was a failure as an ocean-going vessel, altho' she made one trip to the West Indies and back.

She laid at the New York Navy Yard for many years, and was finally given new engines and boilers and important changes made in her general appearance. When completed she was known as FULTON THE THIRD. In 1862 she was destroyed by Confederates at Pensacola, Fla.

LONG ISLAND SOUND STEAMBOAT JOHN W. RICHMOND, 1837.

John W. Richmond:

BUILT 1837, at PROVIDENCE, R.I.

HULL, of wood, designed and built by John S. Eddy. Length of keel 202 feet 2 inches; length on deck 210 feet; breadth of beam 23 feet 10 inches; depth of hold 10 feet 4 inches.

JOINER WORK, by TALMAN & BUCKLIN.

ENGINE, square type, designed and constructed by J. Babcock, Providence Steam Engine Company. Diameter of cylinder 48 inches, by 11 feet stroke.

WHEELS, 25 feet in diameter.

— TONNAGE 520 90/95 —

This steamboat was built for the Atlantic Steamboat Company to run as an independent boat between New York and Providence, on Long Island Sound, making her first trip to New York on June 7, 1838. She was handsomely fitted up and soon became a very popular boat, being of great speed for those times, one trip being made from New York to Providence in a little less than 11 hours. She ran on this route a number of years. In March, 1840, she was sold for $52,250, to Captain Kimberly, for the Boston and Hallowell (Maine) route. She was burned in 1843.

38

HUDSON RIVER STEAMBOAT TROY, 1840.

LAKE ERIE STEAMBOAT INDIANA, 1841.

INDIANA.

BUILT 1841, at TOLEDO, Ohio.

HULL, OF WOOD, 175 feet in length; 26 feet breadth of beam, and 12 feet depth of hold.

ENGINE, VERTICAL BEAM, 48 inches diameter of cylinder by 7 feet stroke

WHEELS, 24 feet in diameter by 8 feet wide.

→ Tonnage 550 ←

The INDIANA was the largest and finest steamboat that had ever been constructed at Toledo in 1841. She was built for the line between that point and Buffalo, upon which route she ran until burned at Conneaut, O., in 1848

NEW ENGLAND COAST IRON PROPELLER BANGOR, 1844.

BANGOR:

BUILT 1844, at WILMINGTON, Del.,
By
Betts, Harlan & Hollingsworth.

Pioneer

Iron

Sea-going

Steamer

HULL, OF IRON, 120 feet between perpendiculars;
131 feet over all, on deck; 23 feet breadth of beam;
depth of hold 9 feet

ENGINES, TWO INDEPENDENT, "LOPER" TYPE;
cylinders each 22 inches in diameter, by
24 inches stroke of piston

BOILER, OF IRON, DROP FLUE TYPE, 20 feet
in length

WHEELS, "LOPER" TYPE, 8½ feet in diameter.

— TONNAGE 231 —

THE BANGOR was constructed for the
route between Boston and Bangor,
Maine, and was the first American
sea steamer built of iron. Her speed
on her trial trip was 15.7 miles per Hour.
On August 31, 1846, she burned, on the coast
of Maine, soon after beginning regular trips,
but was rebuilt and again placed on the route
In December, 1846, she was purchased by the
United States Government, for $29,975, and
used as a war vessel during the Mexican War

DELAWARE RIVER IRON STEAMBOAT JOHN STEVENS, 1844.

JOHN STEVENS.

Designed by Robert L Stevens —
BUILT 1844, at HOBOKEN, N.J.

HULL, OF IRON, CONSTRUCTED BY ROBERT L. STEVENS. Length on deck 245 feet ; breadth of beam 31 feet; over guards 65 feet ; depth of hold 11 feet

ENGINE, STEEPLE, WITH VIBRATING CROSS-HEAD, BUILT BY T.F. SECOR, NEW YORK Diameter of cylinder 75 inches, by 8 feet stroke

BOILERS, TWO, TUBULAR Length 15 feet, width 12 feet; each having 384 tubes 12 feet long and 1¾ inches bore

WHEELS, 31 feet 8 inches in diameter; length of buckets 12 feet ; average dip 2 feet 7 inches.

···GROSS·TONNAGE·1380···

✳   ✳   ✳   ✳

THE first large iron steamboat built in the United States She was constructed for use on the Dela-ware River, commencing trips between Philadelphia and Bordentown in 1846 She was the finest on the river at that time and had remarkable speed — 19 miles an hour. She was burned, at White Hill, near Bordentown, N.J, in 1855.
In 1865 the hull was supplied with propeller engines, and she was placed in the cattle carrying trade by the Pennsylvania Rail-road Co, in New York Harbor —

The JOHN STEVENS as a Propeller.

GREAT LAKES PASSENGER STEAMBOAT EMPIRE, 1844.

EMPIRE:

BUILT 1844, at CLEVELAND, O.

HULL, OF WOOD, CONSTRUCTED BY CAPT. GEORGE W. JONES. Length on water line 251 feet ; over all 260 feet.

ENGINE, INCLINED LOW PRESSURE, BELOW DECK, BUILT BY THE CUYAHOGA STEAM FURNACE CO., CLEVELAND, O. Diameter of cylinder 35 inches, by 10 feet stroke of piston. Horse power 600.

BOILERS, SIX, OF IRON, LOCOMOTIVE TYPE, CONSTRUCTED BY SPANG & CO., PITTSBURGH, PA. Length of each 26½ feet; diameter 4½ feet, each containing 22 flues, 6 inches in diameter, 20½ feet in length, offering a fire surface of 5000 square feet. Fuel, wood.

WHEELS, 28 feet in diameter; buckets 12 feet in length.

~ TONNAGE 1136 ~

A NOTABLE VESSEL, BEING THE FIRST steamboat built in the United States to measure over 1000 tons, and was, at the time she came out, 200 tons larger than any other steam vessel in the World. Instead of the round, bluff bow and square stern of the usual build of lake boats at that period, the EMPIRE had an excellent model, being sharp at both ends. She was the fastest as well as the most elegantly fitted up boat on the Great Lakes.

Her best time during her first year was 20 hours and 25 minutes from Detroit to Buffalo, and 12 hours and 44 minutes from Cleveland to Buffalo.

She ran for many years between Buffalo and Chicago and was afterwards used on the Buffalo and Toledo route. Later she was converted into a propeller.

BOSTON HARBOR STEAMBOAT MAY FLOWER, 1845.

MAYFLOWER:

~ Designed by CURTIS PECK ~

BUILT 1845, AT BROOKLYN, N.Y.

HULL, OF WOOD
Length over all 133 feet; breadth of beam (over guards) 42 feet, depth of hold 8 feet; average draft of water 4½ feet

ENGINE, "SQUARE," CONSTRUCTED BY THE Allaire Works, NEW YORK Diameter of cylinder 30 inches by 10 feet stroke of piston.

BOILER, OF IRON, BUILT BY ALLAIRE WORKS. Length 19 feet; diameter 8½ feet

WHEELS, 21½ feet in diameter, 21 buckets to each wheel, 7½ feet in length; average dip 2 feet

~ TONNAGE 262 $\frac{62}{95}$ ~

THE MAYFLOWER was built for the Boston & Hingham Steamboat Company, to ply between Boston and Hingham. Her contract price was $25,000, and she had a speed of 12 miles an hour. In 1856 Thomas Collyer, shipbuilder, of New York, took her in part payment for a new boat (the NANTASKET), and lengthened her by putting on a new bow, her cylinder was enlarged to 36 inches. She ran between New York, Glen Cove and Northport, and on other routes. Was used as a transport during the War.

44

HUDSON RIVER STEAMBOAT RIP VAN WINKLE, AS REBUILT, 1851.

RIP VAN WINKLE:
BUILT 1845, at NEW YORK.

HULL, OF WOOD, BUILT BY **GEORGE COLLYER.** Lengthened 1851, to 242 feet 3 inches, over all; breadth of beam 25½ feet, depth of hold. 8 feet 9 inches.

ENGINE, HORIZONTAL HALF-BEAM, CONSTRUCTED BY **W.A.LIGHTHALL.** Diameter of cylinder 50 inches, by 10 feet stroke.

BOILERS, TWO, OF IRON, ON GUARDS. Length of each 28 feet, by 7½ feet diameter of shell.

~TONNAGE 640?~

THE RIP VAN WINKLE, was built for the Hudson River route between New York and Albany, for the day line, but not being able to compete in speed with the other boats, she was used as a night boat. In 1846 she ran on the Delaware River, between Philadelphia and Cape May, and the next year ran again as a night boat to Albany. Rebuilt 1851 and continued to run to Albany. In 1852 she was sold to J.H.Tremper and ran between New York and Rondout, and afterwards plied on various routes about New York.

On April 16, 1872, while on her way from Troy to New York, she ran against the railroad bridge at Albany and was so badly damaged as to be of no further use.

45

GREAT LAKES PROPELLER PRINCETON, 1845.

PRINCETON:
BUILT 1845, by SAML. HUBBELL, at PERRYSBURG, OHIO.
Designed by Amos Pratt Hubbell.

Length 185 feet; Breadth, 27 feet (over guards 39 feet); Depth of hold, 10 feet. Two twin-screw Engines, 24 inch cylinders, by 24 inches stroke; built by the Auburn, New York, States Prison. Two boilers, 6 by 14 feet. Speed, 11 miles.

THE Princeton was the first propeller on the Great Lakes that had an Upper Cabin. She was one of a fleet of 14 steamers forming the line of passenger boats from Buffalo to Chicago.

The PRINCETON.

LONG ISLAND SOUND STEAMBOAT ATLANTIC, 1846.

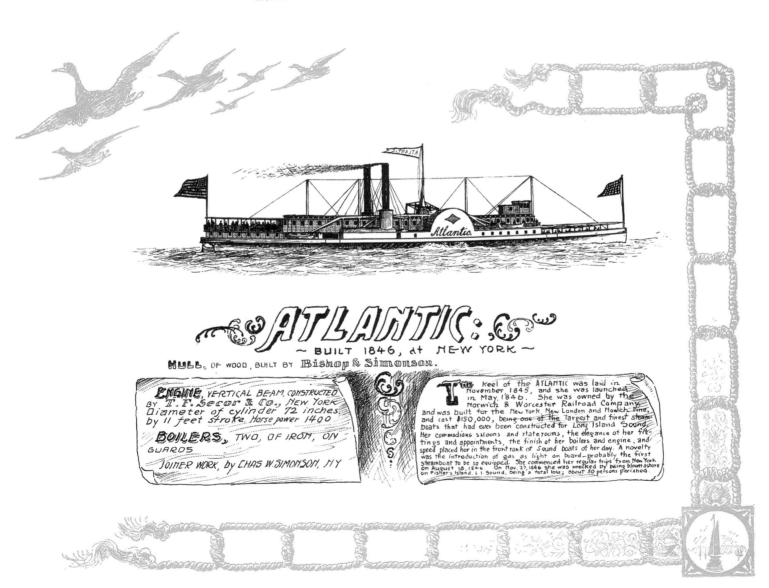

ATLANTIC
~ BUILT 1846, at NEW YORK ~
HULL, OF WOOD, BUILT BY Bishop & Simonson.

ENGINE, VERTICAL BEAM, CONSTRUCTED BY T. F. Secor & Co., NEW YORK. Diameter of cylinder 72 inches by 11 feet stroke. Horse power 1400

BOILERS, TWO, OF IRON, ON GUARDS

JOINER WORK, by CHAS. W. SIMONSON, N.Y.

The keel of the ATLANTIC was laid in November 1845, and she was launched in May, 1846. She was owned by the Norwich & Worcester Railroad Company, and was built for the New York, New London and Norwich line, and cost $150,000, being one of the largest and finest steamboats that had ever been constructed for Long Island Sound. Her commodious saloons and staterooms, the elegance of her fittings and appointments, the finish of her boilers and engine, and speed placed her in the front rank of Sound boats of her day. A novelty was the introduction of gas as light on board—probably the first steamboat to be so equipped. She commenced her regular trips from New York on August 18, 1846. On Nov. 27, 1846 she was wrecked by being blown ashore on Fisher's Island, L. I. Sound, being a total loss; about 50 persons perished.

HUDSON RIVER STEAMBOAT ISAAC NEWTON, AS REBUILT, 1855.

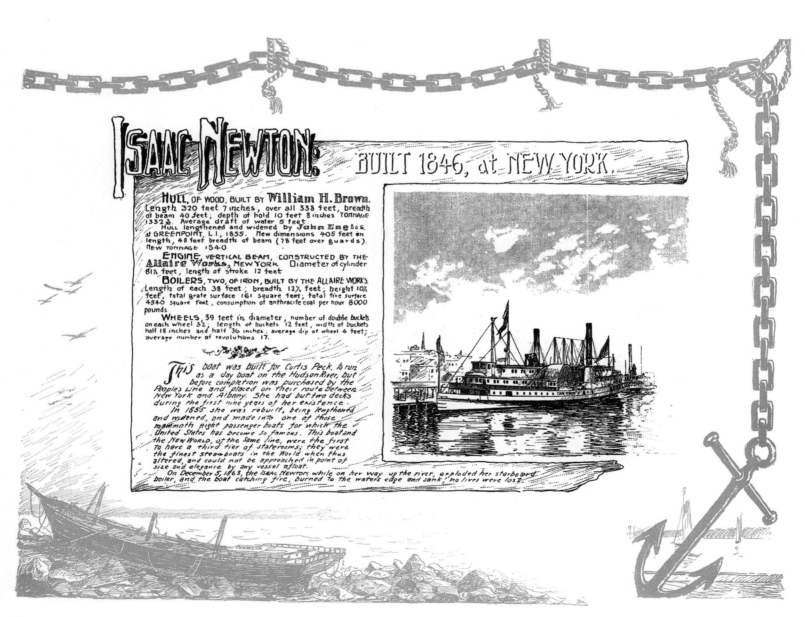

ISAAC NEWTON.
BUILT 1846, at NEW YORK.

HULL, OF WOOD, BUILT BY William H. Brown.
Length 320 feet 7 inches, over all 338 feet, breadth
of beam 40 feet; depth of hold 10 feet 8 inches TONNAGE
1332⅜. Average draft of water 5 feet.
Hull lengthened and widened by John Englis,
at GREENPOINT, L.I., 1855. New dimensions 405 feet in
length, 48 feet breadth of beam (78 feet over guards).
NEW TONNAGE 1540

ENGINE, VERTICAL BEAM, CONSTRUCTED BY THE
Allaire Works, NEW YORK. Diameter of cylinder
81½ feet, length of stroke 12 feet

BOILERS, TWO, OF IRON, BUILT BY THE ALLAIRE WORKS.
Length of each 38 feet; breadth 12½ feet; height 10½
feet, total grate surface 161 square feet; total fire surface
4540 square feet, consumption of anthracite coal per hour 8000
pounds

WHEELS, 39 feet in diameter, number of double buckets
on each wheel 32; length of buckets 12 feet, width of buckets
half 18 inches and half 36 inches; average dip of wheel 4 feet;
average number of revolutions 17.

This boat was built for Curtis Peck, to run
as a day boat on the Hudson River, but
before completion was purchased by the
People's Line and placed on their route between
New York and Albany. She had but two decks
during the first nine years of her existence.
In 1855 she was rebuilt, being lengthened
and widened, and made into one of those
mammoth night passenger boats for which the
United States has become so famous. This boat and
the NEW WORLD, of the same line, were the first
to have a third tier of staterooms; they were
the finest steamboats in the World when thus
altered, and could not be approached in point of
size and elegance by any vessel afloat.
On December 5, 1863, the ISAAC NEWTON, while on her way up the river, exploded her starboard
boiler, and the boat catching fire, burned to the water's edge and sank; no lives were lost.

HUDSON RIVER STEAMBOAT THOMAS POWELL, 1846.

THOMAS POWELL.

BUILT 1846, at NEW YORK.

HULL, OF WOOD, BUILT BY Lawrence & Sneden. Length 231 feet 2 inches; breadth of beam 28 feet 11 inches; depth of hold 9 feet.

ENGINE, VERTICAL BEAM, CONSTRUCTED BY T. F. Secor & Co., New York. Diameter of cylinder 48 inches, by 11 feet stroke. Average number of revolutions 24 per minute; average pressure of steam 50 lbs. to square inch; cutting off at 8 feet.

BOILERS, TWO, OF IRON, ON GUARDS, BUILT BY T. F. SECOR & Co. Length 27¼ feet; diameter 7 feet. Whole amount of fire surface 2244 square feet; whole amount of grate surface 88 square feet, consumption of anthracite coal per hour 600 lbs.

WHEELS, RADIAL. Diameter 29 feet 6 inches; 24 buckets each wheel; length of buckets 9 feet; width of buckets 2 feet; average dip of wheels 2 feet.

~ TONNAGE 585 ⁷⁄₉₅ ~

This vessel was one of those famous Hudson River craft of the halcyon days of steamboating that were unrivalled in any other part of the World in point of completeness, speed and perfect adaptability for the purpose for which they were intended. She was built for Thomas Powell and Homer Ramsdell, to take the place of steamboat HIGHLANDER, on the route between Newburgh and New York, and no expense was spared to make her one of the finest then afloat. She was one of the fastest steamboats ever built; on June 18, 1846, she ran from New York to Cauldwells, 43 miles, in 2 hours, and to Newburgh, 60 miles, in 2 hours and 40 minutes, the quickest on record, up to that period.

She ran between New York and Newburgh a number of years and then to Piermont, in connection with the Erie Railroad. In 1851 she commenced to run to Poughkeepsie, but was sold the same year, to run on the Delaware River, between Philadelphia and Cape May. Returning to New York she again ran to Poughkeepsie, and later to Rondout, being relieved on the latter route by the steamboat MARY POWELL, in 1862. Afterwards ran to Catskill and to Troy, as a night boat. Was broken up at Port Ewen, on the Hudson, in 1881.

HUDSON RIVER STEAMBOAT ARMENIA, 1847.

ARMENIA:
BUILT 1847, at NEW YORK.

HULL, OF WOOD, BUILT BY **THOMAS COLLYER.** Length on deck 185 feet; breadth of beam 26 feet; depth of hold 8 feet. Average draft of water 3 feet 9 inches. Tonnage 421. Afterward lengthened to 212 feet; tonnage 528.

ENGINE, VERTICAL BEAM, CONSTRUCTED BY **HENRY R. DUNHAM & CO.,** New York. Diameter of cylinder 40 inches; stroke of piston 14 feet. Average pressure of steam 35 pounds, cutting off at 10 feet. Average number of revolutions 23 per minute.

BOILER, ONE, OF IRON; BELOW DECK, BUILT BY **HENRY R. DUNHAM & CO.** Whole amount of fire surface 1402 square feet; whole amount of grate surface 57 square feet. Consumption of anthracite coal per hour 2500 pounds. TWO NEW BOILERS in 1850, each 31 feet in length by 6½ feet wide.

WHEELS, 29 feet 4 inches in diameter; length of buckets 8 feet 3 inches; width of buckets 2 feet 4 inches; number of buckets each wheel, 26; average dip of wheel 2 feet 4 inches.

THE ARMENIA, although not of the largest size, was one of the most widely known and popular steamboats that ever ran on the Hudson River. She was built originally for the New York and Peekskill route, but proving as fast a craft she was placed on the day line to Albany and she ran between these two points many years. For a short time in 1853 she ran daily to Keyport, N.J. In 1860 she made the run from New York to Albany in 7 hours and 42 minutes, making eleven landings. Distance 144 miles.

The ARMENIA was founded in depot and there years but continued to be used as a spare boat on the day line, and lastly when laid aside she burned on the Hudson River. on Jan. 9, 1886, while laid up at Alexandria Va., she caught fire and burned to the water's edge.

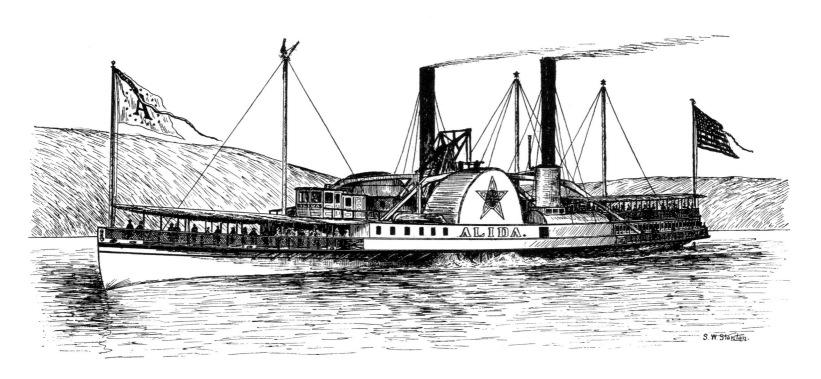

HUDSON RIVER STEAMBOAT ALIDA, 1847.

ALIDA

BUILT 1847, at NEW YORK

AMONG the famous and popular Hudson River steamers of the early days the ALIDA may be said to have occupied a leading place. In regard to speed she stand out prominently, and during her entire career as a passenger boat was the greatest of favorites with the traveling public.

She was built for the day line between New York and Albany, being launched on January 9, 1847, and commenced regular trips to Albany on April 16 of that year. Her speed was over 20 miles an hour.

The ALIDA was used as a passenger boat many years, and was then converted into a towboat. She went out of service in 1875, and was afterwards broken up at Port Ewen, N.Y.

HULL, OF WOOD, BUILT BY WILLIAM H. BROWN. Length on water line 249 feet 5 inches; over all 265 feet; breadth of beam 28 feet 6½ inches; depth of hold 9 feet 9 inches. By the addition of a new bow her extreme length was afterwards 276 feet. Tonnage 680½; afterwards 741.

ENGINE, VERTICAL BEAM, CONSTRUCTED BY HENRY R. DUNHAM & CO., New York. Diameter of cylinder 56 inches, by 12 feet stroke. Average number of revolutions, 25 per minute.

BOILERS, TWO, OF IRON, ON GUARDS, BUILT BY HENRY R. DUNHAM & CO. Length of each 52 feet 6 inches, by 8 feet 6 inches wide. Whole amount of fire surface 2706 square feet; whole amount of grate surface 100 square feet. Consumption of anthracite coal per hour 6600 pounds. Average pressure of steam 40 pounds to square inch.

WHEELS, 32 feet 8 inches in diameter; length of buckets 9 feet 6 inches; width of buckets 2 feet 9 inches; number of buckets to each wheel 30. Average dip of wheel 2 feet 11 inches.

LAKE ERIE STEAMBOAT ATLANTIC, 1848.

ATLANTIC:

Built for E.B.& S.Ward, by J.L.Wolverton, at Newport, Mich., 1848.
Length 267 feet; 33 feet beam, and 13 feet 4 inches depth of hold. 1,155.18 tons.
Engine, by Hogg & Delamater, N.Y., cylinder 60 inches by 11 ft stroke.
2 Boilers, each 10 feet diameter by 34 feet long.
Cost $110,000.

THE Atlantic was chartered as soon as finished to run between Buffalo and Detroit with steamers Mayflower and Ocean, in connection with the Michigan Central Railroad, and continued on this route from 1849 until 1852. On August 20, 1852, while on passage from Buffalo to Detroit with 110 first class and 270 steerage passengers, and a crew of 40, was run into by the propeller Ogdensburg, off Long Point, (Canada) Lake Erie, and sunk in 15 minutes. 150 persons perished

The Atlantic in point of beauty, elegance and convenience, in finish and accommodation, was not surpassed by any boat on the Lakes. On June 7, 1849 she reached Detroit from Buffalo in 16½ hours, the quickest passage up to that time.

HUDSON RIVER STEAMBOAT NEW WORLD, 1855.

NEW WORLD.

BUILT 1848 AT NEW YORK

HULL, CONSTRUCTED BY WILLIAM H. BROWN. Original length on deck, 371 feet; breadth of beam 36 feet; over guards 69 feet; depth of hold 10½ feet; average draft 5½ feet; tonnage 1418. In 1855 the hull was widened to 43 feet, by JOHN ENGLIS, at GREENPOINT, making tonnage 1675.

ENGINE, VERTICAL BEAM, BUILT BY T.F. SECOR & CO., New York. Diameter of cylinder 76 inches, by 15 feet stroke, cutting off at 8 feet. Average revolutions 17 per minute.

BOILERS, TWO, OF IRON, BY T.F. SECOR & Co. Each 40½ feet in length, by 11 feet in diameter, with 13 feet width of front of shell. Total fire surface 5332 square feet; total grate surface 212 square feet; average pressure of steam 45. New boilers in 1855, same size, allowed 37 lbs. to square inch.

WHEELS, 46 feet in diameter; number of buckets each wheel 33, length of buckets 12 feet; width of buckets 13 inches; average dip of wheel 3 feet 4 inches.

ONE of the most celebrated of American river steamboats. The NEW WORLD was the wonder of her day, being larger in size of hull, engine, wheels, etc., than any boat that had heretofore been constructed. She was first used as a day boat on the Hudson, and had an average speed of over 20 miles an hour. In 1855 she was rebuilt into a night boat, being the first of the great inland steamers to have double tiers of staterooms above the main deck.

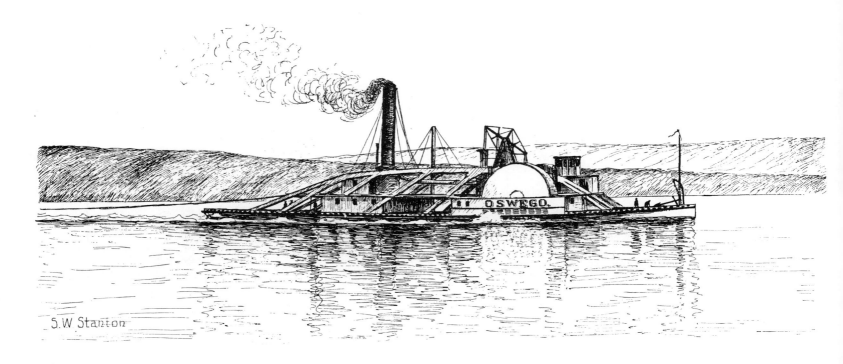

HUDSON RIVER TOWBOAT OSWEGO.

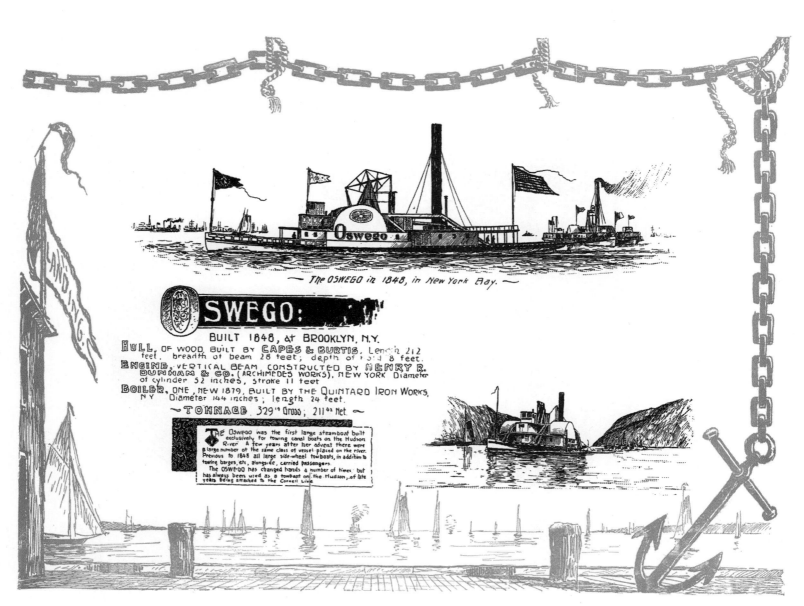

— The OSWEGO in 1848, in New York Bay. —

OSWEGO:

BUILT 1848, at BROOKLYN, N.Y.

HULL, OF WOOD, BUILT BY CAPES & BURTIS, Length 212 feet, breadth of beam 28 feet; depth of hold 8 feet.

ENGINE, VERTICAL BEAM, CONSTRUCTED BY HENRY R. DUNHAM & CO. (ARCHIMEDES WORKS), NEW YORK Diameter of cylinder 52 inches, Stroke 11 feet.

BOILER, ONE, NEW 1879, BUILT BY THE QUINTARD IRON WORKS, N.Y. Diameter 144 inches; length 24 feet.

~ TONNAGE 329⁴⁹ Gross; 211⁴³ Net. ~

THE OSWEGO was the first large steamboat built exclusively for towing canal boats on the Hudson River. A few years after her advent there were a large number of the same class of vessel placed on the river. Previous to 1848 all large side-wheel towboats, in addition to towing barges, etc., alongside, carried passengers.

The OSWEGO has changed hands a number of times, but has always been used as a towboat on the Hudson, of late years being attached to the Cornell Line.

NEW ENGLAND COAST STEAMBOAT STATE OF MAINE, 1848.

STATE OF MAINE.

BUILT 1848, at NEW YORK

HULL of wood, constructed by J. Simunson. Length 236½ feet, breadth of beam 31⅗ feet, depth of hold 11⅘ feet

ENGINE, vertical beam. Diameter of cylinder 54 inches, by 11 feet stroke

BOILERS, two, of iron, return tubular. Length 26 feet diameter 8 feet

~ TONNAGE 806 ⁷⁄₉₅ ~

The STATE OF MAINE was built for the line between Boston and Bangor, Maine, but proved to be too large and expensive a boat for the route at that period. She was placed on Long Island Sound the next year, running from Stonington to New York, and the year following was purchased by the "Bay State Line" (afterwards Fall River line), and for many years plied between New York and Fall River. She underwent numerous changes up to the year 1863 when she was taken to the South and used as a hospital boat on the James River.

She afterwards returned to New York where she was used as an excursion boat, finally being sold for service in the West Indies.

LONG ISLAND SOUND STEAMBOAT BAY STATE, 1848.

BAY STATE

BUILT 1848, at NEW YORK.

HULL, OF WOOD, BUILT BY SAMUEL SNEDEN
Length on water line 300 feet; on deck 317 feet; breadth of beam 39 feet; depth of hold 13 feet 2 inches; average draft of water 8 feet; Tonnage 1,554.
Lengthened 1854 to 352 feet; 82 feet over guards; New tonnage 2,200.

ENGINE, VERTICAL BEAM, BUILT BY THE ALLAIRE WORKS, NEW YORK.
Diameter of cylinder 76 inches, by 12 feet stroke Average revolutions 18 per minute.

BOILERS, TWO, OF IRON, ON GUARDS, BY THE ALLAIRE WORKS. Steam pressure 25 lbs. to square inch. Whole amount of fire surface 4554 square feet; whole amount of grate surface 173 square feet; consumption of fuel (anthracite coal) per hour 6500 pounds

WHEELS, 38 feet in diameter; length of buckets 10 feet 3 inches; width of buckets 2 feet 8 inches; number of buckets each wheel 30; average dip of wheel 3 feet 6 inches.

ONE of the most celebrated of the early steamboats was the BAY STATE; probably the finest specimen of marine architecture of her day She was built for the Fall River Line, and was the first of a wonderful fleet of inland steamers, of this company which from that day continued to be the leading line on Long Island Sound, a sheet of water always noted for its palatial steamers.
Her extensive passenger accommodations and superb fittings at once made her a favorite with the travelling public, and her great speed placed her in the front rank of the Sound flyers. The fastest trip of the BAY STATE occurred in 1857, when she made the run from New York to Fall River in 8 hours and 42 minutes, including a stop at Newport
The BAY STATE was employed continuously up to 1864 when she was dismantled and her engine placed in the new steamboat OLD COLONY.

PUGET SOUND TOWBOAT GOLIAH.

GOLIAH:
BUILT 1849, at NEW YORK
HULL BY WM. H. WEBB
ENGINE BY T.F. SECOR

HULL, of wood Length 154 feet over all, breadth of beam 30 feet, over guards 51 feet, depth of hold 9¾ feet

ENGINE, vertical beam Diameter of cylinder 50 inches, by 8 feet stroke of piston Indicated horse power 250

BOILER, one of iron Original one remained in her until 1877, when it was replaced by one made in San Francisco, 14 feet in length and 15 feet diameter

TONNAGE 235 86 GROSS

Built for towing purposes on New York Bay and adjacent waters. Sold, and left New York for California on April 1, 1850, reaching San Francisco in January 1, 1851. Ran on the Sacramento river a short time, then lengthened 44 feet and rebuilt into a passenger boat, running down the coast to San Diego and as far north as Portland, Oregon, being at this time called AVENGER. She was again changed into a tugboat, the 44 feet being taken out, and was used as a water boat at San Francisco many years, by Goodall, Perkins & Co. Purchased in 1871 by the Puget Mill Co., at Port Gamble, Wash., and used since that date in towing ships and rafts of logs on Puget Sound

57

TRANSATLANTIC STEAMSHIP ARCTIC, 1849.

ARCTIC:

BUILT 1849, by WM. H. BROWN, AT NEW YORK.

HULL: Length of keel 277 feet; overall, 286 feet; breadth of beam 45 feet 8 inches; depth of hold, from main deck, 24 feet; from spar deck 32 feet. Tonnage 2772. Average draught of water 19 feet.

ENGINES: Two side-lever, designed and constructed by Stillman, Allen & Co. (Novelty Iron Works), New York; Diameter of cylinders 95 inches, 10 feet stroke.

PADDLE WHEELS: Diameter 35 feet 6 inches; length of buckets 12 feet 2 inches; depth of buckets 2 feet 2 inches; 36 buckets to each wheel; dip of wheel, 7 feet 5 inches; average number of revolutions 13¾, or, 14 lbs. steam pressure, cutting off at 4 feet, and burning 6615 pounds of bituminous coal.

BOILERS: Two, of iron (back to back), designed by John Faron. 21,160 square feet fire surface; 15,066 square feet tube surface.; 655 square feet grate surface.

THIS steamer belonged to the famous Collins Line of steamships between New York and Liverpool, and was one of the most magnificent of her day. She was built under the superintendence of George Steers and was launched January 28, 1849. In February, 1852, she made the passage from New York to Liverpool in 9 days, 17 hours and 12 minutes, which was the fastest on record up to that time.

The Arctic was sunk by collision with the French steamer Vesta, 40 miles off Cape Race, September 27, 1854, and 567 persons perished.

DELAWARE RIVER STEAMBOAT RICHARD STOCKTON, 1851.

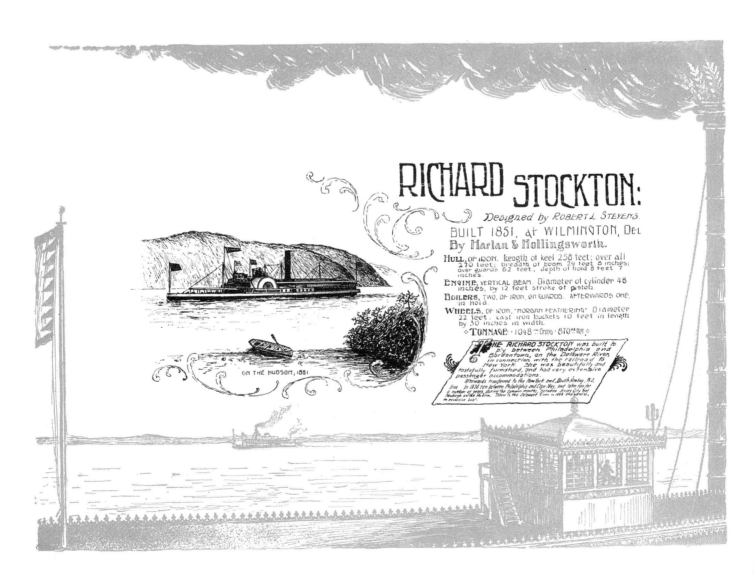

ATLANTIC COAST STEAMSHIP EL DORADO, 1851.

EL DORADO

BUILT 1851, at NEW YORK.

HULL, OF WOOD, BUILT BY THOMAS COLLYER.
Length on water line 225 feet, over all 235 feet,
breadth of beam 31 feet, depth of hold 23 feet

ENGINES, TWO, VERTICAL BEAM, CONSTRUCTED by
CUNNINGHAM, BELKNAP & CO., NEW YORK. Diameter of
cylinders 50 inches, by 10 feet stroke Average pressure
of steam 10 lbs cutting off at 5 feet

BOILERS, TWO, OF IRON, SINGLE RETURN FLUE, built
by CUNNINGHAM, BELKNAP & CO., Length 30 feet, height of front
10 feet, diameter 11 feet Steam pressure 20 lbs. to square inch,
Whole amount of fire surface 3838 square feet, whole amount of
grate surface 143 square feet, consumption of bituminous coal per hour
2600 pounds

WHEELS, 29 feet 4 inches in diameter; length of
buckets 8 feet 10 inches, width of buckets 2 feet, number of
buckets each wheel 30, average dip of wheels 5 feet

~ TONNAGE 1049¾ ~

BUILT for the New York and
Chagres (Isthmus of Panama)
route When first built it was
found necessary to add sponsons
to her sides, both forward and aft
of the wheels, in order that she might
maintain an upright position without
which 300 tons of Kentledge, for
ballast, was found insufficient to
secure vertical equilibrium

The EL DORADO was not a success, but being a spare boat was not
remodeled. Ran most of the time she
was in existence between Aspinwall, Havana and New Orleans
She was broken up and engines put
in new steamship MOSES TAYLOR

HUDSON RIVER STEAMBOAT FRANCIS SKIDDY, 1851.

THE FRANCIS SKIDDY AS A NIGHT BOAT

FRANCIS SKIDDY.

— BUILT 1851, at NEW YORK. —

HULL, of wood, by GEORGE COLLYER. Length over all 322 feet; width of hull 38 feet; depth of hold 10 feet 4 inches. Draft of water 5 feet 6 inches

ENGINE, vertical beam, by JAMES CUNNINGHAM & Co., (PHŒNIX Foundry), New York. Diameter of cylinder 70 inches, by 14 feet stroke

BOILERS, four, of iron, by JOHN F. RODMAN, New York. Each 24 feet in length, by 9 feet in diameter, allowed 70 lbs of steam. Total grate surface 208 square feet; total heating surface 5132 square feet; consumption of fuel (anthracite coal) 2000 lbs per hour. Blowing engine attached to each boiler 12 inch cylinder by 12 inch stroke.

WHEELS, by JOHN F. RODMAN. Each 40 feet in diameter. Twenty-eight buckets to each wheel, 11 feet in length by 36 inches wide.

— TONNAGE 1235 99/95 —

THE FRANCIS SKIDDY was one of the largest and finest steamboats that had ever been built for the Hudson River. When she was finished she was considered the acme of steamboat architecture; her model was one of the most beautiful and faultless ever constructed. Built for the day line between New York and Albany, speed was the requisite quality, and she regularly made the run, 146 miles, with 6 landings, in 7¾ hours.

Her cabins were spacious and sumptuously fitted up, being finished in mahogany and all the beauty for which the steamboats of that day were noted. The main cabin was in the hull exceeding its entire length, and the dining tables could seat 500 people.

She began trips in June, 1852, and for a time left New York every morning, and returning from Albany at night. A few years afterward she was greatly altered, being rebuilt as a night boat, and for a number of years ran between New York and Troy, the steamboats RIP VAN WINKLE, COMMODORE, HENDRICK HUDSON and C. VANDERBILT running at different periods with her. On the night of November 5, 1864, while coming down the river she ran ashore and sunk. The hull was broken up and the engine placed in the new steamboat DEAN RICHMOND.

ATLANTIC COAST STEAMSHIP MARION, 1851.

MARION.

— BUILT 1851, at NEW YORK —

HULL, OF WOOD, BUILT BY Jacob Bell. Length 198 feet 6 inches; breadth of beam 30 feet 10 inches; depth of hold 15 feet 5 inches.

ENGINE, SIDE LEVER, CONSTRUCTED BY Stillman, Allen & Co. (NOVELTY IRON WORKS), NEW YORK Diameter of cylinder 70 inches by 8 feet stroke.

BOILERS, TWO, OF IRON Each 24 feet long, by 11 feet in diameter.

— TONNAGE 900 62 —

THE MARION was built for Spofford & Tileston, for the route between New York and Savannah, Ga. She was a first-class steamship in every respect and was the fastest of the line Was afterwards placed on the line to Charleston On Sept. 5, 1854 she reached New York in 58 hours from Charleston, being quickest trip on record She was lost in April, 1863, having been used as a Confederate transport during the Civil War

ATLANTIC COAST STEAMSHIP ILLINOIS, 1851.

ILLINOIS:

BUILT 1851 at NEW YORK.

HULL, of wood, by Smith & Dimon. Dimensions: Length of keel, 255 feet; Length on deck, 267 feet 9 inches; Breadth of beam 40 feet 3 inches; Depth of hold, to main deck, 22 feet 6 inches; to spar deck, 31 feet.

TWO OSCILLATING ENGINES, constructed by the Allaire Works, New York. Diameter of cylinders 85 inches, stroke of pistons 9 feet. FOUR RETURN TUBULAR IRON BOILERS, each 12 feet in length by 13 feet in height. Whole amount of fire surface 12,052 square feet; whole amount of tube surface (tubes 3 inches bore) 8,396 square feet; whole amount of grate surface, 367 square feet.

PADDLE WHEELS: Diameter 33 feet 6 inches; Breadth 10 feet 6 inches; Length of buckets, 11 feet; 28 paddles to each wheel. — TONNAGE 2,100 tons —

THE ILLINOIS was launched in the Spring of 1851, under the name of Louisiana, but was purchased before she was finished, by George Law, who put her on the New York and Chagres (Isthmus of Panama) route. She plied on this line for a number of years, and was finally dismantled in 1862.

The maximum performance of this vessel, as taken from a log of her trip from New York to Chagres and back via Havana, in May, 1852, was as follows:- Average pressure of steam 17 pounds; average revolutions 11; average consumption of coal, 60 tons per day; average speed 11 miles per hour; maximum speed 13⅛ mils. Running time from Havana to New York 94½ hours, from dock to dock; distance run 1032 miles; greatest run per day (in Gulf Stream) 337 miles.

At another time the Illinois ran from Chagres to New York (distance estimated at 1980 miles) in 6 days and 16 hours, this being an average of nearly 12½ miles per hour the whole voyage.

NEW ENGLAND COAST STEAMBOAT EASTERN CITY, 1852.

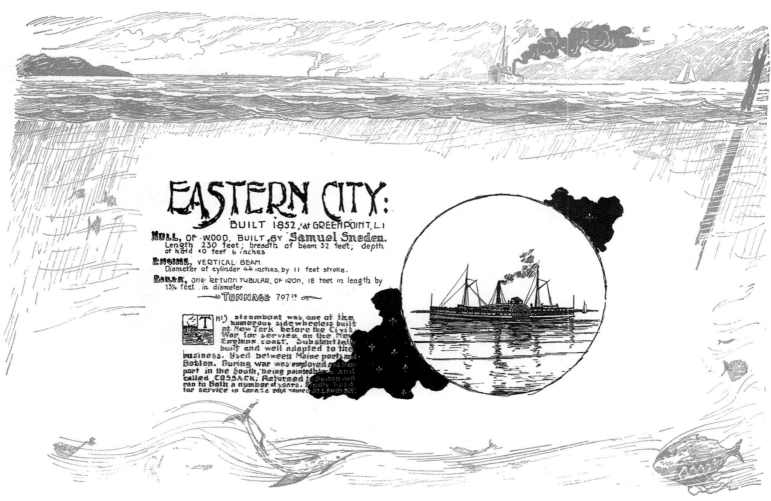

EASTERN CITY:
BUILT 1852, at GREENPOINT, L.I

HULL, OF WOOD, BUILT BY **Samuel Sneden**.
Length 230 feet; breadth of beam 32 feet; depth
of hold 10 feet 6 inches.

ENGINE, VERTICAL BEAM.
Diameter of cylinder 44 inches, by 11 feet stroke.

BOILER, ONE RETURN TUBULAR, OF IRON, 18 feet in length by
13½ feet in diameter

— TONNAGE 797 —

THIS steamboat was one of the numerous side wheelers built at New York before the Civil War for service on the New England coast. Substantially built and well adapted to the business. Used between Maine ports and Boston. During war was employed and took part in the South, being painted black and called COSSACK. Returned to Boston and ran to Bath a number of years. Finally sold for service in Canada and named ST LAWRENCE.

ATLANTIC COAST STEAMSHIP BLACK WARRIOR, 1852.

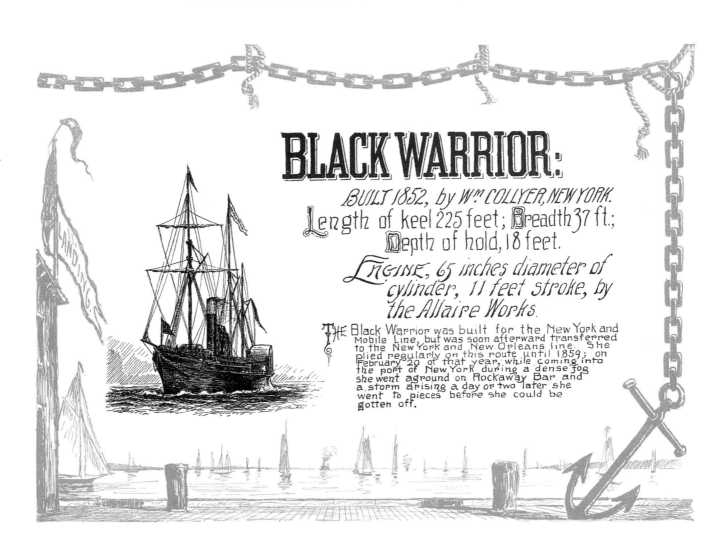

BLACK WARRIOR:

BUILT 1852, by W.ᵐ COLLYER, NEW YORK.
Length of keel 225 feet; Breadth 37 ft.;
Depth of hold, 18 feet.

Engine, 65 inches diameter of cylinder, 11 feet stroke, by the Allaire Works.

THE Black Warrior was built for the New York and Mobile Line, but was soon afterward transferred to the New York and New Orleans line. She plied regularly on this route until 1859; on February 20 of that year, while coming into the port of New York during a dense fog she went aground on Rockaway Bar and a storm arising a day or two later she went to pieces before she could be gotten off.

DELAWARE RIVER STEAMBOAT MAJOR REYBOLD, 1852

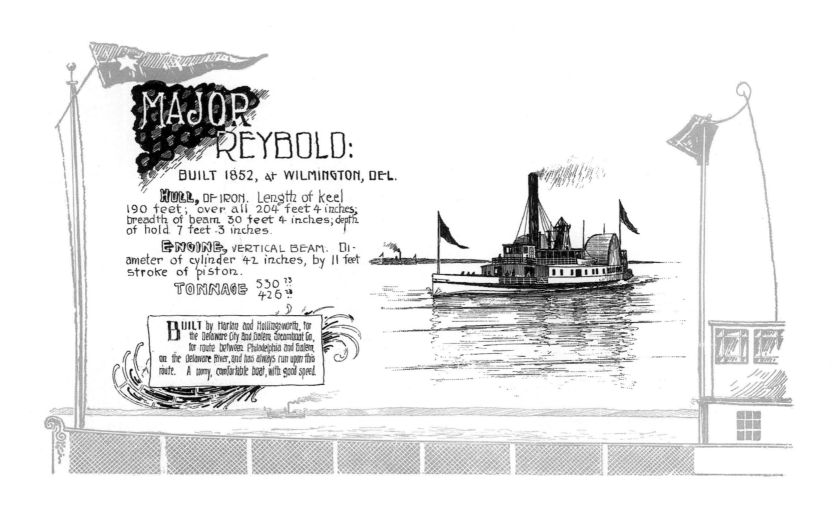

MAJOR REYBOLD:

BUILT 1852, at WILMINGTON, DEL.

HULL, OF IRON. Length of keel 190 feet; over all 204 feet 4 inches; breadth of beam 30 feet 4 inches; depth of hold 7 feet 3 inches.

ENGINE, VERTICAL BEAM. Diameter of cylinder 42 inches, by 11 feet stroke of piston.

TONNAGE 530 $\frac{73}{95}$
426 $\frac{89}{95}$

BUILT by Harlan and Hollingsworth, for the Delaware City and Salem Steamboat Co, for route between Philadelphia and Salem on the Delaware River, and has always run upon this route. A roomy, comfortable boat, with good speed.

UNITED STATES NAVAL STEAMER POWHATAN, 1852.

POWHATAN.

BUILT 1848-50 at
~ PORTSMOUTH, Virginia ~

ENGINES AND BOILERS DESIGNED BY Charles H. Haswell,
(at that time Engineer in Chief, United States Navy) and constructed by
MEHAFFY & CO, PORTSMOUTH, VA.

HULL, OF WOOD:—
LENGTH ON DECK .... 251 feet
BREADTH OF BEAM .... 45 "
DEPTH OF HOLD .... 26½ "
MAXIMUM DRAFT OF WATER .... 18¾ "

ENGINES, TWO, INCLINED:—
DIAMETER OF CYLINDERS ...... 70 inches
LENGTH OF STROKE .... 10 feet
HORSE POWER 1172

BOILERS, FOUR, OF COPPER (back to back):—
WHOLE AMOUNT OF FIRE SURFACE 7784 square feet
    "   "   GRATE "   353   "   "

WHEELS, RADIAL:—
DIAMETER (23 BUCKETS ON EACH WHEEL) ..... 31 feet
LENGTH OF BUCKETS .... 10 "
WIDTH OF BUCKETS, 14, 16 and .... 30 inches
AVERAGE DIP OF WHEEL .... 5½ feet

~ DISPLACEMENT 3980 tons ~
~ REGISTERED TONNAGE, 2182 ~

THE POWHATAN was one of the best
of the earlier war vessels of
the United States. She took
part in the Civil War and afterward remained
in service for many years

OHIO RIVER STEAMBOAT JACOB STRADER, 1853.

JACOB STRADER:

BUILT 1853, at CINCINNATI, Ohio.

THIS steamboat was built for the Ohio River route between Cincinnati and Louisville. She cost $200,000, and was the largest that had ever been built to run above the Falls of the Ohio. She had sleeping accommodations for 400 passengers, the cabins were richly furnished and all of her appointments were first class.

The JACOB STRADER had two engines, on the low pressure principle, each having cylinders 60 inches in diameter by 10 feet stroke of piston. The original boilers were two in number, built by Anthony Harkness, at Cincinnati, each 11 feet in diameter by 38 feet in length. In 1860 these were replaced by five cylindrical fire-flued boilers, each 38 feet in length, by 63 inches in diameter.

LAKE ERIE STEAMBOAT MISSISSIPPI, 1853.

MISSISSIPPI:
BUILT 1853
By F.W. & B.B. JONES, at BUFFALO, N.Y.

Length 335 feet; Beam 40 feet; Depth of hold 14 ft
Tonnage 1829
One Beam Engine, by J.P. Morris & Co, of Philadelphia, 82 inch cylinder by 12 ft stroke;
(Walking beam 12 feet wide by 24 feet long)
Three Boilers, each 50 feet long by 11 ft diameter.

THIS steamboat, during her day, was one of those floating palaces of Lake Erie, which became so widely known and popular with travelers on account of their luxurious appointments and great speed. She was built for the Buffalo and Sandusky line, and ran with the steamer St. Lawrence.

The Mississippi went out of commission in 1859 and after lying idle at Detroit until 1863 was dismantled, the hull being remodeled into a dry dock, portions of the cabins and joiner work transferred to the steamboat Racine, and the engine taken to New York and placed in the new steamship Guiding Star.

GREAT LAKES STEAMBOAT NORTH STAR, 1854.

North Star:

BUILT AT CLEVELAND, OHIO, 1854.

Length 274 feet; beam 33½ feet; hold 15½ feet; 1,106 tons.

The NORTH STAR was built for the Cleveland and Lake Superior Line, and was launched on May 20, 1854. She was considered one of the most beautiful boats of her class and was splendidly furnished throughout. She had a speed of between 16 and 17 miles an hour. She ran regularly each season between Cleveland, Detroit and the ports on Lake Superior. She was burned at her dock in Cleveland, February 21, 1862.

LONG ISLAND SOUND STEAMBOAT PLYMOUTH ROCK, 1854.

PLYMOUTH ROCK.

BUILT 1854, at NEW YORK

HULL, OF WOOD, BUILT BY JEREMIAH SIMONSON.
Length of keel 312 feet; over all 330 feet; breadth of beam 38 feet;
over guards 74 feet; depth of hold 12 feet.

ENGINE, VERTICAL BEAM, CONSTRUCTED BY THE ALLAIRE WORKS,
New York. Diameter of cylinder 76 inches; length of stroke 12 feet.

BOILERS, TWO, OF IRON, ON GUARDS, each 38 feet in length, by 12
feet 6 inches wide, and 11 feet 8 inches high.

WHEELS, 37 feet in diameter; 30 buckets to each wheel, 10 feet
in length and 2 feet 6 inches wide.

TONNAGE, Old Measurement, 1742 71/95

TONNAGE, New Measurement; 1810.16 gross; 1607.58 net tons.

A CELEBRATED STEAMBOAT, built for Commodore Vanderbilt, for the New York and Stonington route,
and when she began trips, October 17, 1854, was
the largest and most costly running on Long Island
Sound. She was a well-built vessel, luxuriously furnished and
of fine speed.   She ran on the Stonington Line for several years,
and then to Groton, Conn.   When this line was closed up the PLY-
MOUTH ROCK was sold, for $94,000, to the owners of the steamboats
BRISTOL and PROVIDENCE, to be used as a spare boat. She was then
very much strengthened and thoroughly overhauled, and ran to Bristol
a short time. When this line came into the hands of Fisk & Gould the PLY-
MOUTH ROCK was remodeled into an excursion boat, and over $100,000 spent
on her in fittings, etc. She plied between New York and Sandy Hook, 1870,
and afterward ran for many years on the Newburgh, Long Branch and
other routes. In 1885 she ran excursions out of Boston, and returned
to New York in 1886.   She was hauled out on Nutt Island, Boston Harbor,
and on the night of May 14, 1887, burned for her old metal.

CHESAPEAKE BAY STEAMBOAT LOUISIANA, 1854.

LOUISIANA:

BUILT 1854, at BALTIMORE, MD

HULL, of wood, built by COOPER & BUTLER. Length 266 feet, 2½ inches; breadth 36 feet, depth of hold 12 feet 2½ inches.

ENGINE, vertical beam, constructed by Chas. Reeder, of Baltimore. Diameter of cylinder 60 inches, by 11 feet stroke.

TONNAGE 1126 ⁹⁵⁄₉₅

THE LOUISIANA was built for the Baltimore Steam Packet Company, to run with the steamboat North Carolina on Chesapeake Bay, between Baltimore and Norfolk, and was a very substantial, handsome and splendidly equipped vessel.

On November 14, 1874, the Louisiana was sunk by collision with the steamship Falcon, off Smith Point, Chesapeake Bay. She was afterwards raised and the hull broken up. The engine and boiler were put in the new steamboat Carolina, in 1878.

NEW ENGLAND COAST STEAMBOAT DANIEL WEBSTER, 1854.

DANIEL WEBSTER.

BUILT 1854, at GREENPOINT, L.I.

HULL, OF WOOD, BUILT BY SAMUEL SNEDEN. Length 240 feet; breadth 34 feet; depth 11 feet. JOINER WORK by H. P. PERRY.

ENGINE, VERTICAL BEAM, CONSTRUCTED BY THE WEST POINT FOUNDRY. Diameter of cylinder 52 inches, by 11 feet stroke of piston.

BOILERS, TWO OF IRON. In 1871, one new boiler in hold, by STAPLES & SON, Portland, Me.

WHEELS, 33 feet in diameter.

— TONNAGE 910 —

The Daniel Webster was built for the Maine Steam Navigation Company, for the Boston and Bangor line, and was the finest boat that had ever run upon that route. She was strongly built and elegantly fitted out.

She was used during the War as a transport under the name of Expounder. She afterwards ran between Baltimore and West Point, Va.

In 1884 the Daniel Webster left Boston for the St. Lawrence River, and her name was changed to Saguenay.

73

LONG ISLAND SOUND STEAMBOAT COMMONWEALTH, 1854.

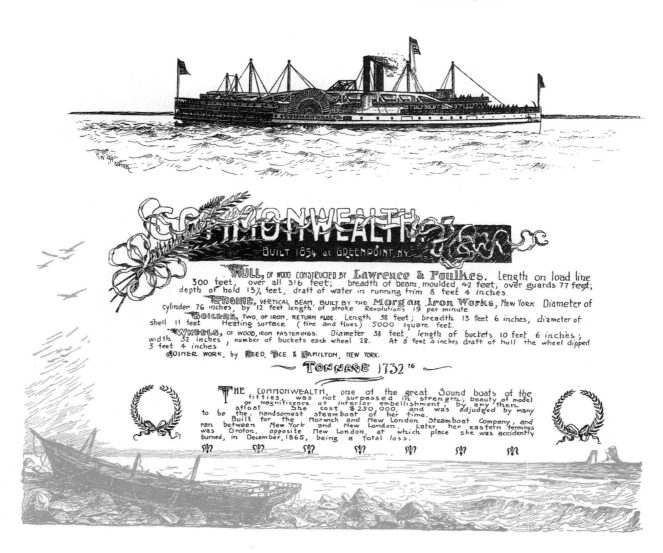

COMMONWEALTH
BUILT 1854 at GREENPOINT, NY

HULL, OF WOOD CONSTRUCTED BY Lawrence & Foulkes. Length on load line 300 feet, over all 316 feet; breadth of beam, moulded 42 feet; over guards 77 feet; depth of hold 13½ feet, draft of water in running frim 8 feet 4 inches.

ENGINE, VERTICAL BEAM, BUILT BY THE Morgan Iron Works, New York Diameter of cylinder 76 inches, by 12 feet length of stroke Revolutions 19 per minute

BOILERS, TWO, OF IRON, RETURN FLUE. Length 58 feet; breadth 13 feet 6 inches, diameter of shell 11 feet Heating surface (fire and flues) 5000 square feet.

WHEELS, OF WOOD, IRON FASTENINGS. Diameter 38 feet, length of buckets 10 feet 6 inches; width 32 inches, number of buckets each wheel 28. At 8 feet 4 inches draft of hull the wheel dipped 3 feet 4 inches

JOINER WORK, by REED, TICE & HAMILTON, NEW YORK.

TONNAGE 1732 ⁷⁶

THE COMMONWEALTH, one of the great Sound boats of the fifties, was not surpassed in strength, beauty of model or magnificence of interior embellishment, by any then afloat She cost $250,000, and was adjudged by many to be the handsomest steamboat of her time. Built for the Norwich and New London Steamboat Company, and ran between New York and New London. Later her eastern terminus was Groton, opposite New London, at which place she was accidently burned, in December, 1865, being a total loss.

LAKE ERIE STEAMBOAT WESTERN WORLD, 1854.

WESTERN WORLD

— BUILT 1854, at BUFFALO, N.Y —

HULL, OF WOOD, CONSTRUCTED BY **John Englis**, AT GREEN-POINT, (Long Island), N.Y., AND PUT TOGETHER IN SHIPYARD OF **Bidwell & Banta**, BUFFALO. Extreme length 348 feet, breadth of beam 45 feet, over guards 72½ feet; depth of hold 15 feet

ENGINE, VERTICAL BEAM, BUILT BY **Secor & Co.** (ALLAIRE WORKS), NEW YORK Diameter of cylinder 81 inches, length of piston stroke 12 feet Horse power 1500

BOILERS, THREE OF IRON, TUBULAR

WHEELS, EACH 38 FEET IN DIAMETER, Length of buckets 11 feet; breadth of buckets 22 inches

JOINER WORK, BY **L. & H. Crampton.**

— TONNAGE 2002.42 —

Two of the very finest sidewheel steamboats ever constructed for use on the Great Lakes were the WESTERN WORLD and PLYMOUTH ROCK. These vessels were duplicates and were built to run between Buffalo and Detroit, in connection with the New York Central and the Michigan Central Railroads. The WESTERN WORLD and her mate were constructed under the supervision of Isaac Newton, each costing $250,000. The WESTERN WORLD was launched on Tuesday, April 11, 1854, and arrived at Detroit on her first trip on July 7 of that year No expense was spared to make these boats as perfect as possible, and when finished they combined the strength of a sea-going steamer with the comfort and elegance of a river boat The hull timbers were diagonally braced with iron; the floors were solid and there were four water-tight compartments. The decoration of the saloons was rich and elegant, the joinery varying from light Gothic to the Ionic and Doric order of architecture There were handsome stained-glass domes and playing fountains; gorgeous satin and lace drapery and splendid mirrors, with furniture of rosewood The dining room seated 200 persons; the silver service was made to order and cost $15,000 for each boat

During the winter following their advent both boats had the position of the boilers altered, they being placed further forward, which served to increase their speed. On May 27, 1855, THE WESTERN WORLD arrived at Buffalo in 14 hours running time from Detroit; her sister ship, PLYMOUTH ROCK was even still faster These boats ran for a few years only, and were laid up at Detroit, where they remained idle a number of seasons. On June 28, 1863 the WESTERN WORLD was towed to Buffalo and here dismantled. Her engine was taken to New York and placed in the new steamer FIRE QUEEN.

LONG ISLAND SOUND STEAMBOAT METROPOLIS, 1854.

METROPOLIS:

BUILT 1854, at GREENPOINT, L.I.

HULL, OF WOOD, CONSTRUCTED BY SNEDEN & WHITLOCK. Length of keel 325 feet; over all 342 feet; width of hull 42 feet; over guards, 51 feet 2 inches; depth of hold 16 feet; average draft of water 10 feet 6 inches.

ENGINE, VERTICAL BEAM, BUILT BY STILLMAN, ALLEN & CO. (Novelty Iron Works), NEW YORK. Diameter of cylinder 105½ inches by 12 feet stroke of piston; average revolutions 15½ per minute.

BOILERS, FOUR, OF IRON, ON THE GUARDS, TWO ON EITHER SIDE, SET BACK TO BACK. Length of each 20 feet 8 inches; breadth of after boilers 13 feet 3 inches; height of after boilers 13 feet 3 inches; breadth of forward boilers 11 feet 3 inches; height of forward boilers 11 feet 3 inches. Total grate surface 294 square feet, total heating surface 12,000 square feet.

WHEELS, OF IRON, 41 feet in diameter; length of buckets 13 feet, width of buckets 2 feet 6 inches; dip, average load 5 feet.

TONNAGE 2210 ⁸⁄₉₅

THE METROPOLIS was one of the most celebrated of American steamboats, being of such size, in hull, engine and boilers, and of such advanced ideas in construction as to become almost world renowned immediately upon her launching, which occurred Thursday, April 20, 1854. For many years she was the largest of the Long Island Sound fleet. She was constructed on the plan of the ocean steamers of the period, the hull timbers being carried to the saloon deck, strongly braced and iron strapped diagonally, thus doing away with the hog frame. Her engine had the largest cylinder that had ever been cast, being at that time more than one-third larger than any other single marine engine in the world. She was capable of running at an average speed of 20 miles an hour. Her interior fittings and furnishings were of the most elegant description, there were sleeping accommodations for more than 600 persons.

She was built for the Fall River Line and ran very successfully many years. Her best time was made June 8, 1855, when she ran from New York to Fall River a distance of 175 miles, in 8 hours and 21 minutes. She was burned at Boston, for her iron, in 1879.

TRANSATLANTIC STEAMSHIP ARAGO, 1855.

ARAGO

BUILT 1855, at NEW YORK.

HULL, OF WOOD, BUILT BY JACOB A. WESTERVELT & SONS. Length on load-line 281 feet; length on deck 295 feet; beam 40 feet 8 inches, and 31 feet depth of hold.

ENGINES, TWO OSCILLATING, CONSTRUCTED BY STILLMAN, ALLEN & CO. (Novelty Iron Works), New York. Diameter of cylinders 65 inches; stroke 10 feet. PADDLE WHEELS of iron, 33 feet in diameter.

BOILERS, TWO IRON FLUE, ONE FORWARD AND THE OTHER AFT OF ENGINES, each affording 4000 square feet of fire and heating surface. Forward boiler 24 feet 3 inches in length, double return drop flues, two tiers of furnaces, grate bars 5 feet 6 inches, and 7 feet 6 inches long. After boiler 28 feet 5 inches long, single up return flues, two tiers furnaces, grates in each 6 feet 6 inches long. Surface of grate bars 650 square feet. Consumption of coal 45 tons per 24 hours.

→ TONNAGE 2260.

THE ARAGO was one of the finest ocean steamships in her day. She was built for the New York, Southampton and Havre line, to take the place of the wrecked steamship HUMBOLDT. Her fittings were of the very best, and she could comfortably accommodate 250 passengers. Her carrying capacity was 400 tons of cargo and 1400 tons of coal, on a draft of 17½ feet. She made her first trip across the Atlantic in June, 1855. Sold in 1860 to the Peruvian Government.

TRANSATLANTIC STEAMSHIP FULTON, 1855.

FULTON:

— BUILT 1855 at NEW YORK. —

WOODEN HULL, built by SMITH & DIMON, Length on deck 290 feet; breadth of beam 42 feet 4 inches (over guards 65 feet 6 inches); depth of hold 31 feet 6 inches   JOINER WORK, by ANDREW MILLS, New York
   ENGINES, two inclined oscillating, by the MORGAN IRON WORKS, New York   Diameter of cylinders 65 inches, length of stroke 10 feet   **BOILERS,** two, of iron, "Martin's Patent," with vertical brass tubes   Length 12 feet; width 30 feet height 14 feet; total amount of fire and heating surface 9,100 square feet, total amount of grate surface 343 square feet
   WHEELS, 31 feet in diameter; 28 buckets to each wheel, 9 feet in length and 18 inches in width   Tonnage 2,061 25

THE FULTON was built for the "New York and Havre Steamship Company." She was launched on September 4, 1855 and left New York for Southampton and Havre on her first trip February 9, 1856 Her interior joiner work was of satin, rose and zebra woods, and rich furnishings, paintings and gilt ornamentation went to make her a palatial vessel She could accommodate 300 passengers and 700 tons of freight on a draught of water of 17 feet 6 inches She was broken up in 1870

TRANSATLANTIC STEAMSHIP VANDERBILT, 1855.

VANDERBILT:

BUILT 1855, at NEW YORK

HULL, OF WOOD, BUILT BY **Jeremiah Simonson.** Length on deck 331 feet; breadth of beam 47½ feet, depth of hold 24½ feet - from spar deck 32½ feet.

ENGINES, TWO, VERTICAL BEAM, CONSTRUCTED BY THE **Allaire Works,** NEW YORK. Diameter of cylinders 90 inches, by 12 feet stroke.

BOILERS, FOUR, OF IRON, HORIZONTAL RETURN TUBULAR. Length of each 28½ feet, breadth 13 feet 11 inches; height 13½ feet, grate surface 600 square feet; heating surface 18,000 square feet, Steam pressure 18 lbs.

WHEELS, 41 feet in diameter, number of buckets each wheel 36, length of buckets 10 feet, width of buckets 24 inches.

TONNAGE 3,360 ^{59}

This famous steamship was built for Com. Vanderbilt to ply between New York, Southampton (England) and Havre (France). She was launched on December 10 1855, and was the largest and finest of her day. She ran for a number of years across the Atlantic, and during the Civil War was presented to the United States Government by Com Vanderbilt, and was used as a war vessel. After the war she was sold, in San Francisco, for $42,000, to Geo Howes & Co., who converted her into a sailing ship, in 1873, and named her THREE BROTHERS. She was used in the New York and California, and Liverpool trade, making some of the quickest voyages on record.

LAKE ERIE STEAMBOAT WESTERN METROPOLIS, 1856.

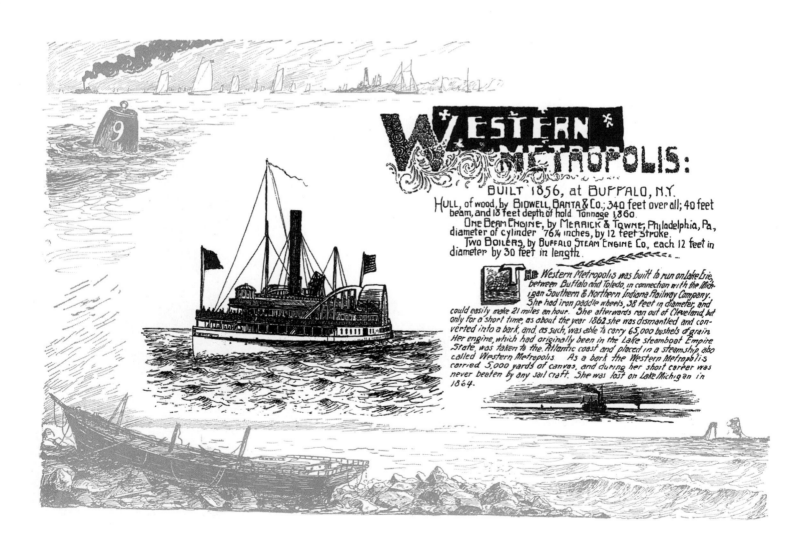

WESTERN METROPOLIS:

BUILT 1856, at BUFFALO, N.Y.

HULL, of wood, by BIDWELL, BANTA & Co.; 340 feet over all; 40 feet beam, and 18 feet depth of hold. Tonnage 1,860.

One BEAM ENGINE, by MERRICK & TOWNE, Philadelphia, Pa., diameter of cylinder 76¼ inches, by 12 feet stroke.

Two BOILERS, by Buffalo Steam Engine Co, each 12 feet in diameter by 30 feet in length.

THE Western Metropolis was built to run on Lake Erie, between Buffalo and Toledo, in connection with the Michigan Southern & Northern Indiana Railway Company. She had iron paddle wheels, 38 feet in diameter, and could easily make 21 miles an hour. She afterwards ran out of Cleveland, but only for a short time, as about the year 1862 she was dismantled and converted into a bark, and, as such, was able to carry 65,000 bushels of grain. Her engine, which had originally been in the Lake steamboat Empire State, was taken to the Atlantic coast and placed in a steamship also called Western Metropolis. As a bark the Western Metropolis carried 5,000 yards of canvas, and during her short career was never beaten by any sail craft. She was lost on Lake Michigan in 1864.

MISSISSIPPI RIVER STEAMBOAT PACIFIC, 1857.

PACIFIC.

BUILT 1857, at NEW ALBANY, IND.

HULL, OF WOOD. Length 290 feet; breadth of beam 40 feet; depth of hold 8 feet.

ENGINES, TWO, HIGH PRESSURE. Diameter of cylinders 28 inches; length of stroke 9 feet

BOILERS, SIX, OF IRON; Diameter of each 40 inches; length 28 feet. Working pressure 135 lbs. steam to sq. inch

The PACIFIC was one of the finest and fastest Western River steamboats of her day. She was built for the Louisville and New Orleans line, and was owned by J. Bragdon & Co. Her model was a fine one and the cabins were richly furnished, the style of finish being of the semi-Gothic and Corinthian order of architecture.

LAKE MICHIGAN SIDEWHEEL STEAMSHIP MILWAUKEE, 1859.

MILWAUKEE.

BUILT 1859, at BUFFALO, N.Y.
HULL, 247 feet in length, 34 feet beam; 17 feet
depth of hold. 1100 tons.
ONE BEAM ENGINE, built by the SHEPARD IRON WORKS
of BUFFALO, N.Y., 60 inches diameter of cylinder by 12 feet
stroke, and of 1050 horse power.

The MILWAUKEE and her mate the Detroit, were
constructed by Mason & Bidwell, at Buffalo,
and employed as passenger boats on Lake Michigan,
running between Milwaukee and Grand Haven. They were designed by H. O. Perry, and were the only ocean style sidewheel
steamships ever put afloat upon the Great Lakes.
The Milwaukee ran successfully until 1868. On the
9th of October, that year while attempting to enter the
harbor at Grand Haven during a gale of wind, struck on
the bar, and becoming unmanageable, was forced toward
the beach, where she grounded, half a mile from shore, and
lay exposed to the fury of the storm. She soon after parted
amidships, the forward half going to pieces. All on board
were saved.

ATLANTIC COAST STEAMSHIP S. R. SPAULDING, 1859.

SAN SALVADOR:
FORMERLY "S·R·SPAULDING."

BUILT 1859, at WILMINGTON, DEL
By HARLAN & HOLLINGSWORTH & COMPANY

HULL, OF IRON. Length over all 210 feet; breadth of beam 33 feet;
depth of hold 15 feet 6 inches; from spar deck 23 feet 4¼ inches;
draft of water at load line 12 feet.

ENGINE, VERTICAL BEAM. Diameter of cylinder 56 inches by
11 feet stroke of piston.

BOILER, OF IRON, RETURN TUBULAR. Length 16 feet; breadth 16 feet
6 inches; heating surface (fire and flue) 3222 square feet.

WHEELS, diameter 30 feet; number of buckets each wheel 26; length
of buckets 7¼ feet; width of buckets 19 inches.

~ TONNAGE 1100 ~

THE S. R. SPAULDING was built for
the Merchants and Miners' Transportation Company, for route between Baltimore and Boston,
and was a well-built and comfortable boat in her day. She was used as
a transport during the Civil War. Afterwards had name changed to SAN SALVADOR
and ran as a cattle boat in the West Indies.

JOHN A. WARNER:

BUILT, 1857, at WILMINGTON, Delaware.

CONSTRUCTED BY MESSRS. HARLAN & HOLLINGSWORTH.

HULL, OF IRON. Length over all 220 feet, breadth of beam 27 feet 9 inches, over guards 53 feet, depth of hold 9 feet. Hull rebuilt 1876.

ENGINE, VERTICAL BEAM. Diameter of cylinder 44 inches, length of stroke 11 feet; nominal horse power 200.

BOILER, OF IRON, Width 168 inches; length 16½ feet.

WHEELS, 30 feet in diameter, 26 buckets each wheel, length of buckets 8 feet, width of buckets 2 feet; average dip of wheel 3 feet 9 inches.

TONNAGE—592⁴⁷ GROSS — 520⁷⁰ NET

OWNED by the "Upper Delaware River Transportation Co." has been employed as a passenger and excursion boat on the Delaware River since built. Of large carrying capacity and good speed.

HENRY E. BISHOP: *Formerly JOSEPHINE.*

BUILT 1852, at NEW YORK.

HULL, OF WOOD, BUILT BY Lawrence & Foulkes. Length between perpendiculars 200 feet, breadth of beam 30½ feet, depth of hold 9 feet 7 inches.

ENGINE, VERTICAL BEAM, CONSTRUCTED BY THE Morgan Iron Works, NEW YORK. Diameter of cylinder 40½ inches, by 14 feet stroke.

TONNAGE 631⁴⁷ GROSS 508⁷² NET

This steamboat was built for George Law, and was launched on September 11, 1852. For over 30 years she was employed as a passenger boat on various routes around the port of New York. Afterwards sold to run between Philadelphia and Lincoln Park, on the Delaware River.

EDWIN FORREST:

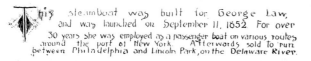

BUILT 1865 at CHESTER, PA.

HULL, OF IRON, CONSTRUCTED BY REANY, SON & ARCHBOLD. Length 196 feet 9 inches; breadth of beam 27 feet 9 inches; depth of hold 7 feet 7 inches.

ENGINE, VERTICAL BEAM, FROM OLD STEAMBOAT EDWIN FORREST, REBUILT BY REANY, SON & ARCHBOLD, CHESTER, PA., 1865. Diameter of cylinder 34 inches, by 12 feet stroke; nominal horse power 109.

BOILER, ONE, BY THE I. P. MORRIS CO., PHILADELPHIA, 1872. Length 15 feet, diameter 156 inches.

JOINER WORK, by WAPLES & WHEATON, PHILADELPHIA.

TONNAGE, 607⁰¹ Gross, 502⁹⁵ Net

THIS steamboat succeeded the old Edwin Forrest, receiving from that boat her engine, much of the joiner work, etc.

Route: Upper Delaware River, from Philadelphia to Trenton.

FLORENCE:

FORMERLY "SILVER STAR."

BUILT 1864, at EAST HADDAM, CONN.

HULL, OF WOOD, BUILT BY O. E. & W. H. GOODSPEED. Length between perpendiculars 120 feet 6 inches; over all 128 feet; breadth of beam 22 feet; depth of hold 8 feet.

ENGINE, VERTICAL BEAM, CONSTRUCTED BY FLETCHER, HARRISON & CO., NEW YORK. Diameter of cylinder 32 ins., by 8 feet stroke of piston.

BOILER, ONE, OF IRON, BUILT 1883, BY THE HARLAN & HOLLINGSWORTH CO., WILMINGTON, DEL. Diameter 9½ inches; length 14 feet.

TONNAGE 245⁸⁵ Gross; 155⁴⁰ Net.

BUILT for service on the Connecticut River. Sold 1883 to George F. Tyler, name changed to "Florence," and placed on the Delaware River route between Philadelphia and Bordentown.

MISSISSIPPI RIVER STEAMBOAT PEYTONA, 1859.

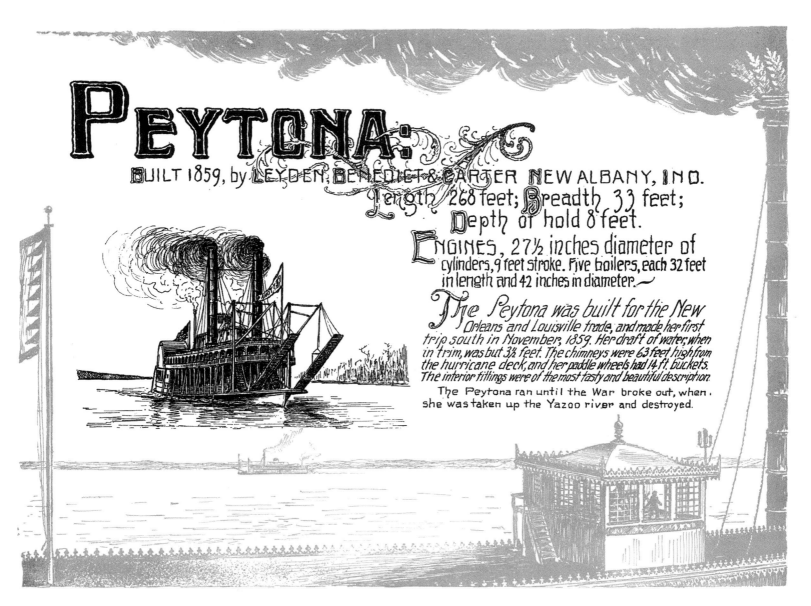

PEYTONA:

BUILT 1859, by LEYDEN, BENEDICT & CARTER NEW ALBANY, IND.
Length 268 feet; Breadth 33 feet;
Depth of hold 8 feet.

ENGINES, 27½ inches diameter of cylinders, 9 feet stroke. Five boilers, each 32 feet in length and 42 inches in diameter.

The Peytona was built for the New Orleans and Louisville trade, and made her first trip south in November, 1859. Her draft of water, when in trim, was but 3½ feet. The chimneys were 63 feet high from the hurricane deck, and her paddle wheels had 14 ft. buckets. The interior fittings were of the most tasty and beautiful description.

The Peytona ran until the War broke out, when she was taken up the Yazoo river and destroyed.

HUDSON RIVER STEAMBOAT JAMES W. BALDWIN.

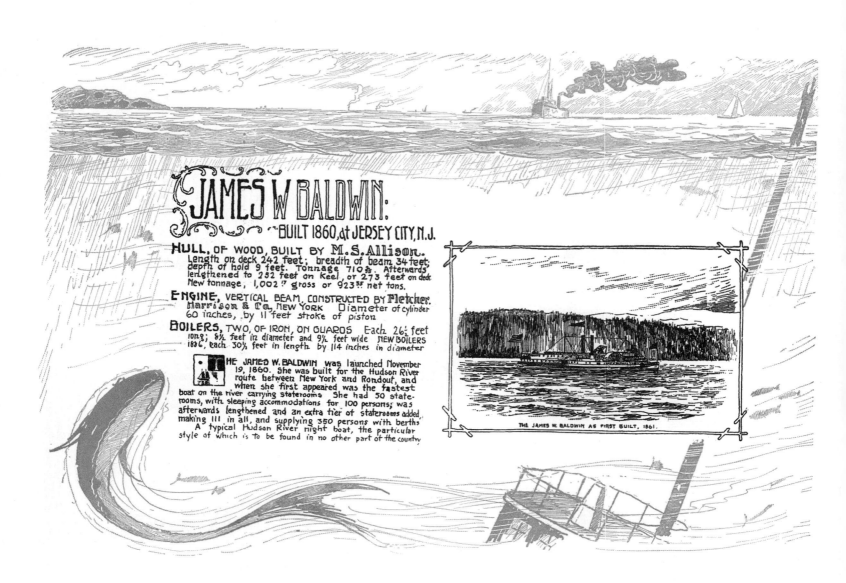

JAMES W BALDWIN.
BUILT 1860, at JERSEY CITY, N.J.

HULL, OF WOOD, BUILT BY **M.S. Allison.**
Length on deck 242 feet; breadth of beam 34 feet:
depth of hold 9 feet. Tonnage 710. Afterwards
lengthened to 252 feet on keel, or 273 feet on deck.
New tonnage, 1,002 gross or 923 net tons.

ENGINE, VERTICAL BEAM, CONSTRUCTED BY **Fletcher.**
Harrison & Co, New York Diameter of cylinder
60 inches, by 11 feet stroke of piston

BOILERS, TWO, OF IRON, ON GUARDS Each 26½ feet
long; 8½ feet in diameter and 9½ feet wide NEW BOILERS
1886, each 30½ feet in length by 114 inches in diameter

THE JAMES W. BALDWIN was launched November
19, 1860. She was built for the Hudson River
route between New York and Rondout, and
when she first appeared was the fastest
boat on the river carrying staterooms She had 50 staterooms, with sleeping accommodations for 100 persons; was
afterwards lengthened and an extra tier of staterooms added,
making 111 in all, and supplying 350 persons with berths
A typical Hudson River night boat, the particular
style of which is to be found in no other part of the country

THE JAMES W. BALDWIN AS FIRST BUILT, 1861.

UNITED STATES WAR VESSEL KEARSARGE.

Kearsarge

BUILT 1861, at KITTERY, Maine

HULL, of wood, 1550 tons displacement, built by the United States Government. Length between perpendiculars 198½ feet, extreme breadth 52 feet, mean draught 15¾ feet —

ENGINES, HORIZONTAL TWO CYLINDER BUILT BY WOODRUFF & BEACH, HARTFORD. Diameter of cylinders, by 18 inches stroke —

BOILERS, TWO, TUBULAR, with 88 square feet of grate surface and 2700 square feet of heating surface —

— TONNAGE 695 —

The KEARSARGE was built by the United States Government for use during the Civil War. She was launched on September 11, 1861 and was completed January 18, 1862, her entire cost being $272,514.00

Her greatest service was the sinking of the Confederate cruiser ALABAMA, with which she had an encounter, off Cherbourg, France on June 19, 1864

After the close of the War she continued in use as a war steamer, and while there were changes made in her from time to time, she remained practically the same vessel up to the year she was lost. On February 2, 1894, she ran on Roncador Reef, in the Caribbean Sea, and became a total loss

THE KEARSARGE AS FIRST RIGGED

LONG ISLAND SOUND STEAMBOAT CITY OF NEW YORK, 1861.

City of New York:

Designed by CHARLES W. COPELAND.

BUILT 1861, at GREENPOINT, L.I.

HULL, OF WOOD, CONSTRUCTED BY **Sneden & Rowland.** Length on load water-line 300 feet; breadth of beam 40 feet; depth of hold 12½ feet; average draft of water 8 feet 3 inches.

ENGINE, VERTICAL BEAM, BUILT BY THE **Novelty Iron Works,** New York. Diameter of cylinder 80 inches, by 12 feet stroke of piston. Indicated horse power 1800. Maximum revolutions 19¾ per minute.

BOILERS, TWO, OF IRON, ON GUARDS, BUILT BY NOVELTY IRON WORKS. Grate surface 192 square feet; heating surface 8920 square feet.

WHEELS, 37 feet 8 inches in diameter.

TONNAGE 1591 $\frac{??}{100}$ Gross; 1467 $\frac{??}{100}$ Net

"REMARKABLE specimens of American architecture" is what the CITY OF NEW YORK and CITY OF BOSTON (sister ships) are called in the great English work "The Modern System of Naval Architecture," by J. Scott Russell, F.R.S.
Built for the Norwich & New York Transportation Company, to run between New York and New London. Acknowledged to be the finest vessels of their class on Long Island Sound, the perfection of the old style large sidewheel steamboat for night traffic, being very speedy, having comfortable passenger accommodations, large freight capacity, economical in coal consumption, as well as handsome boats. Saloons elegantly fitted up. Hulls built of white oak throughout, with frames strapped with diagonal and double laid iron braces. The fastest trip of the CITY OF NEW YORK between New York and New London was 6 hours and 5 minutes, — distance 120 miles.

MISSISSIPPI RIVER IRON CLAD GUNBOAT CARONDELET, 1861.

CARONDELET:

BUILT 1861, at CARONDELET, MO.

HULL, OF WOOD, plated with iron [DESIGNED BY JOHN LENTHALL, CHIEF OF THE BUREAU OF CONSTRUCTION OF THE NAVY], built by CAPTAIN JAMES B. EADS Length 175 feet; breadth of beam 51½ feet; depth of hold (from top of floor to top of gun deck beams) 6 feet; draft of water 5 feet.

ENGINES, TWO, HORIZONTAL NON-CONDENSING (FROM SPECIFICATIONS BY THOMAS MERRITT, CINCINNATI, OHIO). Diameter of cylinder of each 22 inches, by 6 feet length of stroke

BOILERS, FIVE, each 36 inches in diameter and 24 feet in length, with 7½ inch flues.

WHEEL, RADIAL, 22 feet in diameter.

TONNAGE 512

THE CARONDELET was a type of Mississippi River gunboat used during the Civil War, performing excellent service. She was built by Capt. James B. Eads, and mounted 13 guns The sides were inclined at an angle of 35 degrees and were iron plated She was sold November 30, 1865, for $3,600

HUDSON RIVER STEAMBOAT MARY POWELL.

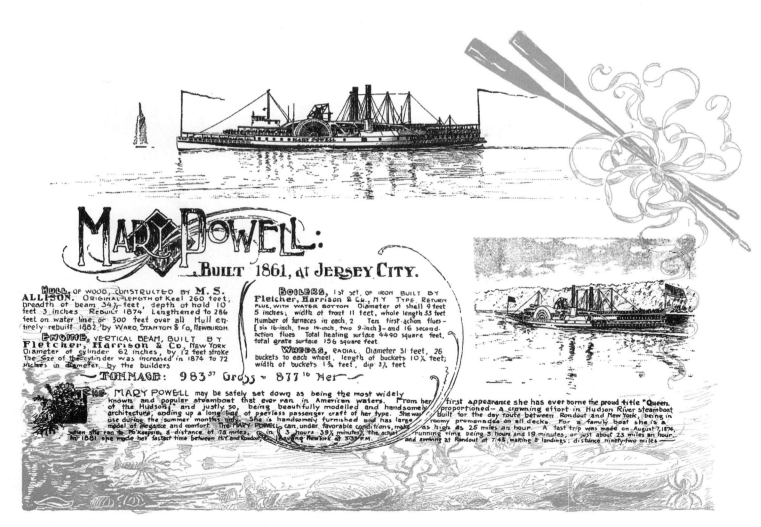

MARY POWELL:

BUILT 1861, at JERSEY CITY.

HULL, OF WOOD, CONSTRUCTED BY **M. S. ALLISON.** ORIGINAL LENGTH OF KEEL 260 feet, breadth of beam 34½ feet, depth of hold 10 feet 3 inches. REBUILT 1874. Lengthened to 286 feet on water line, or 300 feet over all. Hull entirely rebuilt 1882, by WARD, STANTON & Co. NEWBURGH.

ENGINE, VERTICAL BEAM, BUILT BY **Fletcher, Harrison & Co**, NEW YORK. Diameter of cylinder 62 inches, by 12 feet stroke. The Size of the cylinder was increased in 1874 to 72 inches in diameter by the builders.

BOILERS, 1st Set, OF IRON BUILT BY Fletcher, Harrison & Co., N Y TYPE RETURN FLUE, WITH WATER BOTTOM. Diameter of shell 9 feet 5 inches; width of front 11 feet, whole length 33 feet. Number of furnaces in each, 2. Ten first-action flues (six 16-inch, two 14-inch, two 9-inch) - and 16 second-action flues. Total heating surface 4490 square feet, total grate surface 156 square feet.

WHEELS, RADIAL. Diameter 31 feet. 26 buckets to each wheel, length of buckets 10¾ feet; width of buckets 1¾ feet, dip 3½ feet.

TONNAGE: 983⁵⁷ Gross - 877¹⁶ Net

THE MARY POWELL may be safely set down as being the most widely known and popular steamboat that ever ran in American waters. From her first appearance she has ever borne the proud title "Queen of the Hudson" and justly so, being beautifully modelled and handsomely proportioned — a crowning effort in Hudson River steamboat architecture, ending up a long line of peerless passenger craft of her type. She was built for the day route between Rondout and New York, being in use during the summer months only. She is handsomely furnished and has large, roomy promenades on all decks. For a family boat she is a model of elegance and comfort. The MARY POWELL can, under favorable conditions, make as high as 25 miles an hour. A fast trip was made on August 7, 1874, when she ran to Po'Keepsie, a distance of 75 miles, in 3 hours 39½ minutes, the actual running time being 3 hours and 19 minutes, or just about 23 miles an hour. In 1861 she made her fastest time between N.Y. and Rondout, leaving New York at 3:35 P.M. and arriving at Rondout at 7:45, making 8 landings; distance ninety-two miles —

GREAT LAKES PASSENGER PROPELLER BADGER STATE, 1862.

BADGER STATE:

BUILT 1862, AT BUFFALO, N.Y.

HULL, OF WOOD, BUILT BY MASON & BIDWELL. Length 213 feet; beam 33 feet, depth of hold 12 feet

ENGINE, ORIGINALLY "SINGLE", CONSTRUCTED BY SHEPARD IRON WORKS, BUFFALO. Diameter of cylinder 44 inches (afterwards changed to "STEEPLE COMPOUND, with cylinders 25¼ and 54 inches in diameter), by 42 inches stroke.

BOILER, OF IRON, BUILT BY SHEPARD IRON WORKS. Diameter 12 feet; length 20 feet; working pressure 51 lbs steam to square inch.

—— TONNAGE - 1,115 ⁵² GROSS - 917 ⁰³ NET ——

BUILT for the Peoples Line of passenger propellers running between Buffalo and Chicago. A well-built and comfortably furnished boat of the typical style of passenger propellers of her time. Afterwards used as a passenger boat in the Lake Superior Transit Co's line between Buffalo and Duluth.

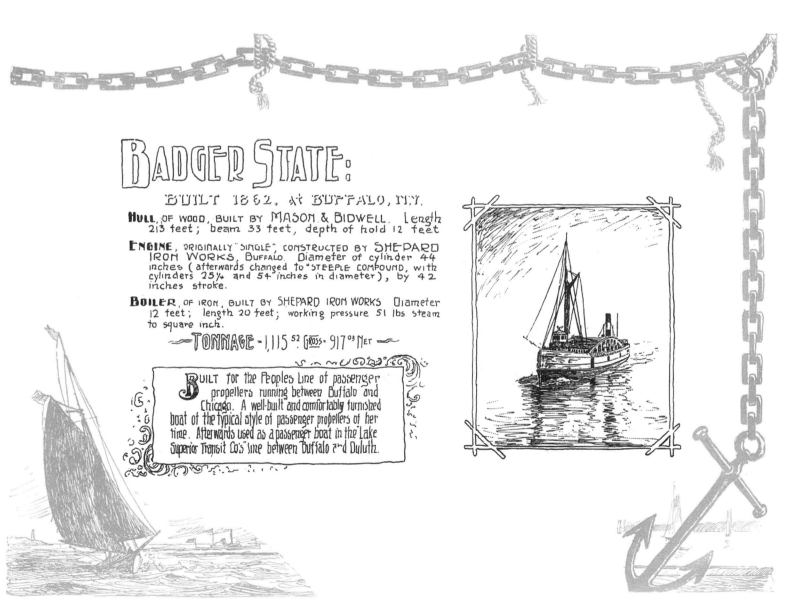

ENGAGEMENT BETWEEN MONITOR AND MERRIMAC, MARCH 9TH, 1862.

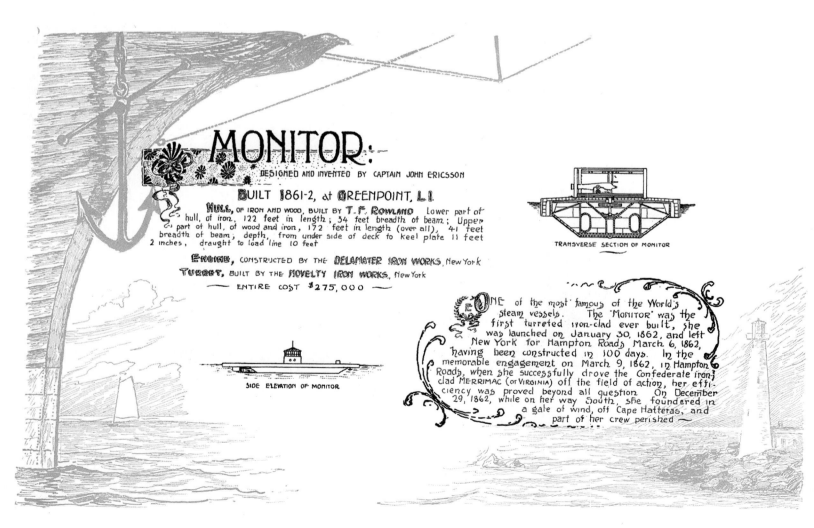

MONITOR:

DESIGNED AND INVENTED BY CAPTAIN JOHN ERICSSON

BUILT 1861-2, at GREENPOINT, L.I.

HULL, OF IRON AND WOOD, BUILT BY T.F. ROWLAND Lower part of hull, of iron, 122 feet in length; 34 feet breadth of beam; Upper part of hull, of wood and iron, 172 feet in length (over all), 41 feet breadth of beam; depth, from under side of deck to keel plate 11 feet 2 inches; draught to load line 10 feet

ENGINE, CONSTRUCTED BY THE DELAMATER IRON WORKS, New York

TURRET, BUILT BY THE NOVELTY IRON WORKS, New York

— ENTIRE COST $275,000 —

TRANSVERSE SECTION OF MONITOR

SIDE ELEVATION OF MONITOR

ONE of the most famous of the World's steam vessels. The "Monitor" was the first turreted iron-clad ever built, she was launched on January 30, 1862, and left New York for Hampton Roads March 6, 1862, having been constructed in 100 days. In the memorable engagement on March 9, 1862, in Hampton Roads, when she successfully drove the Confederate iron-clad MERRIMAC (or VIRGINIA) off the field of action, her efficiency was proved beyond all question. On December 29, 1862, while on her way South, she foundered in a gale of wind, off Cape Hatteras, and part of her crew perished —

GREAT LAKES PROPELLER MERCHANT, 1862.

PIONEER IRON LAKE PROPELLER.

MERCHANT.

BUILT 1862, at BUFFALO, N.Y.
By DAVID BELL.

HULL, OF IRON. Length of keel 192 feet; over all 200 feet; breadth of beam 29 feet; depth of hold 14 feet; average draft of water 12 feet. The hull was afterwards lengthened 30 feet.

ENGINE, SINGLE CYLINDER, CONDENSING. Diameter of cylinder 40 inches by 36 inches stroke. Indicated horse power 600.

BOILER, ONE, OF IRON, RETURN FLUE. Total grate surface 60 square feet; total heating surface 1800 square feet.

WHEEL, 4 BLADES. 10 feet in diameter and 14 feet pitch.

JOINER WORK, by HITCHCOCK & GIBSON.

~ TONNAGE 861 [15] ~

THE first iron propeller on the Great Lakes. Built for J. C. & E. T. Evans, for the Buffalo and Chicago passenger and freight business, and she ran between these two points very successfully thirteen seasons. Cost $90,000. Speed 14 miles per hour.

On October 6, 1875, the MERCHANT ran onto Racine Reef, Lake Michigan, and became a total loss.

93

CHESAPEAKE BAY EXCURSION STEAMBOAT LOUISE.

LOUISE.
BUILT 1863 at WILMINGTON, Del.

HULL, OF IRON; 231 feet 6 inches in length; 33 feet breadth of beam, 10 feet depth of hold.

ENGINE, VERTICAL BEAM. Diameter of cylinder 50 inches; length of stroke 11 feet; horse power 1280.

BOILER, ONE, OF IRON, 21 feet in length, by 16 feet in diameter. Working pressure 30 lbs.

TONNAGE GROSS 1023 ½
NET 718 ⁶⁵

The LOUISE was built by Harlan & Hollingsworth & Company for Charles Morgan, for the New Orleans and Mobile route. In 1874 she was purchased by the York River Line, and placed on the route between Baltimore and West Point, Va. In 1891 she began running as an excursion boat between Baltimore and Tolchester Beach.

HUDSON RIVER STEAMBOAT ST. JOHN, 1863.

ST. JOHN:

BUILT 1863, at GREENPOINT, L.I.
— TONNAGE, 2645 10 GROSS, 2443 73 NET —

HULL, OF WOOD, BUILT BY JOHN ENGLIS. Length of keel 393 feet, overall 417 feet; breadth of beam 51 feet, over guards 84 feet; depth of hold 10 feet

ENGINE, VERTICAL BEAM, BUILT by T. F. SECOR & CO., N.Y., 1848, and first used in steamboat NEW WORLD. Diameter of cylinder 76 inches, by 15 feet stroke.

WHEELS, RADIAL. Diameter 48 feet; number of buckets on each wheel 30; length of buckets 10½ feet; width 32 inches.

The ST JOHN was one of the fleet of mammoth and palatial steamboats of the river Hudson, belonging to the People's Line; she cost $600,000, and ran each season after being built between New York and Albany until 1884. She was the longest steamboat that ever ran on the river, had extensive passenger accommodations, and was magnificently fitted up.

At 2 a.m., Friday, January 24, 1885, she caught fire while lying at her wharf, foot of Canal St., N.Y., and was burned. At the time of her loss she was valued at $475,000.

PACIFIC OCEAN STEAMSHIP GOLDEN CITY, 1863.

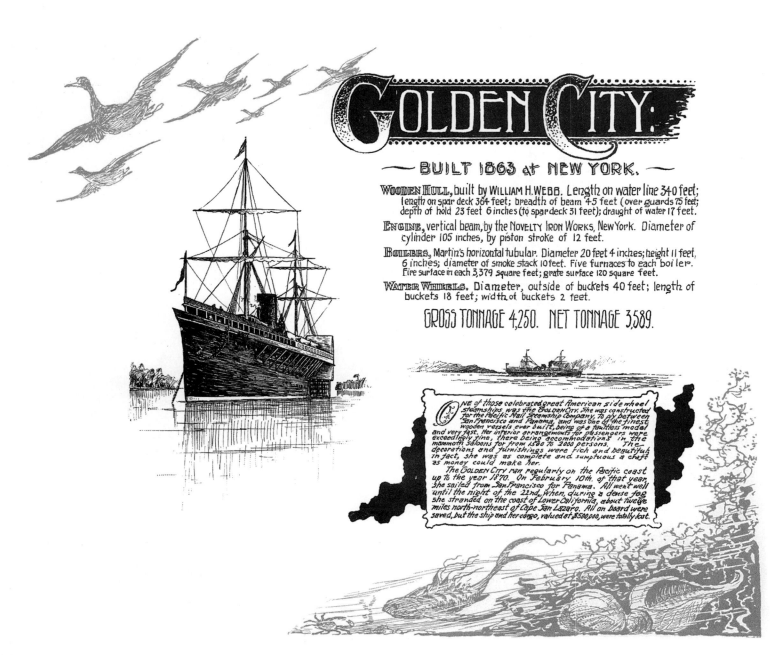

GOLDEN CITY:

— BUILT 1863 at NEW YORK. —

WOODEN HULL, built by WILLIAM H. WEBB. Length on water line 340 feet; length on spar deck 364 feet; breadth of beam 45 feet (over guards 75 feet; depth of hold 23 feet 6 inches (to spar deck 31 feet); draught of water 17 feet.

ENGINE, vertical beam, by the NOVELTY IRON WORKS, New York. Diameter of cylinder 105 inches, by piston stroke of 12 feet.

BOILERS, Martin's horizontal tubular. Diameter 20 feet 4 inches; height 11 feet, 6 inches; diameter of smoke stack 10 feet. Five furnaces to each boiler. Fire surface in each 3,379 square feet; grate surface 120 square feet.

WATER WHEELS. Diameter, outside of buckets 40 feet; length of buckets 18 feet; width of buckets 2 feet.

GROSS TONNAGE 4,250. NET TONNAGE 3,589.

ONE of those celebrated great American side wheel steamships was the GOLDEN CITY. She was constructed for the Pacific Mail Steamship Company, to ply between San Francisco and Panama, and was one of the finest wooden vessels ever built, being of a faultless model and very fast. Her interior arrangements for passengers were exceedingly fine, there being accommodations in the mammoth saloons for from 1500 to 2000 persons. The decorations and furnishings were rich and beautiful; in fact, she was as complete and sumptuous a craft as money could make her.

The GOLDEN CITY ran regularly on the Pacific coast up to the year 1870. On February 10th of that year, she sailed from San Francisco for Panama. All went well until the night of the 22nd, when, during a dense fog, she stranded on the coast of Lower California, about twelve miles north-northeast of Cape San Lazaro. All on board were saved, but the ship and her cargo, valued at $500,000, were totally lost.

HUDSON RIVER STEAMBOAT BERKSHIRE, 1864.

BERKSHIRE:
BUILT 1863-4, at ATHENS, N.Y

HULL, OF WOOD, CONSTRUCTED BY MORTON & EDMONDS.
Length of keel 250 feet, over all 263 feet ; breadth of hull 37
feet ; depth of hold 10 feet ; draft of water 6½ feet

ENGINE, VERTICAL BEAM, ORIGINALLY IN STEAMBOAT SOUTH AMERICA;
REBUILT BY FLETCHER, HARRISON & CO., NEW YORK Diameter of
cylinder 54 inches, by piston stroke of 11 feet.

BOILERS, FOUR, OF IRON, RETURN TUBULAR. TWO BY
COBANKS & THEALL, and TWO BY SLATER & O'HARA,
New York Diameter of shell of each 7 feet; width of
front 7 feet ; length 17 feet 4 inches Total grate surface
152 square feet, total heating surface 4820 square feet.

WHEELS, 30 feet in diameter ; number of buckets each
wheel 26, length of buckets 9 feet ; width of buckets
24 inches ; dipping 36 inches.
~ JOINER WORK by JOHN BROWN, N.Y. ~

The BERKSHIRE was built for the route between
New York and Hudson, being owned by George H. Power and
others. She was a well built and comfortably furnished
boat, designed for night service. Her speed was 18 miles
per hour.
On June 8, 1864 the BERKSHIRE was burned on
the Hudson River, while on her passage to New York;
forty persons lost their lives.
The next year the hull was rebuilt by J.R. and
H.S. Baldwin, at New Baltimore, N.Y. and a propeller
engine placed in it. Her new name was NUAHA, which
was afterwards changed to METROPOLITAN.

GREAT LAKES PROPELLER IRONSIDES, 1864.

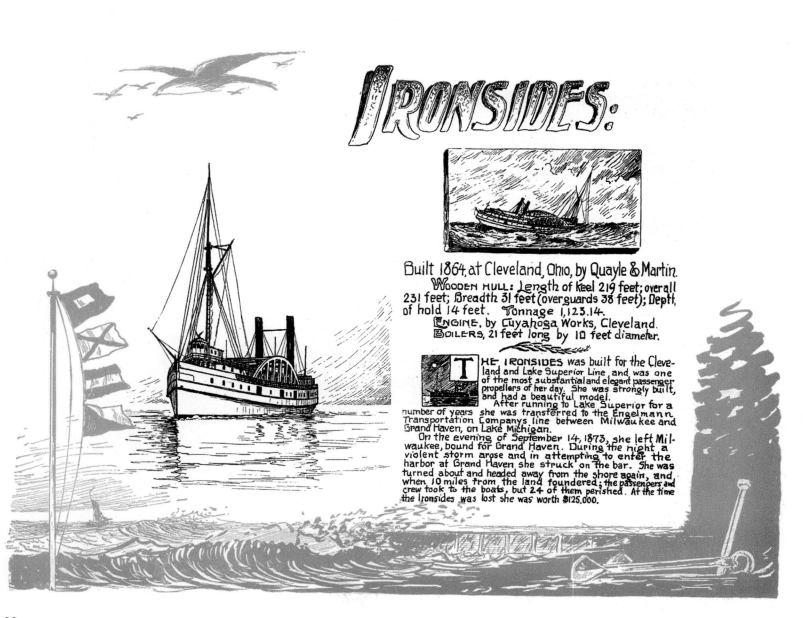

IRONSIDES.

Built 1864, at Cleveland, Ohio, by Quayle & Martin.
WOODEN HULL: Length of keel 219 feet; overall 231 feet; Breadth 31 feet (overguards 38 feet); Depth of hold 14 feet.   Tonnage 1,123.14.
ENGINE, by Cuyahoga Works, Cleveland.
BOILERS, 21 feet long by 10 feet diameter.

THE IRONSIDES was built for the Cleveland and Lake Superior Line, and was one of the most substantial and elegant passenger propellers of her day. She was strongly built, and had a beautiful model.
After running to Lake Superior for a number of years she was transferred to the Engelmann Transportation Companys line between Milwaukee and Grand Haven, on Lake Michigan.
On the evening of September 14, 1873, she left Milwaukee, bound for Grand Haven. During the night a violent storm arose and in attempting to enter the harbor at Grand Haven she struck on the bar. She was turned about and headed away from the shore again, and when 10 miles from the land foundered; the passengers and crew took to the boats, but 24 of them perished. At the time the Ironsides was lost she was worth $125,000.

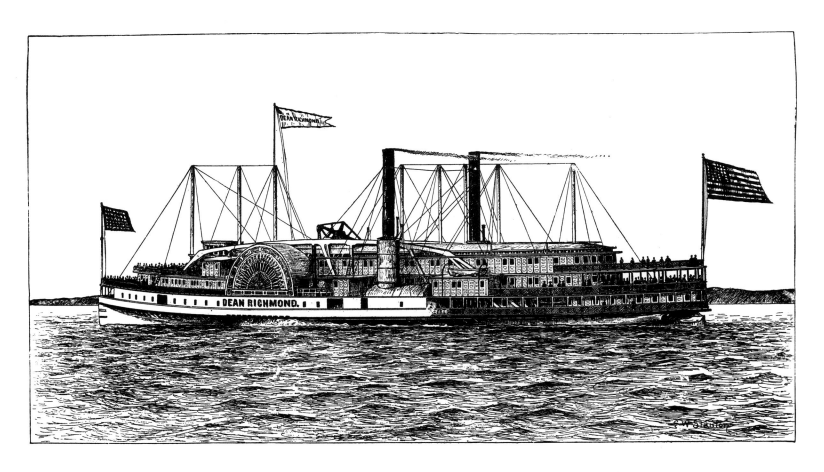

HUDSON RIVER STEAMBOAT DEAN RICHMOND, 1865.

DEAN RICHMOND:

BUILT 1865, at GREENPOINT, L.I.

HULL, OF WOOD, BUILT BY John Englis & Son. Length 348 feet between perpendiculars, breadth of beam 46 feet; depth of hold 10.6 feet.

ENGINE, VERTICAL BEAM, RE-BUILT BY THE ALLAIRE WORKS, NEW YORK Diameter of cylinder 75 inches, by 14 feet stroke; built originally by CUNNINGHAM & Co, 1852, and used in steamboat FRANCIS SKIDDY.

BOILERS, TWO OF STEEL, BY HORACE THEALL, N.Y. 1889, each 26 feet in length and 152 inches in diameter; steam pressure 40 lbs.

~ TONNAGE 2525⁵⁵ GROSS 2322⁹⁷ NET ~

A great Hudson River night-boat, with sleeping accommodations for nearly 1000 passengers One of the "People's Line" of steamers running between New York and Albany and among the largest ever built. Mammoth saloons, exquisitely embellished with frescoing, gilding, carving and elaborate paneling, luxurious furniture and rich hangings, a great dining cabin, etc., etc., go to make the DEAN RICHMOND one of the most wonderful steam vessels afloat.

NEW YORK HARBOR TOWBOAT ANDREW FLETCHER, 1864.

ANDREW FLETCHER:

BUILT 1864, at ATHENS, New York.

WOODEN HULL, by MORTON & EDMONDS: Length of keel 125 feet; width of hull 25 feet; depth of hold 8 feet 6 inches. ENGINE, by FLETCHER, HARRISON & CO., of New York, vertical beam, cylinder 36 inches by 8 feet stroke. BOILER, lobster return flue type, diameter of shell 7 feet 4 inches; width of front 9 feet; whole length 27 feet.

TONNAGE 160.78.

THIS steamboat was launched, completed on November 3, 1864. She was built for and owned by Fletcher, Harrison & Co to be used in New York Harbor, towing transporting, etc. She was sold to the Quarantine Commissioners, of New York and employed by them. She cost $65,000, and had a speed, in dead water, of 17½ miles an hour. On December 20, 1872, she was burned while lying at her wharf, Staten Island. Hull, joiner work, etc., a total loss. Engine was repaired and put in the new boat Nelson K. Hopkins (afterwards called Crystal Stream) by Fletcher, Harrison & Co, 1873.

LONG ISLAND SOUND STEAMBOAT NEWPORT, 1865.

NEWPORT:

BUILT 1865, at GREENPOINT, L I

HULL, *of wood,* by JOHN ENGLIS & SON
  Length of keel........350 feet
  ”   over all.........361 ”
  Width ....43½ ”
  ”   over guards... 80. ”
  Depth of hold....,...14 ”
ENGINE, *vertical beam,* by NOVELTY IRON WORKS, N Y
  Diameter of cylinder 85 inches
      Stroke 12 feet
BOILERS, *four,* of iron. Two on each Guard
  Length ....20 and 24½ feet
    Diameter..... 10¾ and 11½ feet.
WHEELS, 42 feet in diameter; buckets 13 feet long.
JOINER WORK, by JOHN E. HOFFMIRE, New York.
~TONNAGE GROSS 2151.⁵¹~
         NET 1862.⁸⁴

A LARGE and palatial Long
Island Sound steamboat,
built for the route between
New York and Fall River. Of
very superior construction,
being strongly put together and having
the heaviest hog-frame ever placed
in a steamer. In 1889 the NEWPORT
was dismantled and hull converted
into a coal barge.

101

LONG ISLAND SOUND STEAMBOAT BRISTOL, 1865.

BRISTOL.

BUILT 1865, at NEW YORK.

HULL, OF WOOD, BUILT BY WILLIAM H. WEBB. Length of keel 362 feet; over all 373 feet; breadth of beam 48 feet 4 inches (over guards 83 feet); depth of hold 16¼ feet; average draft water 10 feet 3 inches.

ENGINE VERTICAL BEAM, CONSTRUCTED BY THE MORGAN IRON WORKS, NEW YORK. Diameter of cylinder 110 inches; stroke 12 feet; maximum revolutions per minute, 19

BOILERS, THREE, OF IRON, FLUE AND TUBULAR, each 35 feet in length and 13 feet in diameter. Grate surface 510 square feet; fire surface 13,850 square feet; average steam pressure 18 lbs., cutting off at 4 feet

WHEELS, 38 feet 8 inches in diameter, 12 feet wide; with stepped buckets, to prevent jarring and shaking

~ TONNAGE 2,962 ⁷⁰ Gross 2,064 Net ~

THE BRISTOL was one of the most celebrated steamboats ever built, and, with her sister-ship, the PROVIDENCE, became world renowned, being the most magnificent vessels known in the history of steam navigation, and the largest, most complete and finest for many years. The BRISTOL cost, when new, $1,250,000, and was built for service on Long Island Sound; had accommodations for 1200 night passengers, room for a large quantity of deck freight, and great speed. Water-tight compartments, floors of solid white oak; every beam bolted fore and aft and cross braced with iron from the keel to the tops of the paddle boxes, in addition to being strengthened by heavy hog-frames. Internal fittings of the most complete and elaborate description, beautified with carved work, frescoing, gilding and the richest of carpets, furniture and hangings.

The BRISTOL ran during the first years of her existence from New York to Bristol, R.I., a new steamboat route being formed on June 17, 1867. In 1869 was inaugurated daily concerts on board. The Narragansett Bay Steamboat Company afterward controlled this line, and in 1874 sold the steamers, among them the BRISTOL, to the Old Colony Steamboat Company (Fall River Line), in which line the BRISTOL ran until accidentally burned at the bridge near Newport, December 30, 1888.

JAMES RIVER STEAMBOAT JOHN SYLVESTER, 1866.

JOHN SYLVESTER:

BUILT 1866, at JERSEY CITY, N.J.

HULL, OF WOOD, BUILT BY M.S.Allison. Length between perpendiculars 193 feet; over all 207 feet; breadth of beam 30 feet; over guards 50 feet; depth of hold 9 feet 7 inches.

ENGINE, VERTICAL BEAM, CONSTRUCTED BY Murphy, McCurdy & Warden, NEW YORK. Diameter of cylinder 44 inches by 10 feet stroke.

BOILERS, TWO OF IRON. Diameter 7 feet; length 22 feet.

TONNAGE 495 GROSS 338 NET

One of the handsomest sidewheel steamboats of the medium size ever turned out in the United States. With an excellent model, fine proportions, easy lines and graceful appearance the JOHN SYLVESTER challenges admiration. Speed 18 miles an hour.

The SYLVESTER was built for the day line on the James River, between Norfolk and Richmond, carrying passengers and mails. She commenced trips on April 7, 1866, and remained on this route until March 22, 1878. She was then placed on the Delaware River, where she ran for a short time. Since then she has been employed as an excursion boat at New York, during the summer months, running on the Newburgh, Sands Point and Bay Ridge routes, and in the winter used as a day boat on the St. Johns River, in Florida. This boat made the fastest time on record between Jacksonville and Palatka — distance 75 miles, — time 4 hours and 15 minutes.

MISSISSIPPI RIVER STEAMBOAT ROBERT E. LEE, 1866.

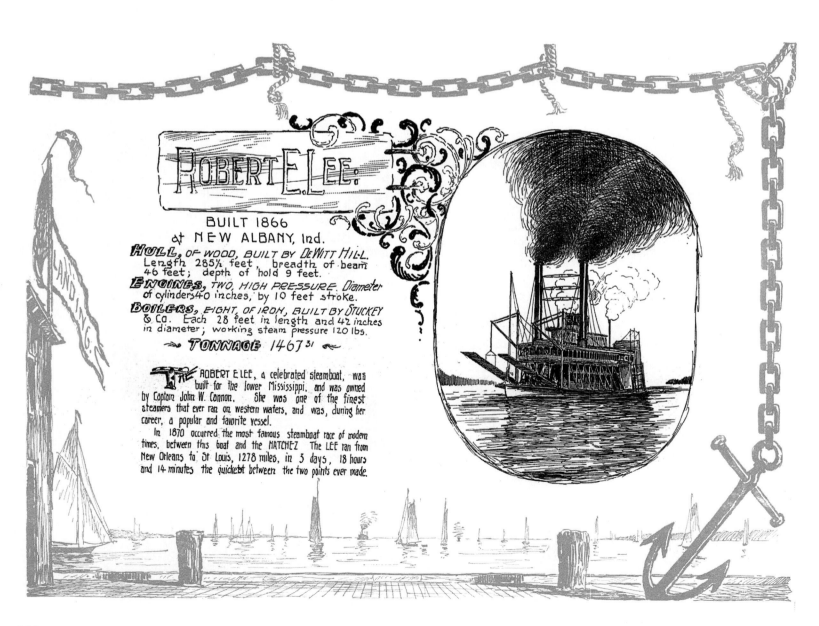

ROBERT E LEE.

BUILT 1866
at NEW ALBANY, Ind.

HULL, OF WOOD, BUILT BY DeWitt Hill.
Length 285½ feet, breadth of beam
46 feet; depth of hold 9 feet.

ENGINES, TWO, HIGH PRESSURE. Diameter
of cylinders 40 inches, by 10 feet stroke.

BOILERS, EIGHT, OF IRON, BUILT BY Stuckey
& Co. Each 28 feet in length and 42 inches
in diameter; working steam pressure 120 lbs.

TONNAGE 1467 31

THE ROBERT E LEE, a celebrated steamboat, was
built for the lower Mississippi, and was owned
by Captain John W. Cannon. She was one of the finest
steamers that ever ran on western waters, and was, during her
career, a popular and favorite vessel.

In 1870 occurred the most famous steamboat race of modern
times, between this boat and the NATCHEZ. The LEE ran from
New Orleans to St. Louis, 1278 miles, in 3 days, 18 hours
and 14 minutes the quickest between the two points ever made.

104

TRANSPACIFIC STEAMSHIP GREAT REPUBLIC, 1866.

LONG ISLAND SOUND STEAMBOAT SEAWANHAKA, 1866.

SEAWANHAKA.

BUILT 1866, at KEYPORT, N.J.

HULL, OF WOOD, BY BENJAMIN C. TERRY. Length 200 feet; breadth of beam 26 feet 7 inches; depth of hold 10 feet.

ENGINE, VERTICAL BEAM, CONSTRUCTED BY HUBBARD & WHITAKER, at BROOKLYN. Diameter of cylinder 50 inches, by 10 feet stroke.

BOILER, ONE, OF IRON, BUILT BY HUBBARD & WHITAKER. Diameter 7 feet; length 21 feet.

— TONNAGE 611.70 —

THE SEAWANHAKA was built for the day passenger route between New York City and Glen Cove, L.I. She was one of the finest boats of her class that had been constructed and was quite a speedy vessel. Plied on the line she was built for continuously up to 1880.

On June 28, 1880, while on her afternoon trip from New York to Glen Cove, she caught fire, off Ward's Island, and was burned. Forty lives were lost, and steamer entirely consumed.

GREAT LAKES STEAMBOAT NORTHWEST, AS REBUILT, 1876.

NEW ENGLAND COAST STEAMBOAT CAMBRIDGE, 1867.

CAMBRIDGE.
BUILT 1867 at GREENPOINT, L.I.

HULL, OF WOOD, BUILT BY JOHN ENGLIS & SON. Length over all 250 feet; breadth of beam 38 feet; depth of hold 13 feet.

ENGINE, VERTICAL BEAM, CONSTRUCTED BY THE MORGAN IRON WORKS, NEW YORK. Diameter of cylinder 60 inches, by 11 feet stroke of piston.

BOILERS, TWO, OF IRON; Each 30 feet in length. Total grate surface 125 square feet.

TONNAGE 1327 22 GROSS
1098 65 NET

BUILT for the Sanford Line, for route between Boston and Bangor, Maine, and was a staunch, sea-going steamboat, finely fitted up and with spacious saloons and state-rooms, as well as ample freight space. Ran continuously on the route between Boston and Bangor (except during the Winter of 1872, when she ran on Long Island Sound, between New York and Providence). Fastest trip, Boston to Bangor, 17 hours 30 minutes.
On February 10, 1886, when bound for Winter-port, Me., she struck on "Old Man" Ledge, off George's Island, coast of Maine, and became a total loss. She was valued at this time at $100,000.

LAKE MICHIGAN STEAMBOAT SHEBOYGAN, 1869.

SHEBOYGAN:

BUILT 1869, at MANITOWOC, WIS.
HULL, of wood built by G.S. RAND. Length of keel
208 feet; width of hull 32 feet; over guards
54 feet; depth of hold 12 feet.
ENGINE, vertical beam; diameter
of cylinder 50 inches, by 12 feet stroke.
TWO BOILERS, by BUFFALO ENGINE WORKS, 1857 (rebuilt 1891) each 8 feet diameter by 21 feet in length.
WHEELS, 27 feet in diameter; 24 buckets
each wheel. Length of buckets 7 feet;
width 16 to 26 inches; dip 32 inches.
GROSS TONNAGE 623.90. NET TONNAGE 461.36.

THE SHEBOYGAN
arrived in Milwaukee, Wis.
on May 5, 1869, and commenced
running on the route between
Chicago and points on the west
shore of Lake Michigan in the
Goodrich Line, the same month.
The engine of this steamer was that
formerly used in the lake steamboats
City of Cleveland and Garden City.

NEW ENGLAND COAST STEAMBOAT FALMOUTH, 1872.

FALMOUTH.
BUILT 1872, at GREENPOINT, L.I.

HULL, of wood, built by JOHN ENGLIS & SON. Length from stem to stern 232 feet; over all 240 feet; breadth of beam 36½ feet; depth of hold 14½ feet.

ENGINE, vertical beam, constructed by the QUINTARD IRON WORKS, New York. Diameter of cylinder 54 inches, by 11 feet stroke of piston.

BOILERS, two, round shell return tubular, each 19 feet in length, 10 feet wide and 10 feet high. 122 square feet of grate surface; 3000 square feet of heating surface.

~ TONNAGE 1156 3⁄100 gross; 849 66⁄100 net ~

THE FALMOUTH was built for the New England & Nova Scotia Steamship Company, to run between Portland, Me. and Halifax, N.S., being designed especially for sea service very strongly put together, with narrow guards, etc. She was afterwards sold to the International S.S. Co. and run to St. John, N.S.
On April 29, 1884, while lying at a wharf at Portland, undergoing repairs, caught fire and became a total loss.

NEW YORK HARBOR STEAMBOAT SYLVAN DELL, 1872.

SYLVAN DELL.

~ BUILT 1872, at GREENPOINT, N.Y. ~

HULL, OF WOOD, BUILT BY LAWRENCE & FOULKES. Length of keel 172 feet; over all 185 feet; breadth of beam 26 feet; over the guards 46½ feet; depth of hold 8 feet 9 inches. Draft of water 4 feet 9 inches.

ENGINE, VERTICAL BEAM, CONSTRUCTED BY FLETCHER, HARRISON & CO., NewYork. Diameter of cylinder 51 inches, by 8 feet stroke.

BOILER, ONE, OF IRON, LOBSTER RETURN FLUE. Total grate surface 66 square feet; total heating surface 1433 square feet.

WHEELS, RADIAL. Diameter 25 feet 10 inches; 22 buckets each wheel; width of buckets 18 inches, length 8 feet; dip 32 inches.

JOINER WORK, by KING & EELS, N.Y.

~ TONNAGE 440⁴⁵ Gross – 330⁴⁵ Net ~

A REMARKABLY handsome and swift steamboat of the medium class. The last of the fleet of the Harlem and New York Navigation Company. Used on the East River for many years, also on the Glen Island, Newburgh and Bay Ridge routes, and known as the "Queen of New York Harbor." Sold, 1866, to run on the Philadelphia and Gloucester Ferry. Speed 19½ miles per hour.

111

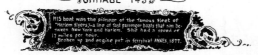

SYLVAN SHORE:
BUILT 1856 at MORRISANIA, N.Y.

HULL, OF WOOD, BUILT BY F. BOOLE. Length of keel 125 feet; over all 136 feet; width 23 feet; over all 40 feet; depth of hold 7½ feet; draft of water 4½ feet. JOINER WORK by DECKER & BROWN, New York.

ENGINE, VERTICAL BEAM, CONSTRUCTED BY FLETCHER, HARRISON & CO., New York. Diameter of cylinder 30 inches; stroke 8 feet.

BOILER, ONE, OF IRON, RETURN FLUE, BUILT BY FLETCHER, HARRISON & CO. Length 22 feet; height 6½ feet; width 7½ feet. Total grate surface 42 square feet; total heating surface 1012 square feet.

WHEELS, DIAMETER 23 feet 8 inches; 22 buckets, each 6 feet in length, 20 inches wide, dipping 30 inches.

TONNAGE 143 88

THIS boat was the pioneer of the famous fleet of "Harlem flyers,"—a line of fast passenger boats that ran between New York and Harlem. She had a speed of 17 miles per hour.
Broken up and engine put in ferryboat ANNEX, 1877.

Sylvan Grove:
BUILT 1858, at NEW YORK.

HULL, OF WOOD, BUILT BY THOMAS COLLYER. Length of keel 134 feet; over all 146 feet; width 25 feet; over guards 43 feet; depth of hold 8 feet; draft of water 4 feet 10 inches. JOINER WORK by Decker & Brown, New York.

ENGINE, VERTICAL BEAM, CONSTRUCTED BY FLETCHER, HARRISON & CO., New York. Diameter of cylinder 36 inches; length of stroke 8 feet.

BOILER, RETURN FLUE, OF IRON, BY FLETCHER, HARRISON & CO. Length 26 feet, 7 feet high and 8½ feet wide. Total grate surface 50 square feet; total heating surface 1290 sq. feet.

WHEELS, 25 feet in diameter; 22 buckets, each 6½ feet long by 20 inches wide; dip 29 ins.

GROSS TONNAGE 320 28   NET TONNAGE 219 03

THE SYLVAN GROVE was the second of the fleet of boats of the Harlem & New York Navigation Company. Her speed was 17½ miles per hour. Was also used on the Rockaway, Bay Ridge, Roslyn and other routes about New York. Taken to the Cape Fear River, in North Carolina, in 1887, and was run by the New Hanover Transit Company, between Wilmington and Carolina Beach. Totally destroyed by fire at wharf Wilmington, Jan. 19, 1891.

EMPIRE STATE.
Formerly SYLVAN STREAM.
BUILT 1863, at NEW YORK

HULL, OF WOOD, BUILT BY THOMAS COLLYER. Length of keel 148 feet; over all 157 feet; width of hull 26 feet; over guards 44½ feet; depth of hold 8 feet 6 inches; draft of water 5 feet 8 inches. JOINER WORK by DECKER & BROWN, N.Y.

ENGINE, VERTICAL BEAM, CONSTRUCTED BY FLETCHER, HARRISON & CO., New York. Diameter of cylinder 40 inches; stroke 8 feet.

BOILER, LOBSTER RETURN FLUE, OF IRON. Total grate surface 62 feet; total heating surface 1363 square feet. Built by FLETCHER, HARRISON & CO.

WHEELS, Diameter 26 feet; 22 buckets to each wheel, 6 feet 8 inches long and 20 inches wide; dip 31 inches.

TONNAGE: Gross 349 83   Net 240 95

THE SYLVAN STREAM was built for the route on the East River, between New York and Harlem. Speed 17½ miles per hour. Sold 1865 for service on St. Lawrence River. Name changed 1893 to EMPIRE STATE.

SYLVAN GLEN:
BUILT 1869, at BROOKLYN, N.Y.

HULL, OF WOOD, CONSTRUCTED BY LAWRENCE & FOULKES. Length of keel 148 feet; over all 160 feet; width of hull 26 feet; over guards 45 feet; depth of hold 8 feet 6 inches; draft of water 4 feet 6 inches.

ENGINE, VERTICAL BEAM, BUILT BY FLETCHER, HARRISON & CO., NEW YORK CITY. Diameter of cylinder 40 inches; stroke 8 feet.

BOILER, LOBSTER RETURN FLUE, OF IRON, BY FLETCHER, HARRISON & CO., N.Y. Total grate surface 54 square feet; total heating surface 1158 square feet.

WHEELS, 24 feet in diameter; 20 buckets to each wheel, 7 feet long, 18 inches wide, 27 inches dip. Speed 17¾ miles per hour.
JOINER WORK by DECKER & BROWN, New York.

GROSS TONNAGE 330 26   NET TONNAGE 165 13

THE SYLVAN GLEN was built for the Harlem & New York Navigation Company, and ran regularly on the river for a number of years afterwards, to and from various points around New York. Ran on Hudson River also, the Savannah River. Purchased 1890 by the Delaware River Rapid Transit Co. for Philadelphia and Gloucester ferry.

GREAT LAKES PASSENGER PROPELLER PEERLESS, 1872.

PEERLESS.
BUILT 1872,
AT CLEVELAND, OHIO.

HULL, OF WOOD, BUILT BY IRA LAFRANIER Length 211 feet; breadth of beam 39 feet 10 inches; depth of hold 12½ feet.

ENGINE, CONSTRUCTED BY THE GLOBE IRON WORKS Diameter of cylinder 54 inches, by 40 inches stroke

BOILERS, TWO, OF IRON, BY GLOBE IRON WORKS Length 20 feet, diameter 54 inches.

TONNAGE 1199 50 Gross 912 70 Net

A LARGE and well built Great Lakes passenger propeller of the old style. Built for the Lake Superior trade, having a large upper saloon, commodious staterooms and good deck space for freight. Used on the route between Chicago and Duluth in the "Lake Michigan & Lake Superior Trans. Co's Line" of passenger boats.

LONG ISLAND SOUND STEAMBOAT C. H. NORTHAM, 1872.

C.H. NORTHAM.

BUILT 1872, at GREENPOINT, L.I.

HULL, OF WOOD, CONSTRUCTED BY John Englis & Son. Length of keel 312 feet; over all 323 feet; breadth of beam 44½ feet; depth of hold 13 feet. Frame, hackmatack, oak and cedar; outside plank, oak. Two sets of keelsons, each 36 inches in height, of Georgia pine. Diagonally strapped on the outside with iron straps 4 by ½ inches, fastened to head straps, both sides of the frame the full length of the hull. Average draft 7½ feet.

ENGINE, VERTICAL BEAM RE-BUILT by the QUINTARD IRON WORKS, New York, 1872. Diameter of cylinder 80 inches, by 12 feet stroke. Originally built 1855 by the MORGAN IRON WORKS, N.Y. for Lake Erie steamboat CRESCENT CITY; transferred from that vessel to the Atlantic coast steamship MORNING STAR, and finally placed in the C. H. NORTHAM.

BOILERS, TWO, ON QUARDS, BUILT by QUINTARD IRON WORKS. Length 28 feet, by 19 feet in diameter.

WHEELS, RADIAL. Diameter 36 feet; 30 buckets each wheel; length of buckets 10½ feet; width 24 inches; dip 4 feet.

JOINER WORK, by John B. Hoffmire, New York.

TONNAGE: Gross 1456 81, Net 1179 99

The finest sidewheel steamboat ever built for the New Haven Line. When she appeared she was considered the best vessel of her type on Long Island Sound; hull, a model of symmetry and beauty; complete in all her fittings; luxurious in her passenger appointments; very roomy, and convenient as to her freighting accommodations, and possessing fine speed — 20 miles an hour. She cost $500,000.

On November 27, 1877, while laid up at the foot of 7th Street, East River, New York, she accidently caught fire and was almost totally destroyed. Damage $200,000. She was rebuilt at once, and immediately placed on the line again.

NEW YORK AND NEW ORLEANS STEAMSHIP NEW ORLEANS, 1872.

LAKE MICHIGAN STEAMBOAT CHICAGO, 1874.

CHICAGO:

BUILT 1874 at MANITOWOC, WIS.

HULL, of wood, built by G.S.RAND. Length of keel 205 feet; width of hull 30 feet; over guards 55 feet; depth of hold 12 feet.

ENGINE, vertical beam; diameter of cylinder 46 inches, by 11 feet stroke

BOILERS, two, of iron; each 9 feet in diameter by 20 feet long.

WHEELS, 26 feet in diameter; 24 buckets to each wheel, 8 feet in length, 16 to 24 inches wide, and 34 inches dip.

GROSS TONNAGE 746.85.   NET TONNAGE 589.48.

THIS steamboat was constructed for the Goodrich Transportation Company for service on the line between Chicago and the western shore ports of Lake Michigan, running in connection with the sidewheel steamers Sheboygan, Muskegon, Corona and Alpena and several propellers, all of the same line.   The engine of the Chicago was taken from the steamer May Queen

NEW YORK AND NEW ORLEANS STEAMSHIP HUDSON, 1874.

HUDSON.

Designed by JOHN BAIRD

BUILT 1874, at WILMINGTON, DEL.
BY PUSEY, JONES & CO.

HULL OF IRON. Length between
perpendiculars 287½ feet; overall 300 feet;
breadth of beam 34 feet; depth of hold 23 feet.

ENGINE, SINGLE SURFACE CONDENSING.
Diameter of cylinder 48 inches; stroke 72 ins.
BOILERS, FOUR, RETURN TUBULAR
(water bottom, semi-circular top). Length 13 feet
8 inches; width 9 feet 4½ ins., height 12½ feet
Total heating surface 7160 square feet; total grate
surface 180 square feet

WHEEL, FOUR BLADES. Diameter
15 feet, pitch 22 feet.

TONNAGE   1872 ¼ Gross
          1309 ⁶⁹ Net

ONE of the Cromwell Line
New York and New
Orleans passenger steamships,
and a sister-ship to the LOUISIANA,
NEW ORLEANS and KNICKERBOCKER. Of
excellent speed and large carrying capacity.

TRANSPACIFIC STEAMSHIP CITY OF PEKING, 1874.

CITY OF PEKING:

DESIGNED BY EDWARD FARON.
BUILT 1874, at CHESTER, Pa,
By JOHN ROACH & SON.

HULL, OF IRON. Length of keel 396½ feet; over all 419 feet; breadth of beam 47 feet 4 inches; depth of hold 19 feet 6 inches; from spar deck 36 feet 2 inches. Loaded draft 22 feet.

ENGINES, TWO, VERTICAL COMPOUND. Diameter of cylinders of each 51 and 88 inches, by 54 inches stroke. Indicated horse power 4000; average horse power 3500, on a consumption of 75 tons of coal per day, making 52 revolutions a minute; steam pressure 60 pounds.

BOILERS, TEN, OF IRON, SCOTCH TYPE, 3 FURNACES IN EACH. Each 10 feet in length, and 13 feet in diameter. Total grate surface 593 square feet; heating surface 17,850 square feet; consumption of coal per day, 75 tons.

WHEEL, 4 BLADES. Diameter 20 feet, 4 inches; pitch 30 feet.

TONNAGE 5079 41/100 GROSS
3128 99/100 NET

THE CITY OF PEKING was launched into the Delaware River on March 18, 1874, in the presence of 30,000 people, and was the largest steamship ever built up to that time, with the exception of the GREAT EASTERN. Fitted up in splendid style, and having very extensive passenger accommodations. Capacity for 88 first- and 30 second-class, and 1407 steerage passengers. Speed 15.27 knots an hour. Her trial trip marked a peculiar event in American history. On board were President Grant, Vice-President Wilson, Cabinet offices, United States senators, etc., and when these dignitaries were three miles out at sea the United States were virtually without an executive head.

Built for the San Francisco and Japan route. She made what was considered a very remarkable run soon after being placed on the Pacific, going from San Francisco to Yokohama, a distance of 4750 miles, in 15 days and 9 hours.

The CITY OF PEKING had a sister ship, launched a month later, named CITY OF TOKIO, which was wrecked at Yokohama.

DELAWARE RIVER FERRYBOAT GENERAL J. S. SCHULTZE, 1875.

GEN! J.S. SCHULTZE:

BUILT 1875, at CAMDEN, N.J.,
By WOOD & DIALOGUE.

HULL, OF IRON. Length 138 feet 7 inches; breadth of beam
36 feet; depth of hold 7½ feet
ENGINE, VERTICAL BEAM, JET CONDENSING. Diameter of cylinder
36 inches, by 10 feet stroke of piston.
BOILER, OF IRON, 23 feet in length by 124 inches diameter
TONNAGE, 461 87 Gross, 361 43 Net

A DELAWARE RIVER
ferryboat, built for
the Philadelphia
and Haighn's Point (Camden)
route. An excellent boat,
serviceable and economical.

DETROIT RIVER FERRYBOAT EXCELSIOR, 1876.

EXCELSIOR:

~ BUILT 1876, at DETROIT, Mich. ~

HULL, OF WOOD, CONSTRUCTED BY THE DETROIT DRY DOCK CO. Length over all 117 feet; breadth of beam 29 feet 4 inches; over guards 45 feet 6 inches; depth of hold 10 feet 10 inches.

ENGINE, VERTICAL, DOUBLE, NON-CONDENSING; TWO CYLINDERS, each 22 inches in diameter with a piston stroke of 24 inches.

BOILER, ONE, 18 feet in length by 96 inches in diameter

TONNAGE 229 tons Gross
129 tons Net

Typical Detroit River ferry-boat; used on the route between Detroit and Windsor, also as an excursion boat to Belle Isle Park. Hull of great strength and built bluff to contend with ice.

DELAWARE RIVER STEAMBOAT COLUMBIA, 1876.

COLUMBIA:

BUILT 1876, at WILMINGTON, Delaware,
By the HARLAN & HOLLINGSWORTH COMPANY

HULL, OF IRON. Length 220 feet, breadth of beam 33
feet, over guards 60 feet, depth of hold 9½ feet
ENGINE, VERTICAL BEAM. Diameter of cylinder 50 inches,
by 11 feet stroke of piston
BOILER, RECTANGULAR OF IRON Length 17 feet; diameter
216 inches
WHEELS, RADIAL. 30 feet in diameter; number of buckets
each wheel 22, length of buckets 9 feet, width 24 inches,
average dip of wheel 30 inches.
TONNAGE 663⁶⁶ Gross, 535⁸⁸ Net

TYPE of light-draught, swift
river passenger steam boat
Built for the navigation
of the Delaware River, and owned
by the Upper Delaware River Transportation Co, of Philadelphia A roomy,
well fitted and successful boat

MISSISSIPPI RIVER STEAMBOAT CHARLES P. CHOUTEAU, 1877.

Charles P. Chouteau:
BUILT 1877, at ST. LOUIS, Mo.

HULL, OF IRON, BUILT BY W. H. Thorwegan. Length 296 feet 8 inches; breadth of beam 54 feet; depth of hold 7½ ft.

ENGINES, TWO HIGH-PRESSURE, CONSTRUCTED BY Dennis Long AND FORMERLY USED IN STEAMBOAT "MARY ALICE". Diameter of cylinders 22 inches, length of stroke 8 feet

BOILERS, FOUR, OF IRON, BUILT BY Joseph Wengler. Diameter of each 42 inches; length 32 feet.

WHEEL, AT STERN. Diameter 27 feet; number of buckets 20, length of buckets 31 feet; width of buckets 24 inches; average dip of wheel 4 feet.

~ TONNAGE 1,304 ½ ~

THIS boat was built for the passenger and cotton-carrying trade, to ply on the Mississippi River, between New Orleans and Memphis. She ran successfully many years. The CHARLES P. CHOUTEAU struck a snag in the Mississippi on Feb.7, 1877, and was damaged to the extent of $10,000. On November 22, 1887, she was burned at Sunflower Landing, about 135 miles below Memphis, and 1 fireman lost his life. Boat was valued at $100,000, and cargo at $180,250, total loss.

NEW YORK OCEAN GOING EXCURSION STEAMBOAT COLUMBIA, 1877.

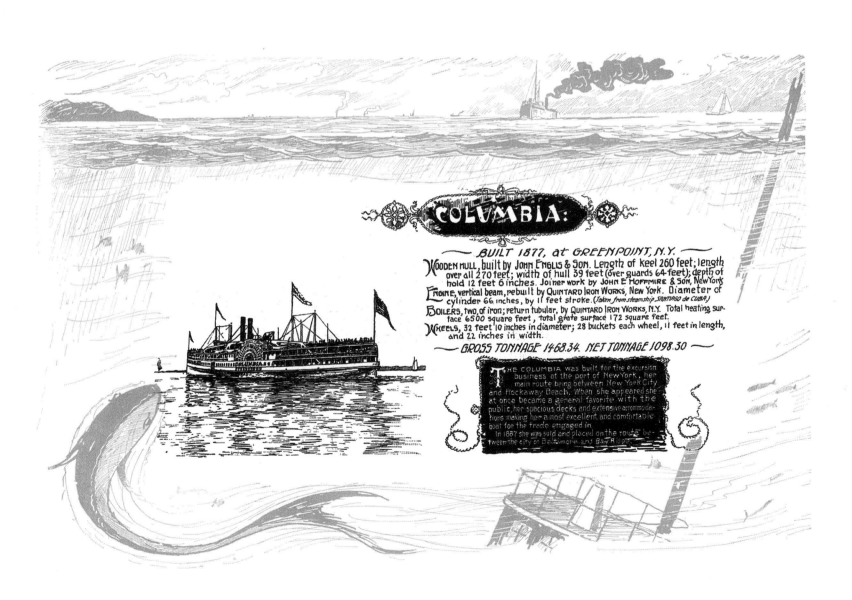

COLUMBIA

BUILT 1877, at GREENPOINT, N.Y.

WOODEN HULL, built by JOHN ENGLIS & SON. Length of keel 260 feet; length over all 270 feet; width of hull 39 feet (over guards 64 feet); depth of hold 12 feet 6 inches. Joiner work by JOHN E HOFFMIRE & SON, New York.

ENGINE, vertical beam, rebuilt by QUINTARD IRON WORKS, New York. Diameter of cylinder 66 inches, by 11 feet stroke. (Taken from steamship SANTIAGO de CUBA.)

BOILERS, two, of iron; return tubular, by QUINTARD IRON WORKS, N.Y. Total heating surface 6500 square feet, total grate surface 172 square feet.

WHEELS, 32 feet 10 inches in diameter; 28 buckets each wheel, 11 feet in length, and 22 inches in width.

GROSS TONNAGE 1468.34. NET TONNAGE 1098.30

THE COLUMBIA was built for the excursion business at the port of New York, her main route being between New York City and Rockaway Beach. When she appeared she at once became a general favorite with the public, her spacious decks and extensive accommodations making her a most excellent and comfortable boat for the trade engaged in.

In 1887 she was sold and placed on the route between the city of Baltimore and Bay Ridge.

MISSISSIPPI RIVER STEAMBOAT NEW MARY HOUSTON, 1877.

THE FANNY BULLITT, in 1854.

NEW MARY HOUSTON:

FORMERLY "MARY HOUSTON" AND "FANNY BULLITT."

BUILT 1877, at JEFFERSONVILLE, IND.

HULL, OF WOOD Length 287 feet; breadth of beam 41 feet; depth of hold 7 feet 4 inches

ENGINES, TWO, HIGH PRESSURE Diameter of cylinders 22½ inches, by 7 feet stroke of piston

BOILERS, FOUR, OF IRON, ON DECK, BUILT BY JOSEPH MITCHELL, LOUISVILLE, KY. Each 30 feet in length by 42 inches in diameter; working pressure 140 lbs

TONNAGE 1,165 93/95

The NEW MARY HOUSTON was formerly the MARY HOUSTON, built 1868, at Jeffersonville, Ind., being at that time constructed out of the steamboat FANNY BULLITT, built at Jeffersonville in 1854. Built for the Ohio River and New Orleans passenger and freight trade. A large size, comfortable boat, having sleeping accommodations for numerous passengers. On January 10, 1893, while lying at wharfboat, Cincinnati, was cut through by ice and sunk. She was afterwards raised, but was dismantled, the hull being converted into a freight barge.

124

HUDSON RIVER STEAMBOAT SARATOGA, 1877.

SARATOGA.

Designed by Joseph Cornell.

BUILT 1877 at GREENPOINT, N.Y.

HULL, of wood, built by John Englis & Son.
   Length of keel 285 feet; over all 300 feet;
   breadth of hull 36 feet (over guards
   70 feet); draft of water 6½ feet.
JOINER WORK, by John E. Hoffmire & Son, New York.
ENGINE, vertical beam, by Secor Iron Works, New
   York; diameter of cylinder 60 inches, by 12 feet
   stroke. Indicated horse power 1050.
TWO STEEL BOILERS, return tubular; total grate surface 164 square feet; consumption of anthracite coal per hour 4000 lbs. Wheels, 32 feet
   in diameter; 26 buckets each wheel, 9 feet
   long by 24 inches wide; dip 30 inches.
➔ GROSS TONNAGE 1438 75 NET TONNAGE 1291 55 ⬅

THE SARATOGA with her consort, the CITY OF TROY, forms part of the
Hudson River Route between New York and Troy, connecting
the Citizens Line . . . through by night. The engine of
the SARATOGA was that formerly in the steamboat SUNNYSIDE.
She cost $175,000, and has . . . . 15 miles per hour.
The interior arrangements . . . . . leave nothing to
be desired. There are sleeping accommodations for 600 persons.

125

DELAWARE RIVER EXCURSION STEAMBOAT THOMAS CLYDE, 1878.

THOMAS CLYDE.

BUILT 1878, at WILMINGTON, Del.,
By the PUSEY & JONES COMPANY

HULL, OF IRON. Length of keel 210 feet; over all 217ft. breadth of beam 30 feet; over guards 54 feet; depth of hold 9 feet, average draft of water 4 feet 3 inches.

ENGINE, VERTICAL BEAM, BUILT BY THE NEPTUNE IRON WORKS, NEW YORK, and formerly used in steamboat STATE OF MARYLAND. Diameter of cylinder 50 inches; stroke 11 feet.

BOILER, RETURN TUBULAR, OF IRON. Total grate surface 82 square feet; total heating surface 3700 square feet; consumption of fuel per hour 2240 pounds.

WHEELS, RADIAL. Diameter 30 feet; 22 buckets to each wheel; length of buckets 9 feet; width 26 inches; dip 27 inches.

TONNAGE 625 $\frac{73}{100}$ GROSS
510 $\frac{83}{100}$ NET

BUILT for the "Delaware City, Salem & Philadelphia Steam Navigation Co" and used as an excursion steamer out of Philadelphia, running to various points down the Delaware River. A well-built, commodious boat, a favorite with the travelling public.

126

MISSISSIPPI RIVER STEAMBOAT ED. RICHARDSON, 1878.

ED. RICHARDSON:

BUILT 1878, at JEFFERSONVILLE, IND.

HULL, OF WOOD, BUILT BY Howard & Company. Length over all 309 feet; breadth of beam 49 feet; over guards 70 feet; depth of hold 12 feet; average draft of water 4 feet 10 inches.

ENGINES, TWO, HIGH PRESSURE LEVER, (FROM STEAMER KATIE), built by JOHN DAVIES, LOUISVILLE

BOILERS, NINE, OF IRON, BUILT BY JOS. MITCHELL, LOUISVILLE. Diameter of each 42 inches, length 32 feet; working pressure 160 lbs.

WHEELS, 41 feet 2 inches in diameter, 21 buckets to each wheel, 18 feet long and 23 inches wide

~ TONNAGE 2 048 ³⁴ ~

ONE of those great Western river passenger and freight steamboats, that have no parallel in their class in any other part of the World, was the ED RICHARDSON She was built for the "New Orleans & Memphis Packet Company," and was capable of carrying 9000 bales of cotton She had a large and handsome saloon beautifully decorated in white and gold, and many spacious and comfortable staterooms The ED RICHARDSON was dismantled in 1888, and her hull burned to recover the old iron

127

COLUMBIA RIVER STEAMBOAT LURLINE, 1878.

LURLINE.

~ BUILT 1878 at PORTLAND, Ore ~

HULL, of wood, built by JOHN F STEFFEN. Length of keel 153 feet; over all 175 feet; breadth of beam 30 feet 7 inches; depth of hold 6½ feet; draft of water 3 feet.

TWO ENGINES, horizontal, constructed by the HARLAN & HOLLINGSWORTH Co. Diameter of cylinders 16 inches, by 6 feet stroke.

BOILER, locomotive tubular, constructed by WARD, STANTON & Co, Newburgh, N.Y.

WHEEL, 18 feet in diameter, 17 buckets, each 16 feet in length, 24 inches wide, dipping 26 inches.

JOINER WORK, by JAMES REED.

~ GROSS TONNAGE 481 62   NET TONNAGE 338 35 ~

THE LURLINE was built for the navigation of the Willamette and Columbia Rivers in Oregon, between Portland and Astoria, the Vancouver Transportation Company being owners. She was designed by JACOB KAMM and cost $40,000. A generally successful boat, being well adapted for the route employed on and having a speed of about 17 miles an hour.

OHIO AND MISSISSIPPI RIVER STEAMBOAT GUIDING STAR, 1878.

GUIDING STAR:

BUILT 1878, at CINCINNATI, Ohio

HULL, OF WOOD, BUILT BY **The Marine Railway & Dry Dock Company**. Length between perpendiculars 303 feet; over all 307 feet; breadth of beam 42 feet; over guards 77 feet; depth of hold 7 feet 8 inches.

ENGINES, TWO, HIGH PRESSURE, NON-CONDENSING, CONSTRUCTED BY **C. T. Dumont**, CINCINNATI. Diameter of cylinders 26 inches by 7¼ feet stroke.

BOILERS, FIVE, OF IRON, ON DECK, BUILT BY THE **Dumont Boiler Works**, CINCINNATI. Diameter of each 42 inches; length 28 feet.

WHEELS, Diameter 30 feet; number of buckets each wheel 22; length of buckets 14 feet, width 26 inches, average dip of wheel 6 inches.

— TONNAGE 1121 ??

The GUIDING STAR was a very fine passenger and freight steamboat built for the Cincinnati and New Orleans trade. She was owned by her commander, Captain J. O. Hegler, and cost $140,000. She was beautifully fitted up, and was a great favorite with the travelling public. Her speed was 12 miles an hour against the Mississippi River current. On January 16, 1893, while on her way from New Orleans she was cut down by the ice, 8 miles below New Madrid, Mo., was beached, and became a total loss.

DELAWARE RIVER EXCURSION STEAMBOAT REPUBLIC, 1878.

REPUBLIC

BUILT 1878, at WILMINGTON, Del.,
By the HARLAN & HOLLINGSWORTH COMPANY.

HULL, OF IRON. Length of keel 272 feet 10
inches; over all 284 feet; breadth of
beam 37 feet; depth of hold 10¾ feet.

ENGINE, VERTICAL BEAM. Diameter of cylinder 66 inches, by 12 feet stroke.

BOILERS, two. Length of each 20 feet; width
180 inches; working pressure 45 lbs. steam to
square inch.

TONNAGE 1285 97/100 Gross
978 13/100 Net

A LARGE DELAWARE RIVER excursion steamboat, built for
the Philadelphia and Cape May
route, between which points she
has run, during the summer season,
each year since constructed. A roomy
well furnished boat, of fine speed.
The REPUBLIC has made the
105 miles of her route in 4 hours
and 55 minutes, which classes her as
one of the fastest excursion boats ever built.

MISSISSIPPI RIVER STEAMBOAT J. M. WHITE, 1878.

J. M. WHITE.

— Designed by Edward J. Howard —
BUILT 1878,
at JEFFERSONVILLE, Ind.

HULL, OF WOOD, BUILT BY HOWARD & CO.
Length of keel 312 feet 7 inches; over all 320 feet;
breadth of beam 47 feet 9 inches; over guards
91 feet; depth of hold 10 feet. Average draft
of water 7 feet 6 inches.

ENGINES, TWO, HIGH PRESSURE, LEVER.
Diameter of cylinders 43 inches, by 11 feet stroke.

BOILERS, TEN, OF IRON, FLUE TYPE, BUILT BY
JOSEPH MITCHELL, LOUISVILLE, KY.
Each 34 feet long by 42 inches wide.
Steam pressure 160 lbs.

WHEELS, 44 feet in diameter, 24
buckets to each wheel; length of
buckets .18 feet 6 inches; width
30 inches.

~ TONNAGE 2027⁷⁶ ~

This was the third boat named J M WHITE that ran on the Mississippi River. All were famous for speed, but neither of her predecessors approached, in size or elegance, the WHITE of 1878. She was built for the navigation of the lower part of the river, running from New Orleans to Vicksburg and Greenville, and has been conceded to be a crowning effort in steamboat architecture in the West. Her saloons were magnificently furnished, and all her fittings were of the most elaborate description. Carrying capacity 7000 bales of cotton, and saloon accommodations for 350 passengers. Her cost was $300,000. On Dec 13, 1886, while lying at the St Maurice Plantation, on the Mississippi River, she took fire and was totally destroyed. From 10 to 15 lives were lost.

131

ARASAPHA:

BUILT 1860, at PHILADELPHIA, PA.

IRON HULL, 110 feet 5 inches in length; 25 feet beam; 8 feet 6 inches depth of hold. Tonnage 232.81.

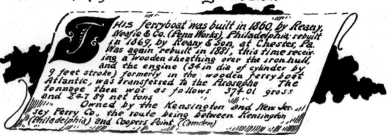

This ferryboat was built in 1860, by Reany, Neafie & Co. (Penn Works), Philadelphia; rebuilt in 1869, by Reany & Son, at Chester, Pa. Was again rebuilt in 1881, this time receiving a wooden sheathing over the iron hull, and the engine (34 in dia of cylinder by 9 feet stroke) formerly in the wooden ferryboat Atlantic, was transferred to the Arasapha. The tonnage then was as follows, 374.01 gross and 247.89 net tons. Owned by the Kensington and New Jersey Ferry Co., the route being between Kensington (Philadelphia) and Coopers Point (Camden).

DELAWARE:

BUILT 1875, BY THE HARLAN & HOLLINGSWORTH CO., WILMINGTON, DEL.

IRON HULL: Length of keel, 136 feet; width of hull, 29 feet; depth of hold 10 feet 3 inches.

ENGINE, 38 inches diameter of cylinder, by 9 feet stroke.

Gross Tonnage 370.84. Net Tonnage 255.34.

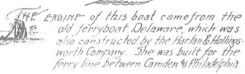

THE ENGINE of this boat came from the old ferryboat Delaware, which was also constructed by the Harlan & Hollingsworth Company. She was built for the ferry line between Camden & Philadelphia.

DAUNTLESS:

BUILT 1875, by the Harlan and Hollingsworth Co., WILMINGTON, Del.

IRON HULL: Length 149 feet; breadth 32 feet; and 8 feet 7 inches depth of hold.

One Engine, inclined, 38 inches diameter of cylinder by 9 feet stroke.

Gross Tonnage 301.17. Net Tonnage 178.77.

Built for the Philadelphia and Gloucester ferry route on the Delaware River.

WENONAH:

BUILT 1882, at WILMINGTON, DEL.

IRON HULL, 145 feet in length; 30 feet beam, and 12 feet depth of hold.

One Beam Engine, 44 inches diameter of cylinder, by 10 feet stroke.

Gross Tonnage 439.00. Net Tonnage 317.32.

THE Wenonah was built by the Harlan and Hollingsworth Company to ply on the ferry between Philadelphia and Camden.

NEW YORK OCEAN GOING EXCURSION STEAMBOAT GRAND REPUBLIC, 1878.

GRAND REPUBLIC.

BUILT 1878, at BROOKLYN, N.Y.
WOODEN HULL, by JOHN ENGLIS & SON. Length of keel 282 feet 6 inches; on deck 300 feet; width of hull 41 feet 6 inches (over guards 72 feet), depth of hold 13 feet
JOINER WORK, by JOHN E HOFFMIRE & SONS, New York.
ENGINE, vertical beam, rebuilt by QUINTARD IRON WORKS, New York. Diameter of cylinder 76 inches by 12 feet stroke.
BOILERS, two, of iron, return tubular, by QUINTARD IRON WORKS, New York. 26¼ feet in length; 11¼ feet diameter of shell.
WHEELS, 36 feet in diameter; 32 buckets each wheel, 10 feet 6 inches in length, by 24 inches in width.
GROSS TONNAGE 1,760 17. NET TONNAGE 1,308 72.

THIS steamboat was the largest ever constructed for excursion purposes exclusively at the port of New York, having a capacity for 4000 passengers. She was built for the Rockaway Beach route and general excursion business, making not only regular trips to sea, but also up the Hudson River and on Long Island Sound. An ideal boat for the trade engaged in, being admirably designed and excellently fitted up, with good speed.

The engine was that formerly used in the steamship MORRO CASTLE, which had originally been built for the Lake Erie steamboat City of Buffalo.

MISSISSIPPI RIVER STEAMBOAT JOHN W. CANNON, 1878.

JOHN W. CANNON.

BUILT 1878, at JEFFERSONVILLE, IND.
— Designed by Edward J. Howard. —

HULL, of wood, built by Howard & Company,
Length of keel 252½ feet; width of hull 43 feet;
depth of hold 9½ feet; draft of water 6 feet.
ENGINES, High Pressure Lever, built by Ainslie
& Cochrane, Louisville, KY. Diameter of cylinders 34½ inches, by 9 feet stroke.
BOILERS, seven, flue type, built by Joseph
Mitchell. Each 34 feet in length by 42 inches diameter; allowed 160 pounds steam.
WHEELS, 38 feet in diameter; 20 buckets each
wheel, 16 feet 2 inches long by 28 inches wide.
TONNAGE 1,144⁵⁰⁄₉₅

One of the most splendid steamboats ever constructed for service on the Mississippi River was the JOHN W. CANNON. She was built for the Coast & Mississippi River Packet Company, and cost $250,000. Her route was from New Orleans to Bayou Sara. Capacity 4500 bales of cotton, and sleeping accommodations for 250 passengers. The cabins of this boat were transferred to the new steamer OLIVER BIERNE.

HUDSON RIVER STEAMBOAT ALBANY.

THE ALBANY AFTER BEING LENGTHENED, 1893.

ALBANY.

BUILT 1880, at WILMINGTON, Delaware.

HULL, OF IRON, BUILT BY The Harlan & Hollingsworth Company. Original length of keel 284 feet — over all 295 feet; breadth of beam 40 feet — over guards 73 feet 2 inches; depth of hold (from base line to top of deck beams amidships) 11 feet 6 inches. Tonnage, gross 1346ᵗᵒⁿ, net 854ᵗᵒⁿ. Hull lengthened 1893, 30 feet, by the HARLAN & HOLLINGSWORTH Company, making the ALBANY 325 feet over all

ENGINE, VERTICAL BEAM, CONSTRUCTED BY Fletcher, Harrison & Company, New York. Diameter of cylinder 73 inches, by stroke of 12 feet.

BOILERS, THREE, OF IRON, IN HOLD, BUILT BY FLETCHER, HARRISON & CO. Length of each 33 feet, by 8 feet 10 inches diameter of shell

WHEELS, RADIAL, OF IRON, 32 feet in diameter and 12 feet wide NEW WHEELS 1893, FEATHERING TYPE

JOINER WORK, by John E. Hoffmire, New York.

A MODERN high-class passenger boat of the river Hudson. The ALBANY was the first-time large iron steamboat built for the day line between New York and Albany. With palatial saloons, extensive promenades and luxurious appointments, she makes an ideal grand passenger vessel. On Friday, October 23, 1885, the ALBANY made the following fast run:—

— THE ALBANY, AS FIRST BUILT, 1880 —

135

GREAT LAKES STEAMBOAT CITY OF CLEVELAND, 1880.

STATE OF OHIO.

FORMERLY "CITY OF ALPENA"
AND "CITY OF CLEVELAND."

BUILT 1880, at WYANDOTTE, MICH.

BY THE DETROIT DRY DOCK COMPANY.

HULL, OF IRON. Length 225 feet, beam 32 feet, depth of hold 12 feet

ENGINE, VERTICAL BEAM, BUILT BY DUNHAM & CO., NEW YORK, 1847. Diameter of cylinder 50 inches, length of stroke 11 feet. Nominal horse power 1800

BOILERS, TWO, OF IRON, BY FLETCHER & HARRISON, N.Y.

WHEELS, FEATHERING, "MORGAN" TYPE. 23 feet in diameter by 9 feet in width

TONNAGE GROSS 1,221 98/100
NET 917 71/100

THE CITY OF CLEVELAND was built for the Detroit & Cleveland Steam Navigation Company, and was one of the handsomest as well as the fastest steamboat on the Great Lakes, when she appeared. Her maximum speed was 19 miles per hour. Her engine was taken from the Lake Champlain steamer UNITED STATES, and the cabins came from the ADIRONDACK also of Lake Champlain. She was used on the route from Detroit to Hancock, on Lake Superior, for two seasons, and was afterwards placed on the line from Detroit to Alpena, having had her name changed to CITY OF ALPENA. In 1893 a new line was inaugurated between Cleveland and Buffalo, and, as the STATE OF OHIO, she ran on this route under the management of the Cleveland & Buffalo Transit Co.

MISSISSIPPI RIVER STEAMBOAT BELLE MEMPHIS, 1880.

BELLE MEMPHIS:-

BUILT 1880, at JEFFERSONVILLE, IND.

HULL, of wood, by HOWARD & COMPANY.
Length of keel..........267 feet
     " over all..........275 "
Width....................42? "
     " over guards.......68 "
Depth of hold..........7? "
Draft of water........44 inches.

ENGINES, two, high pressure lever, constructed by Ainslie, Cochran & Co, Louisville.
Diameter of cylinders, 27 inches
     stroke.. 8 feet

BOILERS, FIVE; OF IRON, ON DECK, BUILT BY MITCHELL & BRO., LOUISVILLE, KY

WHEELS. Diameter. . . . 35 feet.
No. of buckets each wheel..... 20.
Length of buckets..14 feet

TONNAGE 1,222 ?? GROSS
         1,222 ?? NET.

ONE of a large fleet of steamboats operated by the St Louis & New Orleans Anchor Line Company on the Mississippi River. She cost $90,000 and is one of the best boats of her class ever constructed. Speed 10 miles.

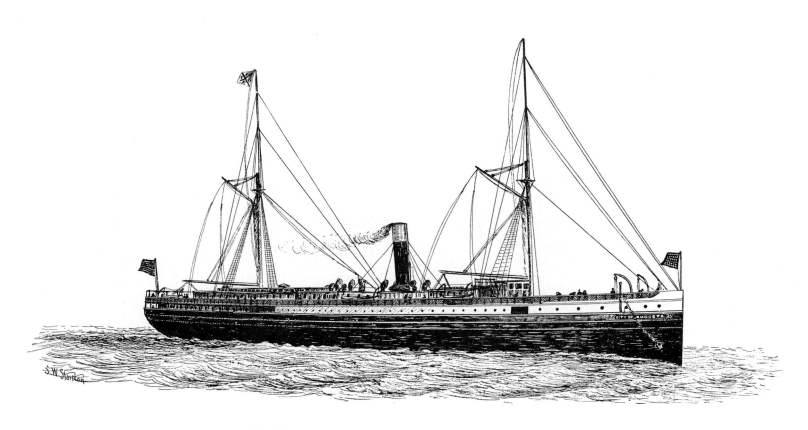

ATLANTIC COAST STEAMSHIP CITY OF AUGUSTA, 1880.

CITY OF AUGUSTA.

—Designed by EDWARD FARON—

BUILT 1880, at CHESTER, PENN.,
BY JOHN ROACH & SON.

HULL OF IRON. Length of Keel 300 feet; over all 320½ feet; breadth of beam 40½ feet; depth of hold 25 feet. Average draft of water 18 feet.

BOILERS SIX OF IRON, Scotch Type. Total grate surface 390 square feet.

ENGINE COMPOUND. Diameter of cylinders 42½ and 82 inches, by 54 inches stroke. Indicated horse power 2200.

WHEEL 4 BLADES, 16 feet 2 inches in diameter; pitch 23½ feet entering; 25½ feet mean, and 27½ feet leaving.

TONNAGE 2869 64/100 Gross 1929 28/100 Net

A LARGE and finely equipped coastwise steamer, built for the Ocean Steamship Company, to ply between New York and Savannah, Ga. Accommodations for 74 1st-class and 24 steerage passengers, and a carrying capacity for 1476 tons of freight. Handsome and well appointed saloons and staterooms, and every comfort and modern contrivance for the convenience of the traveling public. Speed 14 miles an hour

PACIFIC COAST STEAMSHIP COLUMBIA, 1880.

COLUMBIA:

~ Designed by Edward Faron ~

BUILT 1880, at CHESTER, PA.
By JOHN ROACH & SON.

HULL, OF IRON. Length between perpendiculars 309 feet 5 inches,
over all 333 feet; breadth of beam 38½ feet, depth of hold
14 feet 5 inches, to main deck 24 feet.

ENGINE, COMPOUND. Diameter of cylinders 42½ and 82 inches, by
54 inches stroke of piston.

BOILERS, SIX, RETURN TUBULAR, SCOTCH TYPE. Length of each 10½ feet;
diameter 12 feet; total grate surface 378 square feet; total heating
surface 8778 square feet.

WHEEL, FOUR BLADED. Diameter 14 feet, pitch 22 feet 6 inches.

~ TONNAGE 2721 89 Gross 1746 13 Net ~

A FINE large coasting steamship, built for the Oregon
Steamship Company for the
route between San Francisco
and Portland, Oregon. With splendid
furnishings, ample passenger accommodations,
large freight space, and good speed,
the COLUMBIA makes an ideal ship
for the business engaged in

139

LONG ISLAND SOUND STEAMBOAT CITY OF WORCESTER, 1881.

CITY of WORCESTER:

BUILT 1881 at WILMINGTON, Del.

By the HARLAN & HOLLINGSWORTH COMPANY.

HULL, OF IRON, 6 WATER-TIGHT BULKHEADS. Length on water line 325 feet; over all 340 feet; breadth of beam 46 feet (over guards 80 feet); depth of hold 14½ feet

ENGINE, VERTICAL BEAM, SURFACE CONDENSING. Diameter of cylinder 90 inches, by 12 feet stroke of piston

BOILERS, THREE. Each 37½ feet in length by 12 feet diameter and 13 feet face, containing 9,300 feet of fire surface and 550 feet of grate surface

WHEELS, 38 feet in diameter length of buckets 11 feet

TONNAGE - 2,489 GROSS
1,921 NET

THE CITY OF WORCESTER was the first large Long Island Sound passenger boat built of iron. She was launched on March 12, 1881, and began running on the route between New York and New London in September of the same year. Her fine speed and magnificent passenger accommodations at once made her a favorite among travellers, and won for her the title "Belle of Long Island Sound." She was a fast and splendid steamer. Sleeping accommodations for 700 people and freight room for 110 car loads

140

NEW YORK BAY EXCURSION STEAMBOAT CYGNUS, 1881.

CYGNUS.

BUILT 1881 at CHESTER, Pa.

BUILT OF IRON, CONSTRUCTED BY JOHN ROACH & SON.
Length of keel 213½ feet; over all 223½ feet; width of hull 32½ feet; over guards 59¼ feet; depth of hold 10¾ feet; draft of water 7 feet.

ENGINE, VERTICAL BEAM, BUILT BY W. & A. FLETCHER.
Diameter of cylinder 53 inches; stroke 12 feet.

BOILERS, TWO, OF IRON,

WHEELS, 29½ feet in diameter; buckets 9 feet in length, by 20 inches broad, dipping 40 inches.

TONNAGE: GROSS 857.44 NET 555.03.

The CYGNUS was one of a fleet of seven steamers built for the Iron Steamboat Company of New York, for excursion purposes on New York Bay, and adjacent waters. The CYGNUS has been employed on the Coney Island and other routes, and in 1883-4 ran on the St Johns River in Florida.

ATLANTIC COAST STEAMSHIP SAN MARCOS, 1881.

SAN MARCOS.

Designed by Edward Faron.

BUILT 1881, by JOHN ROACH & SON.
AT CHESTER, PA.

HULL, OF IRON.
Length of keel................318 feet
" over all................339 "
Width of hull.................39 "
Depth of hold.................21¾ "
Draft of water, 14 feet.

ENGINE, compound.
Diameter of cylinders...38¾74 inches
Stroke of piston..........54 "
Indicated horse power 1850.

BOILERS, six "SCOTCH" of IRON.
Length....................11 feet
Diameter..................128 inches
Total grate surface, 273 square feet.

PROPELLER WHEEL, 4 BLADES.
Diameter..................15 feet
Mean pitch..........11 feet 6 inches

→ TONNAGE: GROSS 2,839.29
NET 2,197.66

NEW YORK BAY EXCURSION STEAMBOAT TAURUS, 1881.

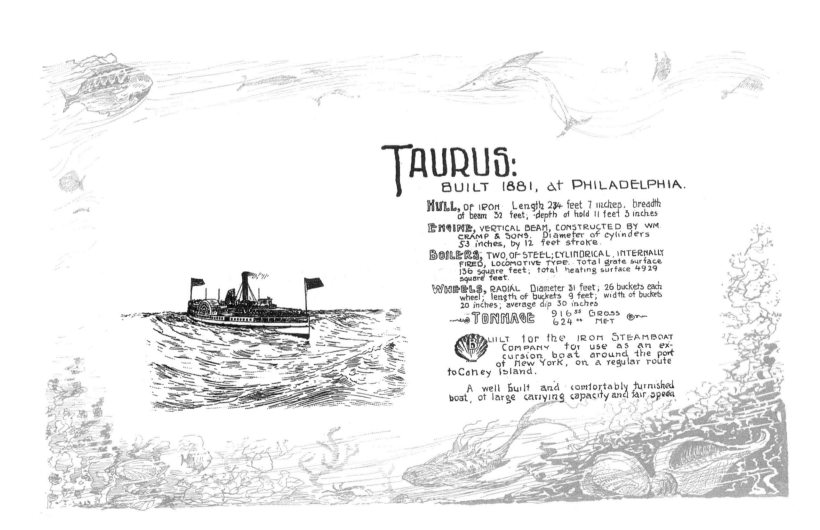

TAURUS:
BUILT 1881, at PHILADELPHIA.

HULL, OF IRON. Length 234 feet 7 inches; breadth of beam 32 feet; depth of hold 11 feet 3 inches.

ENGINE, VERTICAL BEAM, CONSTRUCTED BY WM. CRAMP & SONS. Diameter of cylinders 53 inches, by 12 feet stroke.

BOILERS, TWO, OF STEEL; CYLINDRICAL, INTERNALLY FIRED, LOCOMOTIVE TYPE. Total grate surface 136 square feet; total heating surface 4929 square feet.

WHEELS, RADIAL. Diameter 31 feet; 26 buckets each wheel; length of buckets 9 feet; width of buckets 20 inches; average dip 30 inches.

TONNAGE 916 55 GROSS
624 44 NET

UILT for the IRON STEAMBOAT COMPANY for use as an excursion boat around the port of New York, on a regular route to Coney Island.

A well built and comfortably furnished boat, of large carrying capacity and fair speed.

CHESAPEAKE BAY PASSENGER PROPELLER DANVILLE, 1882.

DANVILLE.

DESIGNED BY JAMES WOODALL

→ BUILT 1882, at BALTIMORE, Md. ←

HULL, OF WOOD CONSTRUCTED BY WILLIAM E. WOODALL & Co. Length of keel 210 feet; over all 228 feet; breadth of beam 38 feet; depth of hold 12 feet 9 inches.

ENGINE, COMPOUND, BUILT BY CHARLES REEDER & SONS, BALTIMORE. Diameter of cylinders 30 and 50 inches by 36 inches stroke. Indicated horse power 850.

BOILERS, TWO, OF STEEL, 'SCOTCH' TYPE, BUILT BY CHARLES REEDER & SONS. Total grate surface 84 square feet; total heating surface 2200 square feet; consumption of fuel per hour 1000 lbs.

WHEEL; FOUR BLADES Diameter 12 feet, pitch 16 feet 6 inches.

TONNAGE, 1297 ⁷³ Gross, 909 ¹⁴ Net.

THE DANVILLE was built for the Baltimore, Chesapeake & Richmond Steamboat Company, or "York River Line," for route between Baltimore and West Point, Va. She cost $150,000, and may be said to be one of the most successful boats of her class in America. Having a speed of 17 miles an hour, being very economical in running, with large and handsome saloons and staterooms and excellent freight carrying capacity, it would be almost an impossibility to excel her.

144

HUDSON RIVER STEAMBOAT KAATERSKILL, 1882.

Kaaterskill.
BUILT 1882, at ATHENS, N.Y.

HULL, OF WOOD, BUILT BY VAN LOAN & MAGEE.
Length of keel 265 feet; over all 285 feet; beam
38 feet; depth of hold 10 feet.

ENGINE, VERTICAL BEAM, CONSTRUCTED BY W.
& A. FLETCHER, New York. Diameter of
cylinder 63 inches, by 12 feet stroke

BOILERS, TWO, each 34 feet in length by 10
feet in diameter.

JOINER WORK, BY JOHN E. HOFFMIRE & SON, N.Y.

TONNAGE, 1361 40/100 Gross, 855 83/100 Net.

ONE OF THE FINEST
Hudson River night
boats of medium size
ever constructed.
A beautiful model
and fine speed. The interior
embellishments of Queen
Anne style and very handsome.
Sleeping accommodations for
300 passengers. Route, New York
to Catskill.

ATLANTIC COAST FREIGHT STEAMSHIP EXCELSIOR, 1882.

EXCELSIOR.

BUILT 1882,
at WILMINGTON, Del.,
By the HARLAN & HOLLINGSWORTH CO.

HULL, OF IRON. Length over all 351 feet; breadth of beam 42½ feet; depth of hold 32½ feet.
ENGINE, COMPOUND. Diameter of cylinders 38 and 76 inches, by 54 inches stroke.
BOILERS, FOUR, CYLINDRICAL, each 48 inches in diameter.
WHEEL, SECTIONAL, 17 feet in diameter.
TONNAGE @ 3,263 95 GROSS @
2,406 72 NET

ONE of the finest freight carrying steamships ever constructed in the United States. Built for the Morgan Line, for route between New York and New Orleans. She made what was considered a wonderful record during the first years of her existence, one round voyage being made in 13 days and 10 hours, which included the discharging and loading of full cargoes, a feat that had before been unparalleled in the history of the service on that route.

146

NEW YORK FERRYBOAT NEWBURGH, 1882.

NEWBURGH.

BUILT 1882, at NEWBURGH, N.Y.,
By WARD, STANTON & COMPANY.

HULL, OF IRON Length between perpendiculars 193½ feet;
over all 205 feet; breadth of beam 36 feet, over guards
65 feet; depth of hold 13 feet 4 inches

ENGINE, VERTICAL BEAM, CONSTRUCTED BY Ward, Stanton
& Co. Diameter of cylinder 50 inches, by 10 feet stroke.

BOILER, OF STEEL, 10½ feet in diameter and 33 feet
long, with two furnaces.

WHEELS, OF IRON, 21 feet in diameter and 8½ feet
wide

TONNAGE, 1053 9¹ Gross; 797 ⁹⁵ Net.

BUILT for the New York, West Shore
& Buffalo Rail Road Company, for
ferry line between New York
and Weehawken. Has mates in
the KINGSTON, ALBANY and OSWEGO.
A large and comfortable boat, with
artistically furnished cabins, and
excellent speed

NEW ENGLAND COAST STEAMBOAT PENOBSCOT, 1882.

PENOBSCOT:
BUILT 1882, at EAST BOSTON, Mass.

HULL, OF WOOD, BUILT BY Smith & Townsend.
Length of keel 225 feet; over all 249 feet; breadth of beam 38 feet; over guards 62 feet; depth of hold 13 feet; average draft of water 9 feet.

ENGINE, VERTICAL BEAM, CONSTRUCTED BY The Atlantic Works, EAST BOSTON. Diameter of cylinder 58 inches by 12 feet stroke.

BOILER, ONE, OF IRON, FLUE TYPE, BY THE ATLANTIC WORKS.

WHEELS, 34 feet in diameter and 8 feet wide

TONNAGE 1414 Gross   1244 Net

A LARGE, substantially built, and handsomely fitted up New England coast steamboat, built for the route between Boston and Bangor, Maine. She cost $200,000 and has a speed of 14 knots an hour, being a large freight carrier and having extensive accommodations for passengers Owned by the Boston & Bangor SS Co

LONG ISLAND SOUND STEAMBOAT PILGRIM, 1882.

PILGRIM:

BUILT 1882, at CHESTER, PA.
By JOHN ROACH & SON.

HULL, OF IRON, DOUBLE BOTTOM Length on load line 375 feet; over all 390 feet; breadth of beam 50 feet; over guards 88 feet, 7 inches; depth of hold 15 feet 7 inches; web frames; 103 water-tight compartments

ENGINE, VERTICAL BEAM, CONSTRUCTED AT THE Morgan Iron Works, New York. Diameter of cylinder 110 inches, by 14 feet stroke of piston

BOILERS, FOUR, OF STEEL, RETURN TUBULAR, EACH boiler having three cylindrical shells, connected, making front of boiler 25 feet 4 inches long, 10½ feet high and 14½ feet deep. Total grate surface 689 square feet. Each boiler has 336 tubes 3½ inches in diameter by 11 feet 6½ inches long.

WHEELS, OF IRON, RADIAL, 41 feet in diameter.

TONNAGE 3483 66 GROSS
 2512 99 NET

THE grandest Long Island steamboat to appear after the BRISTOL and PROVIDENCE, 1866, was the PILGRIM 1883. A veritable floating palace, a really great, a beautiful, marine wonder. Built for the Old Colony Steamboat Company for the route between New York and Fall River. She was the largest inland steam vessel ever constructed when she began running, since which time she has only been equalled by sister ships in the same Line.
Her saloons are of great beauty, everything being on a liberal and massive scale, and yet dainty and artistic to a degree. The PILGRIM cost $1,000,000; she has a speed of 20 miles an hour.

STEAM YACHT ATALANTA, 1883.

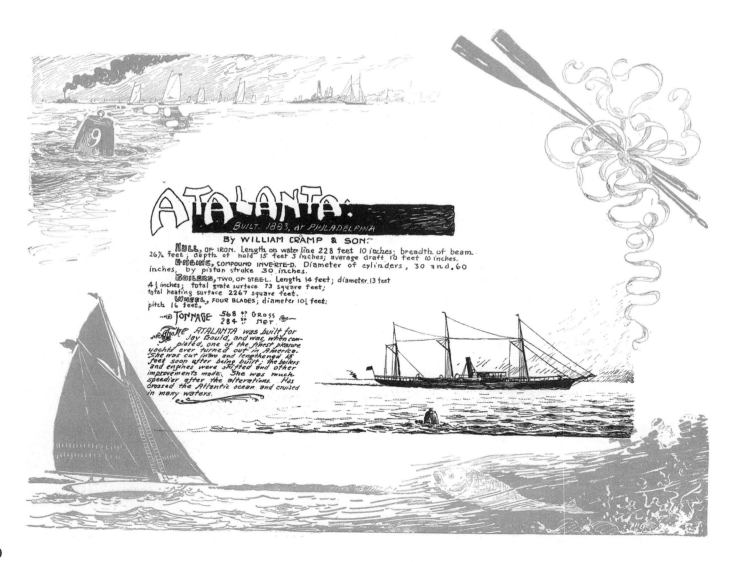

ATALANTA.
BUILT 1883, at PHILADELPHIA
BY WILLIAM CRAMP & SONS.

HULL, OF IRON. Length on water line 228 feet 10 inches; breadth of beam 26½ feet; depth of hold 15 feet 3 inches; average draft 10 feet 10 inches.

ENGINE, COMPOUND INVERTED. Diameter of cylinders, 30 and 60 inches, by piston stroke 30 inches.

BOILERS, TWO, OF STEEL. Length 14 feet; diameter 13 feet 4½ inches; total grate surface 73 square feet; total heating surface 2267 square feet;

WHEEL, FOUR BLADES; diameter 10½ feet; pitch 16 feet.

TONNAGE 568 52 GROSS
284 85 NET

The ATALANTA was built for Jay Gould, and was, when completed, one of the finest pleasure yachts ever turned out in America. She was cut in two and lengthened 18 feet soon after being built; the boilers and engines were shifted and other improvements made. She was much speedier after the alterations. Has crossed the Atlantic ocean and cruised in many waters.

150

NEW YORK AND CUBA STEAMSHIP CIENFUEGOS, 1883.

Stranded February 4, 1895, near Nassau, N. P.

CIENFUEGOS.

DESIGNED BY EDWARD FARON.

BUILT 1883, at CHESTER, PA.
By JOHN ROACH & SON.

HULL, OF IRON. Five bulkheads. Length on water line 292 feet, over all 308 feet; breadth of beam 39½ feet; depth of hold 21 feet 3 inches, average draft 16½ feet.

ENGINE, COMPOUND. Diameter of cylinders 38 and 74 ins, by 54 inches stroke, indicated Horse power 1800.

BOILERS, FOUR, OF IRON, SCOTCH TYPE. Total grate surface 307½ square feet.

WHEEL, FOUR BLADES, 15 feet in diameter; 23 feet mean pitch.

TONNAGE 2865³³ GROSS
2027⁵⁴ NET

The CIENFUEGOS was built for the route between New York and the south side of the island of Cuba, in the line known as the "N. Y. & Cuba Mail Steam Ship Company." An able vessel, and well adapted for the trade engaged in, being a large carrier on a light draft of water, and provided with splendid passenger accommodations.

HUDSON RIVER TUGBOAT JOHN H. CORDTS, 1883.

JOHN H. CORDTS.

BUILT 1883, at NEWBURGH, N.Y.
By WARD, STANTON & CO.

HULL, OF WOOD. Length 114 feet 6 inches; breadth of beam 25 feet; depth of hold 10 feet 6 inches.
ENGINE, COMPOUND. Diameter of cylinders 28 and 52 inches, by 40 inches stroke.
BOILERS, two. Diameter 96 inches; length 18 feet.
TONNAGE Gross 194 79; NET 97 40

THIS tugboat, the first on the coast having two smokestacks, was built for towing on the Hudson River, and when she appeared she immediately became celebrated as being the most powerful on the river. A strong, serviceable vessel, fitted with all modern improvements. FIRST EMPLOYED IN TOWING BETWEEN GLASCO AND NEW YORK, IN THE WASHBURN LINE, AND LATER TRANSFERRED TO THE CORNELL TOWBOAT LINE.

STEAM YACHT ELECTRA, 1884.

Electra

Designed by
GUSTAV HILLMAN

BUILT 1884, at WILMINGTON,
By the HARLAN & HOLLINGSWORTH CO.

HULL, OF IRON. Launched April 14, 1884. Length on water line (with 9½ feet draft) 161½ feet; length on deck, from foreside of rudder post to after side of stem, 172½ feet; breadth of beam, extreme, 23 feet; depth moulded from top of keel to top of beams at side 13 feet 6 inches; depth of hold at center and middle of load line 13 feet 3 inches.

ENGINE, INVERTED, DIRECT-ACTING, SURFACE-CONDENSING COMPOUND, DESIGNED AND BUILT BY SAMUEL STANTON, 1886. Diameter of cylinders 22 and 40 inches, by 26 inches stroke.

BOILERS, TWO, OF STEEL, CYLINDRICAL, EACH 10¾ FEET in diameter by 11 feet in length; 1550 square feet of heating surface in each.

WHEEL, 8 feet in diameter, 13 feet pitch.

TONNAGE - 303 Gross - 190 Net

A HANDSOME steam yacht, belonging to Mr. Elbridge T. Gerry, and for a number of years the flag-ship of the New York Yacht Club. Palatially fitted up and very speedy

PACIFIC COAST STEAMSHIP SANTA ROSA, 1884.

SANTA ROSA:

~ BUILT 1884, at CHESTER, PA., ~
~ By JOHN ROACH & SON ~

HULL, OF IRON. Length of keel 326½ feet; over all 345 feet; breadth of beam 40½ feet; depth of hold 23 feet.

ENGINE, INVERTED COMPOUND. Diameter of cylinders 45 and 86 inches, by 54 inches stroke of piston.

BOILERS, FOUR, DOUBLE-ENDED RETURN TUBULAR, "SCOTCH" TYPE. Length of each 23 feet 2 inches; diameter 11 feet 9 inches; total grate surface 480 square feet; total heating surface 12000 square feet;

WHEEL, FOUR BLADES. Diameter 15 feet; pitch 24 feet.

~ TONNAGE, 2416⁷⁷ Gross; 1335⁴⁰ Net ~

A LARGE, HANDSOME and speedy coastwise steamship, built for the Oregon Railway and Navigation Company, for service on the Pacific Coast. Speed 16½ knots an hour.

TAMPA BAY STEAMBOAT MANATEE, 1884.

MANATEE.

DESIGNED BY
SAMUEL STANTON.
BUILT 1884,
at NEWBURGH, N.Y.,
By WARD, STANTON & CO.

HULL, OF IRON. Length of Keel 107 feet,
10 inches; over all 120 feet; breadth of
beam 20 feet 6 inches, over guards 32
feet, depth of hold 6 feet 4 inches.

ENGINE, VERTICAL BEAM. Diameter of cylinder
20 inches, by 5 feet stroke of piston.

BOILER, ONE OF IRON. Diameter 72 inches;
length 10 feet; working pressure 60 lbs.

TONNAGE 104 69 GROSS
66 17 NET

BUILT for the route
between Tampa and
the Manatee River,
in Florida. Launched
in August, 1884, and
made the run from New
York to Tampa Bay in 7
running days. Afterwards used
on the route between Tampa,
Charlotte Harbor and Fort Myers.
Sold 1886, for service on
the St. Johns River.

155

HUDSON RIVER PASSENGER PROPELLER CITY OF KINGSTON, 1884.

CITY OF KINGSTON

BUILT 1884, at WILMINGTON, Del,
By the HARLAN & HOLLINGSWORTH COMPANY.

HULL, OF IRON Length between perpendiculars 240 feet, over all 250 feet, breadth of beam 33½ feet, depth of hold 12½ feet

ENGINE, COMPOUND Diameter of cylinders 30 and 56 inches, by 36 inches stroke

BOILERS, Two. Diameter 11½ feet, length 12 feet 3 furnaces in each boiler, 38 inches in diameter.

WHEEL, FOUR BLADES, 11 feet in diameter, pitch 18 feet 3 inches

~ TONNAGE - 1113 40/100 Gross - 816 35/100 Net ~

The CITY OF KINGSTON was built for the Cornell Steamboat Company, to ply on the Hudson River between New York and Rondout, and was the pioneer large modern passenger propeller to run on that sheet of water. Her speed was 19 miles an hour and she ran very successfully for a number of years. Finely finished and comfortably furnished, with sleeping accommodations for a large number of persons, and excellent freight carrying capacity.

Sold and left New York for Puget Sound, Washington November 22, 1889, and since 1890 has been employed on the Sound, also making occasional trips to Alaska.

STEAM YACHT NOURMAHAL, 1884.

NOURMAHAL

Designed by GUSTAV HILLMAN

BUILT 1884, at WILMINGTON, Del.,
By the HARLAN & HOLLINGSWORTH COMPANY.

HULL, OF STEEL Length on water line 221 feet, on deck
232 feet 5 inches, breadth of beam, extreme, 30 feet;
depth of hold 18½ feet; extreme 20 feet

ENGINE, VERTICAL, DIRECT ACTING, SURFACE CONDENSING,
COMPOUND Cylinders 34 and 60 inches in diameter
by 36 inches length of stroke.

BOILERS, FOUR, OF STEEL. Each 12 feet in length by
8 feet 3 inches in diameter.

WHEEL, FOUR BLADES; 12 feet in diameter; 19 feet pitch

TONNAGE 745 20/100 GROSS
372 60/100 NET

BUILT for William Astor, of
New York, the NOURMAHAL,
was, at the time of her launching the largest screw steam yacht
ever constructed in America.

A magnificent specimen of
naval architecture, staunch and sea-
worthy, and of fine speed. Interior
finish and embellishments tasty and
elegant.

HUDSON RIVER TUGBOAT POCAHONTAS, 1884.

POCAHONTAS:
BUILT 1884,
at NEWBURGH, N.Y.,
By WARD, STANTON & COMPANY.
HULL, OF WOOD. Length 118 feet; breadth of beam
26 feet 5 inches; depth of hold 9 feet 4 inches.
ENGINE, COMPOUND. Diameter of cylinders 24 and 42
inches by 36 inches stroke.
BOILERS, TWO. Diameter of each 96 inches, length
15 feet.
~ TONNAGE 117 44/100 Gross; 94 18/100 Net ~
THE POCAHONTAS, and her mate the
OSCEOLA, were built for the
Ronan Line, to tow canal boats
on the Hudson River between New York
and Albany. Strongly built, first-class tugs,
admirably adapted to the business.

DELAWARE RIVER PASSENGER PROPELLER BRANDYWINE, 1885.

BRANDYWINE.

BUILT 1885, by THE HARLAN & HOLLINGSWORTH CO,
at WILMINGTON, DEL.
STEEL HULL; Length 177 feet 6 inches; width 25 feet; depth of
hold 9 feet 6 inches.
ONE COMPOUND ENGINE, 24 and 42 inches diameter of
cylinder by 24 inches stroke.
TWO BOILERS, locomotive type, each 24 feet long by 87
inches in diameter, allowed 105 pounds of steam.

GROSS TONNAGE 407.82. NET TONNAGE 215.27.

THE BRANDYWINE was built
to ply between Phila-
delphia and Wilmington on
the Delaware river in conjunction
with the propeller WILMINGTON.
The speed of this vessel is
about 18 miles per hour. Owned
by the Wilmington Steamboat Company.

OHIO RIVER STEAMBOAT HUDSON, 1886.

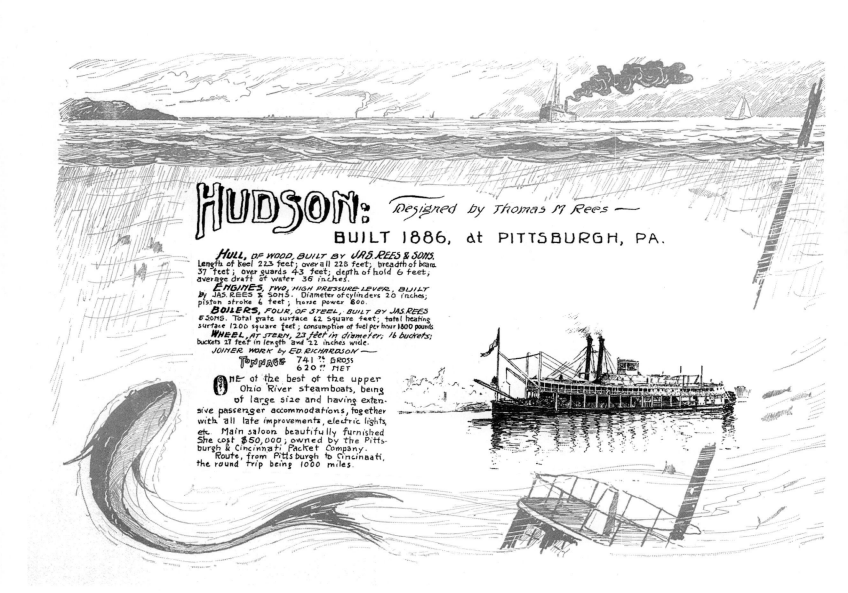

HUDSON: Designed by Thomas M Rees —

BUILT 1886, at PITTSBURGH, PA.

HULL, OF WOOD, BUILT BY JAS. REES & SONS. Length of keel 223 feet; overall 225 feet; breadth of beam 37 feet; over guards 43 feet; depth of hold 6 feet; average draft of water 36 inches.

ENGINES, TWO, HIGH PRESSURE·LEVER, BUILT by JAS. REES & SONS. Diameter of cylinders 20 inches; piston stroke 6 feet; horse power 800.

BOILERS, FOUR, OF STEEL, BUILT BY JAS. REES & SONS. Total grate surface 62 square feet; total heating surface 1200 square feet; consumption of fuel per hour 1800 pounds.

WHEEL, AT STERN, 23 feet in diameter; 16 buckets; buckets 21 feet in length and 22 inches wide.

JOINER WORK by ED. RICHARDSON —

TONNAGE 741 7/10 GROSS
620 5/10 NET

ONE of the best of the upper Ohio River steamboats, being of large size and having extensive passenger accommodations, together with all late improvements, electric lights, etc. Main saloon beautifully furnished She cost $50,000; owned by the Pittsburgh & Cincinnati Packet Company.
Route, from Pittsburgh to Cincinnati, the round trip being 1000 miles.

STEAM YACHT ALVA, 1886.

BUILT 1886, by the HARLAN & HOLLINGSWORTH CO.,
AT WILMINGTON, DEL.
Designed by St Clare Byrne, Liverpool
Owned by William K. Vanderbilt, New York.

DIMENSIONS: Hull, of steel, length from stem to stern post, 256 feet, over all, 285 feet; breadth of hull, 32½ feet, depth of hold, 18 feet 6 inches Gross tonnage 1,151.24 Net tonnage 600.55
ONE ENGINE, compound surface condensing, with three cylinders, 45, 31 and 45 inches in diameter, by 42 inches stroke Two steel boilers, 17 feet in diameter by 10 feet stroke.

ONE of the most beautiful and costly steam yachts ever built in America was the Alva She was launched on October 14 1886, and cost complete, nearly $1,000,000 The longest cruise she ever took was in 1887-88, when she crossed the Atlantic to England thence to the North Sea and afterwards to the Mediterranean, and back to New York via the Canary Islands and Nassau
On July 24, 1892, while lying at anchor near Pollock Rip, Nantucket Shoals the Alva was run into by the steamship H.F. Dimock, during a dense fog, and sunk in 15 minutes. All on board were saved; she could not be raised and became a total loss

GREAT LAKES STEAMSHIP SUSQUEHANNA, 1886.

SUSQUEHANNA:

BUILT 1886, at BUFFALO, N.Y.

By the UNION DRY DOCK COMPANY.

HULL, OF STEEL. Length of keel 302½ feet; over all 320½ feet; breadth of beam 40 feet; depth of hold 24 feet.

ENGINE, TRIPLE EXPANSION. Diameter of cylinders 36, 51 and 51 inches, by 48 inches stroke.

BOILERS, TWO, OF STEEL, "SCOTCH" TYPE, BUILT by the "LAKE ERIE BOILER WORKS, BUFFALO. Length 11 feet; diameter 13 feet. Total grate surface 120 feet.

WHEEL, FOUR BLADES. Diameter 14 feet; pitch at first 21 feet, afterward changed to 18 feet

TONNAGE 2500 ʰ GROSS.
2065 ʰ NET

A MODERN Steamship of the Great Lakes, built for the "Anchor Line," and used in carrying package freight. Was one of the finest ever constructed for service on the Northwestern Lakes when she first came out

CHESAPEAKE BAY STEAMBOAT EMMA GILES, 1887.

163

CHATTAHOOCHEE:

FIRST STEEL HULL AMERICAN STEAMBOAT.

BUILT 1881, at PITTSBURGH, PA.

Length 159 feet; Beam 31 feet (over guards 37½ feet); Depth of hold, 5 feet, 8 inches
HULL, ENGINES and BOILERS, by JAMES REES & SONS, PITTSBURGH.
JOINER WORK, by W. F. RICHARDSON, PITTSBURGH.

TWO ENGINES (HIGH PRESSURE LEVER, POPPET VALVES); 15 inches diameter of cylinders, by 5 feet stroke
THREE BOILERS, of steel, each 42 inches wide by 20 feet in length, 6 flues in each
STERN WHEEL, 18 feet in diameter; 24 foot buckets.
GROSS TONNAGE 436.92; NET TONNAGE 415.08.

THE Chattahoochee was the first all-steel hull American steamboat built to ply in United States waters. She was constructed for the Peoples Line, of Columbus, Ga., for service on the Chattahoochee river, and cost $45,000. The hull (both plates and frames) was of crucible steel, and she drew, light, 21 inches of water, the deepest draught being at the stern. With a cargo of 50 tons, she drew 3 feet; with 200 tons, 3 feet, and when fully loaded, 450 tons of freight, the speed was 13 miles an hour, with 160 lbs. steam pressure. After a few seasons' work on the Chattahoochee she was taken to the St. Johns River, in Florida, where she ran for a number of years; later she was taken to the Mississippi River and ran between Vicksburgh and Greenville. Destroyed by fire while lying at the Kleinstone wharf boat, below Vicksburgh, on December 7, 1893.

CITY of JACKSONVILLE:

BUILT 1882, by the HARLAN & HOLLINGSWORTH CO., WILMINGTON, DEL.

IRON HULL, 165 feet in length; 32 feet 6 inches beam, and 7 feet 6 inches depth of hold.

TWO ENGINES, inclined jet condensing, with 30 inch cylinders by 6 feet stroke.
GROSS TONNAGE 459.85   NET TONNAGE 395.75

THE City of Jacksonville was built for the navigation of the St. Johns River in Florida, for the De Bary Merchants Line, in connection with the Fredk de Bary, and other steamers. Afterwards ran in the Clyde Line. Used during summer seasons on excursion routes at New York, Boston and vicinity.

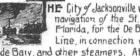

QUEEN of ST. JOHNS:

BUILT 1884, at CINCINNATI, OHIO.

WOODEN HULL: Length 192 feet 6 inches; beam 30 feet 4 inches (over guards 54 feet); depth of hold 7 ft 5 inches.
GROSS TONNAGE 459.03   NET TONNAGE 329.03

This boat was constructed for the Favorite Navigation Company, for service on the St. Johns River, Florida, and was designed by Frank N. Marten. She was originally a propeller, the engines, built by the Covington Machine Works, being high pressure, each cylinder 16 inches in diameter by 16 inches stroke, driving a propeller wheel, 4 blades, 9 feet in diameter. There were 4 steel return flue boilers, built by Robert Jones, at Cincinnati. The hull was constructed by James Mack. She cost $54,000. Soon after arriving on the St. Johns River she was converted, at Jacksonville, into a side-wheel steamer, with engines 28 inches diameter of cylinders by 7 feet stroke, high pressure. Wheels 24 foot diameter, 10 foot buckets, 20 inches wide, 24 inches dip. These engines were out of the Ohio River steamer Bonnie Tyger. The Queen of St. Johns, after running a number of years on the St. Johns, went to the Cape Fear River, in North Carolina, where she was totally destroyed by fire on July 18, 1889.

ROSA:

BUILT 1870, at WILMINGTON, DEL.

IRON HULL: Length of keel, 136 feet; beam 22 ft. (over guards 38 feet); depth of hold 5 feet.

TWO INCLINED ENGINES, with 16 inch cylinders by 5 feet stroke.
ONE BOILER, 6 feet 7 inches width of front, 5 feet 6 inches diameter of shell, and whole length 18 feet 4½ inches.

BUILT by the Pusey & Jones Co. for Capt. I. N. Philpot, and first used on Savannah River, in Georgia. Afterwards transferred to the St. Johns River, Florida, on which she ran for a number of years, from which place she went to the Atrato River, in South America, and renamed *José m Goenngea.*

164

GULF OF MEXICO STEAMSHIP OLIVETTE, 1887.

OLIVETTE:

Built 1887, at PHILADELPHIA, Pa.

IRON HULL: Length, water line, 281 feet 6 inches; over all 291 feet 6 inches; width, 35 feet; depth 19 feet 6 inches.

ENGINE: Inverted triple expansion; diameter of cylinders 23, 36 and 60 inches, by 36 inches stroke; indicated horse power 1700.

BOILERS, four, of steel, cylindrical, internally fired, return tubular; total grate surface 186 sq feet; total heating surface, 5798 sq. feet;

PROPELLER WHEEL, 4 blades, 11 feet in diameter, 15 feet pitch.

~ Gross tonnage 1611.42   Net tonnage 1104.90 ~

THE OLIVETTE was built by the WILLIAM CRAMP SHIP & ENGINE BUILDING COMPANY for Mr. H.B. PLANT, to ply (with the steamship Mascotte) between Tampa, Fla., and Havana, Cuba.
She is a very handsome vessel, being finely furnished and equipped with every modern improvement. Speed, 16 knots.
Used during summer season on the route between Boston, Mass., and Nova Scotia.

HUDSON RIVER PROPELLER HOMER RAMSDELL, 1887.

HOMER RAMSDELL.

~ BUILT 1887, ~
at NEWBURGH, N.Y.

Designed by Thomas E. Marvel

HULL, OF STEEL, CONSTRUCTED BY
T.S. MARVEL & Co. Length of keel 225
feet 8 inches; over all 237 feet; breadth of
beam 32 feet 6 inches; over guards 37 feet 6 inches;
depth of hold 11 feet 9 inches; average draft of water
11 feet 6 inches. Original hull was 25 feet shorter;
lengthened in 1892.

ENGINE, COMPOUND, BUILT by WILLIAM WRIGHT, Newburgh.
Diameter of cylinders 28 and 52 inches; by 36 inches stroke of piston.
Indicated horse power 1022.

BOILERS, TWO OF STEEL, LOBSTER BACK TYPE, BUILT BY
THE W.& A. FLETCHER Co. HOBOKEN, N.J. Consumption
of fuel per hour 4000 lbs.

WHEEL, FOUR BLADES. Diameter 11 feet; pitch
16 feet.

JOINER WORK, by THOMAS SHAWS SONS, NEWBURGH.

TONNAGE 1181 GROSS 822 Net

BUILT for the line between
Newburgh and New York,
and owned by the Homer Ramsdell
Transportation Co. of Newburgh.
A large, speedy, modern passenger propeller of the first
class. Cost $115,000. Speed
16 miles an hour.

HUDSON RIVER STEAMBOAT NEW YORK, 1887.

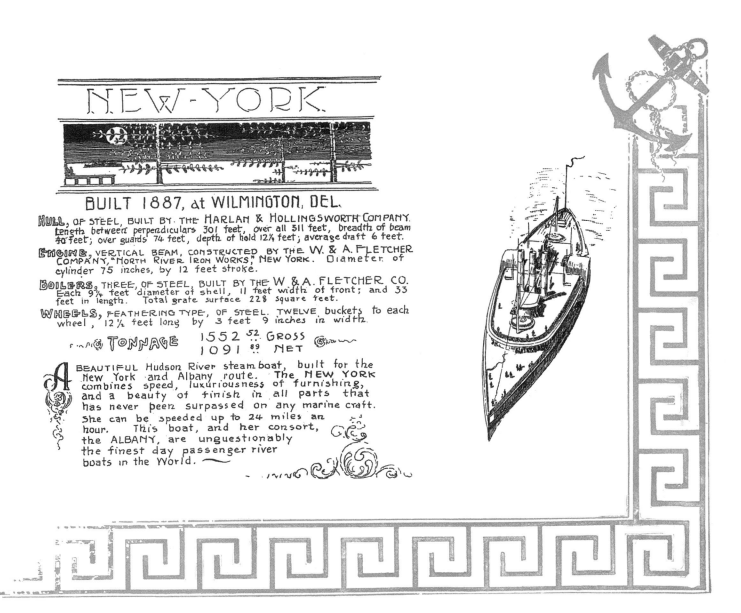

NEW-YORK.

BUILT 1887, at WILMINGTON, DEL.

HULL, OF STEEL, BUILT BY THE HARLAN & HOLLINGSWORTH COMPANY. Length between perpendiculars 301 feet, over all 311 feet, breadth of beam 40 feet; over guards 74 feet, depth of hold 12½ feet; average draft 6 feet.

ENGINE, VERTICAL BEAM, CONSTRUCTED BY THE W. & A. FLETCHER COMPANY, "NORTH RIVER IRON WORKS", NEW YORK. Diameter of cylinder 75 inches, by 12 feet stroke.

BOILERS, THREE, OF STEEL, BUILT BY THE W. & A. FLETCHER CO. Each 9¼ feet diameter of shell, 11 feet width of front; and 33 feet in length. Total grate surface 228 square feet.

WHEELS, FEATHERING TYPE, OF STEEL. TWELVE buckets to each wheel, 12½ feet long by 3 feet 9 inches in width.

TONNAGE $1552 \frac{52}{}$ GROSS
$1091 \frac{89}{}$ NET

A BEAUTIFUL Hudson River steamboat, built for the New York and Albany route. The NEW YORK combines speed, luxuriousness of furnishing, and a beauty of finish in all parts that has never been surpassed on any marine craft. She can be speeded up to 24 miles an hour. This boat, and her consort, the ALBANY, are unquestionably the finest day passenger river boats in the World.

DELAWARE RIVER PASSENGER PROPELLER CITY OF CHESTER, 1887.

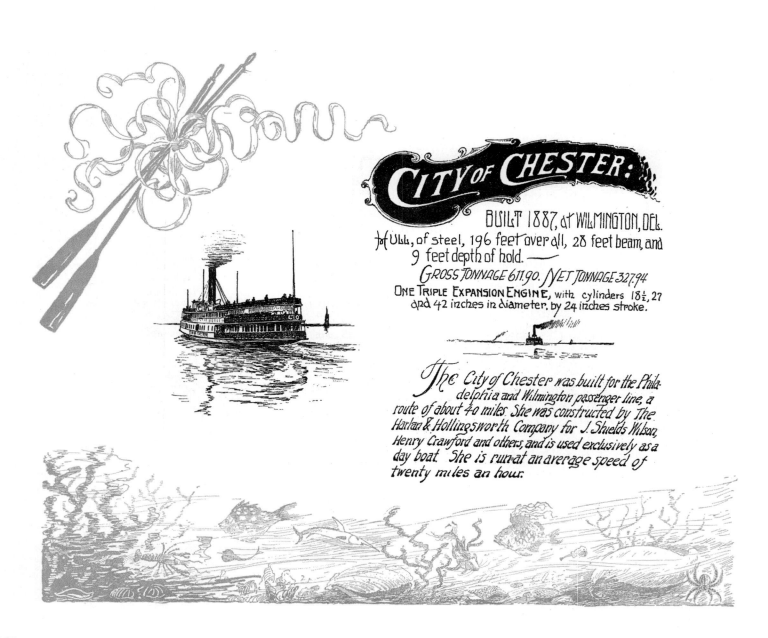

CITY OF CHESTER:

BUILT 1887, at WILMINGTON, DEL.
Hull, of steel, 196 feet over all, 28 feet beam, and 9 feet depth of hold.
GROSS TONNAGE 611.90. NET TONNAGE 327.94
ONE TRIPLE EXPANSION ENGINE, with cylinders 18½, 27 and 42 inches in diameter, by 24 inches stroke.

The City of Chester was built for the Philadelphia and Wilmington passenger line, a route of about 40 miles. She was constructed by The Harlan & Hollingsworth Company for J. Shields Wilson, Henry Crawford and others, and is used exclusively as a day boat. She is run at an average speed of twenty miles an hour.

LAKE MICHIGAN PASSENGER PROPELLER PETOSKEY, 1887.

PETOSKEY:

BUILT 1887, at MANITOWOC, Wis.

HULL, OF WOOD, CONSTRUCTED BY RAND and BURGER Length 171 feet 4 inches; breadth of beam 30 feet 3 inches; depth of hold 3 feet

ENGINE, "TROUT" FORE AND AFT COMPOUND, BUILT BY KING IRON WORKS, BUFFALO, N.Y. Diameter of cylinders 20 and 40 inches, by 36 inches stroke.

BOILER, ONE, 16 feet in length by 10 feet in width.

TONNAGE, GROSS 770 96 NET 544 51

BUILT for the freight and passenger traffic on Lake Michigan, in the Seymour Transportation company's line between Chicago and Harbor Springs, and intermediate points. A staunch and excellent boat for the trade engaged in. Sixty staterooms and sleeping accommodations for two hundred and ten persons. Cabins mahogany finished. Speed thirteen miles an hour.

PACIFIC COAST PROPELLER PREMIER, 1887.

PREMIER:

BUILT 1887, at SAN FRANCISCO, Cal.

HULL, of steel. Length of keel 200 feet; length over all 207 feet; width of hull 42 feet (over guards 43 feet); depth of hold 12 feet 10 inches; draft of water 7 feet 9 inches.

ENGINE, triple expansion. Diameter of cylinders 23, 34 and 56 inches, by 36 inches stroke.

BOILERS, three of steel; total grate surface 108 square feet; total heating surface 4038 square feet

FOUR-BLADED PROPELLER WHEEL, 10 feet 3 inches in diameter; mean pitch 16 feet 6 inches.

~ GROSS TONNAGE 1080 53/100. NET TONNAGE 602 05/100. ~

THE PREMIER was designed by Captain John Irving and constructed by the Union Iron Works. She cost $150,000 and had a speed of 15 knots per hour. She plied on Puget Sound and was a popular boat.

On October 9, 1892, during a dense fog, she collided with the steamship Willamette, on Puget Sound, by which accident four passengers lost their lives. She was badly damaged, but was subsequently repaired, having been placed under the English flag.

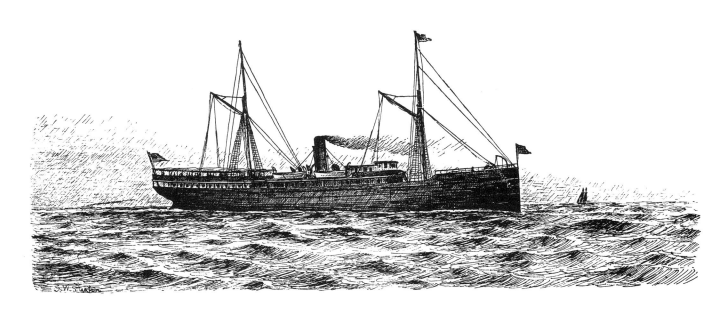

ATLANTIC COAST STEAMSHIP PARTHIAN, 1887.

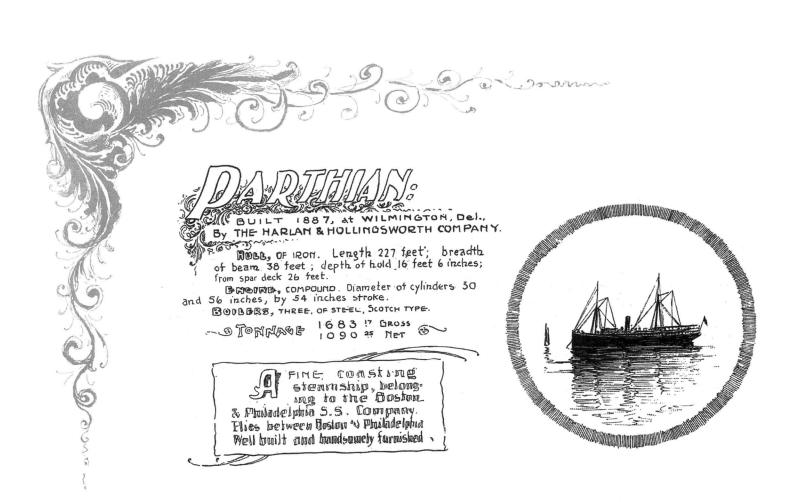

PARTHIAN.

BUILT 1887, at WILMINGTON, Del.,
By THE HARLAN & HOLLINGSWORTH COMPANY.

HULL, OF IRON. Length 227 feet; breadth
of beam 38 feet; depth of hold 16 feet 6 inches;
from spar deck 26 feet.

ENGINE, COMPOUND. Diameter of cylinders 30
and 56 inches, by 54 inches stroke.

BOILERS, THREE, OF STEEL, SCOTCH TYPE.

TONNAGE   1683 17 GROSS
          1090 25 NET

A FINE COASTING steamship, belonging to the Boston
& Philadelphia S.S. Company.
Plies between Boston & Philadelphia.
Well built and handsomely furnished.

 **JOPPA.** BUILT 1885, at WILMINGTON, Delaware

~CONSTRUCTED BY THE HARLAN & HOLLINGSWORTH CO. ~

HULL, OF IRON. Length 190 feet; beam 31 feet; depth of hold 9 feet.
ENGINE, VERTICAL BEAM. Diameter of cylinder 40 inches; stroke 10 feet.
BOILER, ONE. Diameter 135 inches; length 18 feet.

~TONNAGE, 607⁵⁰ Gross; 483⁶³ Net. ~

 BUILT for the Maryland Steamboat Company, for the passenger and freight line from Baltimore to Chesapeake Bay ports. An excellent steamboat, well appointed, of good speed and ample carrying capacity.

B.S.FORD.

BUILT 1877, at WILMINGTON, Delaware.

HULL, OF IRON, 164½ feet in length; 27 feet 3 inches breadth of beam; 8½ feet depth of hold.
ENGINE, VERTICAL BEAM. Diameter of cylinder 38 inches; stroke 9 feet.
BOILER, ONE, ORIGINAL BY THE HARLAN & HOLLINGSWORTH CO. NEW. BOILER BY THE COLUMBIAN IRON WORKS, BALTIMORE. Diameter, 111 inches; length 16½ feet.

~TONNAGE GROSS 417⁴³ NET 318⁸¹ ~

THE B.S.FORD was built by the Harlan & Hollingsworth Company for the Chester River Steamboat Company, of Baltimore, Md. On May 3, 1884, she was partially destroyed by fire, at Chestertown, Md. Was rebuilt and placed on her regular route again.

CAMBRIDGE.

DESIGNED BY JAMES WOODALL.

BUILT 1890, at BALTIMORE, Md.

HULL, OF WOOD, BY WILLIAM E. WOODALL & CO., Length of keel 164 feet; over all 175 feet; width of hull 34 feet; over guards 36 feet 6 inches; depth of hold 9 feet; draft forward 4 feet 8 inches; draft aft 8 feet.
ENGINE, COMPOUND, PROPELLER, BUILT BY JAMES CLARK & CO., Baltimore. Diameter of cylinders 20 and 40 inches, by 26 inches stroke.
BOILERS, TWO "SCOTCH" OF STEEL, BY JAMES CLARK & CO. Grate surface 80 square feet; heating surface 2396 square feet; consumption of fuel per hour ½ ton.
WHEEL, FOUR BLADES, 9 feet in diameter, 12 feet 6 inches pitch.

~TONNAGE: Gross 834.¹⁸ Net 692.⁹³ ~

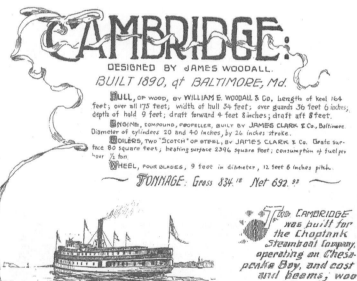

THE CAMBRIDGE was built for the Choptank Steamboat Company, operating on Chesapeake Bay, and cost $90,000. Her hull is of the composite type, having iron frames and beams, wood planked. Capacity 200 night passengers. Speed 18 miles per hour. One of the most successful steamers of her class in America.

~SASSAFRAS:~

BUILT 1892, at BALTIMORE, Md.

HULL, COMPOSITE – IRON FRAMES, WOOD PLANKING – BUILT BY S. W. Skinner & Son. Length 151 feet; beam over guards, 45 feet; depth of hold 8 feet.
ENGINE, VERTICAL BEAM, CONSTRUCTED BY Charles Reeder & Sons, BALTIMORE. Diameter of cylinder 36 inches, by 9 feet stroke.
BOILER, OF STEEL, BUILT BY CHARLES REEDER & SONS. Diameter 120 inches; length 15½ feet.

~TONNAGE: 403⁷⁷ Gross; 329⁷³ Net. ~

 BUILT for the Sassafras River Steamboat Company, and used as a day boat between Baltimore and the Sassafras River. A staunchly built and excellent inland steamboat of the medium size.

NEW YORK HARBOR FERRYBOAT ROBERT GARRETT, 1887.

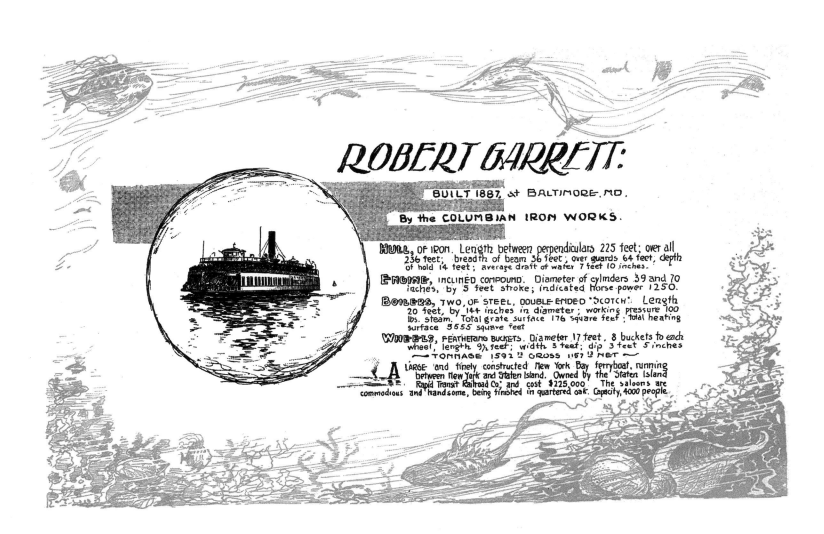

ROBERT GARRETT:

BUILT 1887, at BALTIMORE, MD.

By the COLUMBIAN IRON WORKS.

HULL, OF IRON. Length between perpendiculars 225 feet; over all 236 feet; breadth of beam 36 feet; over guards 64 feet; depth of hold 14 feet; average draft of water 7 feet 10 inches.

ENGINE, INCLINED COMPOUND. Diameter of cylinders 39 and 70 inches, by 5 feet stroke; indicated horse-power 1250.

BOILERS, TWO, OF STEEL, DOUBLE-ENDED "SCOTCH". Length 20 feet, by 144 inches in diameter; working pressure 100 lbs. steam. Total grate surface 176 square feet; total heating surface 5555 square feet.

WHEELS, FEATHERING BUCKETS. Diameter 17 feet, 8 buckets to each wheel; length 9½ feet; width 3 feet; dip 3 feet 5 inches.

— TONNAGE 1592²³ GROSS 1157¹³ NET —

A LARGE and finely constructed New York Bay ferryboat, running between New York and Staten Island. Owned by the Staten Island Rapid Transit Railroad Co., and cost $225,000. The saloons are commodious and handsome, being finished in quartered oak. Capacity, 4000 people.

STEAM YACHT BALLYMENA, 1888.

BALLYMENA:

BUILT 1888, at BRISTOL, R.I.

HULL, OF STEEL, BUILT BY THE HERRESHOFF MANUFACTURING COMPANY. Length of Keel 134 feet; over all 146 feet; breadth of Beam 17 feet; depth of hold 11½ feet.

ENGINE, ONE QUADRUPLE EXPANSION, WITH FIVE CYLINDERS, BUILT BY THE HERRESHOFF MFG. COMPANY. Cylinders 11¾, 16, 22¾, 22½ and 22½ inches in diameter, by 15 inches stroke.

BOILER, WATER-TUBE STEEL PIPE, BUILT by the ALMY WATER-TUBE BOILER COMPANY, PROVIDENCE, R.I. Width 5 feet 1½ inches; length 100 inches; height 96 inches. Total grate surface 51 square feet; total heating surface 1661 square feet.

~ TONNAGE, 145 ⁵⁵ Gross; 72 ⁵⁵ net ~

THE BALLYMENA was the first steel steam yacht built by the HERRESHOFF Mfg. Co. A handsome vessel, with comfortable and airy apartments, and good speed. In 1893 made 168 miles in 10 hours and 55 minutes, with new "Almy" boilers, natural draft. Built for Alexander Brown of Baltimore, and afterwards sold to John H. Brown.

LAKE CHAMPLAIN STEAMBOAT CHATEAUGAY, 1888.

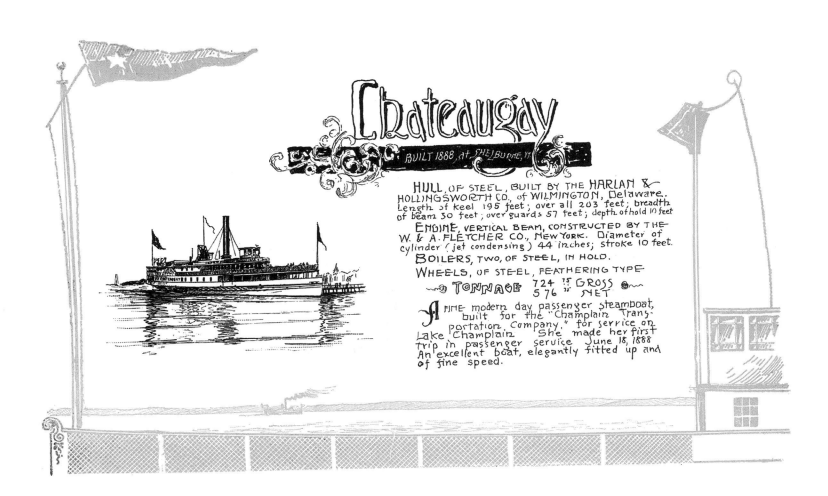

Chateaugay

BUILT 1888, at SHELBURNE, VT

HULL OF STEEL, BUILT BY THE HARLAN & HOLLINGSWORTH CO., of WILMINGTON, Delaware. Length of keel 195 feet; over all 203 feet; breadth of beam 30 feet; over guards 57 feet; depth of hold 10 feet

ENGINE, VERTICAL BEAM, CONSTRUCTED BY THE W. & A. FLETCHER CO., NEW YORK. Diameter of cylinder (jet condensing) 44 inches; stroke 10 feet.

BOILERS, TWO, OF STEEL, IN HOLD.

WHEELS, OF STEEL, FEATHERING TYPE

TONNAGE 724 $\frac{15}{100}$ GROSS 576 $\frac{71}{100}$ NET

A FINE modern day passenger steamboat, built for the "Champlain Transportation Company," for service on Lake Champlain. She made her first trip in passenger service June 18, 1888. An excellent boat, elegantly fitted up and of fine speed.

NEW YORK BAY PASSENGER PROPELLER MONMOUTH, 1888.

MONMOUTH:

BUILT 1888 at PHILADELPHIA
BY THE
William Cramp Ship & Engine Building Co.

HULL, OF IRON, 260 feet 6 inches length of water line; 270 feet 4 inches over all; 35 feet breadth of beam; 13 feet 6 inches depth

ENGINES, TWO INVERTED TRIPLE EXPANSION. Diameter of cylinders of each 19, 30 and 50 inches, by 30 inches stroke. Indicated horse power 5000.

BOILERS, FOUR, OF STEEL, CYLINDRICAL INTERNALLY FIRED RETURN TUBULAR. Total grate surface 230 square feet; total heating surface 7473 square feet

WHEELS, TWIN SCREWS, 3 BLADED, EACH 9 FEET 6 inches in diameter; 13 feet 6 inches pitch

TONNAGE 1440.34 GROSS
931.41 NET

A SPLENDID specimen of the modern fast passenger propeller. Built to the order of the New Jersey Southern Railroad Company for the route between New York and Sandy Hook and cost a quarter of a million of dollars. Draft of water, with a full load 9 feet 6 inches forward and 11 feet aft. Speed over 20 miles per hour. Elegant saloons and all the comforts that modern ingenuity could suggest combine to make the MONMOUTH as fine a craft as any afloat.

GREAT LAKES PROPELLER SOO CITY, 1888.

SOO CITY.

BUILT 1888, at WEST BAY CITY, MICH.

WOODEN HULL, constructed by F. W. WHEELER & Co Length 171 feet, beam 33 feet 6 inches, and depth of hold 12 feet

ONE COMPOUND ENGINE, by SAMUEL F HODGE & Co, Detroit Diameter of cylinders 22 and 42 inches by 36 inches stroke

ONE BOILER, 15 feet in length by 120 inches in diameter

GROSS TONNAGE 670.79 NET TONNAGE 438.36

This handsome propeller was built for the Cheboygan and River Saint Marie trade, upon which route she plied for several seasons. Commodious cabins finely furnished, and all modern conveniences made her a very popular boat. Used during 1893 in carrying excursionists between Michigan City and Chicago.

COLUMBIA RIVER STEAMBOAT T. J. POTTER, 1888.

T.J.POTTER.

BUILT 1888. at NORTH PORTLAND, Ore.

HULL, OF WOOD, BUILT BY John F. Steffen. Length 230 feet; breadth of beam 35 feet; depth of hold 10½ feet.

ENGINES, TWO, NON-CONDENSING. Diameter of cylinders 32 inches; stroke 8 feet. Horse power 1700.

BOILER, "FIRE-BOX," BUILT 1887 by the PUSEY & JONES COMPANY, WILMINGTON, DEL. Length 32 feet; diameter 84 inches.

GROSS TONNAGE 659 4!
NET TONNAGE 589 60

THE T. J. POTTER was built for service on the Columbia River. A well constructed and handsomely furnished boat. In August, 1888 she made the run from Portland to Astoria, 106 miles, in 5 hours and 31 minutes. She has also been used on Puget Sound.

GREAT LAKES STEAMSHIP OWEGO, 1888.

OWEGO.

BUILT 1888, at BUFFALO, N.Y.,
By the UNION DRY DOCK COMPANY.

HULL, OF STEEL. Length of keel 324 feet, over all 350 feet; 7 inches; breadth of beam 41 feet 3 inches, depth of hold 13 feet 8 inches; from spar deck 25½ feet.

ENGINE, TRIPLE EXPANSION. Diameter of cylinders 28, 42½ and 72 inches, by 54 inches stroke

BOILERS, SIX, OF STEEL, each 11½ feet in diameter, by 11½ feet long. Total grate surface 240 square feet.

WHEEL, SECTIONAL. 15½ feet in diameter, pitch 21 feet.

TONNAGE 2611 ⁹⁰ GROSS
1940 ⁰⁰ NET

The OWEGO and her mate, the CHEMUNG, were when built, the two finest inland freight steamships ever turned out, each costing $350,000. They are of the ocean model, strongly built and fine specimens of marine architecture. Built for the Union Steamboat Company, for the package freight trade between Buffalo and Chicago. The OWEGO'S record, two days, 6 hours and 16 minutes, between Buffalo and Chicago, an average of 16⅗ miles an hour was the fastest ever made by a freight boat.

BALTIMORE:

BUILT 1882, at WILMINGTON, Delaware.

HULL, OF IRON, BUILT BY THE HARLAN & HOLLINGSWORTH COMPANY.
Length of keel 192 feet; over all 206 feet; breadth of beam
36 feet; over guards 65 feet; depth of hold 13 feet 9 inches

ENGINE, VERTICAL BEAM, CONSTRUCTED BY THE PENNSYLVANIA RAIL
ROAD CO, at HOBOKEN, N.J. Diameter of cylinder 46 inches; stroke 11 feet

TONNAGE 1007 1⁄8 GROSS; 796 57 NET

ONE of a fleet of ferryboats owned
by the Pennsylvania Railroad Co.,
and plying on the North River, between New
York and Jersey City.

NORTHFIELD:

BUILT 1863, at NEW YORK.

HULL, OF WOOD, CONSTRUCTED BY JEREMIAH SIMONSON.
Length 202 feet, breadth 33½ feet, depth of hold 13 feet.

ENGINE, VERTICAL BEAM.
Diameter of cylinder 50 inches, by 10 feet stroke.

BOILER, ONE, NEW 1874.
Length 32½ feet, by 112 inches in diameter.

TONNAGE - 600 44 GROSS - 388 30 NET

A NEW YORK BAY ferryboat, built
for service between New York and
Staten Island. Accommodations for
a large number of passengers, horses and vehicles.

EDWIN H. MEAD:

BUILT 1892, at NEWBURGH, N.Y.

HULL, OF STEEL, BUILT BY T.S. MARVEL & Co. Length of keel
110 feet; over all 120 feet; breadth of beam 25 feet; depth
of hold 12 feet 3 inches; draft of water 11 feet.

ENGINE, COMPOUND, CONSTRUCTED BY T.S. MARVEL & Co. Diameter
of cylinders 22 and 44 inches, by 32 inches stroke.

BOILERS, TWO "SCOTCH" OF STEEL, BUILT BY P. DELANY & CO.,
NEWBURGH, N.Y.

PROPELLING WHEEL, 4 BLADES; diameter 9 feet 10 inches; pitch
14 feet 3 inches

A large and powerful tug, built for
towing on Hudson River, between
New York and Rondout, and to super-
cede the old style side-wheel towboat. Cost
$52,000.
Owned by Cornell Steamboat Company.
Tonnage: GROSS 248 30
NET 124 18

GEORGE M. WINSLOW:

BUILT 1891, at EAST BOSTON, Mass.

HULL, OF WOOD, BUILT BY RICHARD F. KEOUGH. Length between
perpendiculars 112 feet; over all 125 feet; breadth of beam 23 feet;
depth of hold 13 feet.

ENGINE, INVERTED TRIPLE EXPANSION, CONSTRUCTED BY THE ATLANTIC
WORKS, EAST BOSTON. Diameter of cylinders 14¼, 22 and 36
inches, by 26 inches stroke.

BOILER, ONE, OF STEEL, 12 feet 2 inches in diameter, by 11 feet
in length.

TONNAGE 197 64 GROSS
98 81 NET

THE GEORGE M. WINSLOW is a type of large tugboat
that has come into use in recent years, for towing
along the coast. One of the finest vessels of
her class ever built. Used mainly on route from
New York to New England ports

GREAT LAKES CAR FERRY ST. IGNACE, 1888.

Saint Ignace:

Built 1888, at Detroit, Mich., By the Detroit Dry Dock Company.

Hull, of wood. Length of keel 198½ feet; over all 231 feet; breadth of beam 51 feet; depth of hold 15¾ feet; moulded depth 24 feet; average draft of water 17 feet.

Engines, two, vertical compound, turning a screw on either end. Diameter of cylinders of forward engine, 26 and 48 inches, by 40 inches stroke, after engine, diameter of cylinders 28 and 58 inches, by 48 inches stroke.

Boilers, three, of steel, cylindrical double ended.

Wheels, forward 10½ feet in diameter, with 15 feet pitch; after wheel, 12 feet in diameter and 16½ feet pitch.

— Tonnage 1199 ⁷⁵ Gross; 600 °° Net. —

A powerful ferry steamer, built to transport railroad cars between Mackinaw City and St. Ignace, in the Straits of Mackinac, Mich. The first double screw ferryboat built in America, and used summer and winter. Capacity for 10 freight or 8 passenger cars; speed 15 miles per hour. Owned by the Mackinac Transportation Company.

LONG ISLAND SOUND STEAMBOAT PURITAN, 1888.

PURITAN.

BUILT 1888, CHESTER, PA.

Length, water line, 403 feet, 5 inches; over all 420 feet; Width of hull, 52 feet, 5 inches; over guards 91 feet; Depth of hold 18 feet, 1 inch; amidships, 21 feet 6 inches; base line to top of house over engine, 70 feet; Draft, loaded, 13 feet.

Engine: Compound, vertical beam, surface condensing. High pressure cylinder, 75 inches diameter by 9 feet stroke; low pressure cylinder, 110 inches diameter, 14 feet stroke. 7500 indicated horse power. Boilers: Eight, of steel, Redfield type; total grate surface 830 sq. feet, total heating surface, 25,500 sq. feet.

Feathering side wheels. Each wheel has thirteen steel buckets, 14 feet long, 5 feet wide and ⅜ inch in thickness.

Tonnage, 4,893.36 gross, 3,075.24 net.

Designed and built under direction of George Peirce, of Old Colony Steamboat Co;
HULL, built by Delaware River Iron Shipbuilding & Engine Works, Chester, Pa;
ENGINE and BOILERS, by W. & A. Fletcher Co., New York;
JOINER work, by William Rowland, New York;
DESIGNS for decorations, by Frank Hill Smith, Boston.

The Puritan is one of the fleet of great inland passenger steamboats (she was the largest ever built up to 1893) running on Long Island Sound. She belongs to the Old Colony Steamboat Company and plies between New York and Fall River, a distance of 180 miles, performing the service summer and winter. She has a double hull, of steel, constructed so as to form, with the longitudinal bulkheads, 52 water tight compartments, besides which there are 7 water-tight bulkheads running athwartship. The interior decorations are chaste and elegant. The total number of staterooms is 360; there are sleeping accommodations for nearly 1000 persons. Her average speed is 20 miles an hour.

LAKE ERIE PASSENGER STEAMBOAT CITY OF DETROIT, 1889.

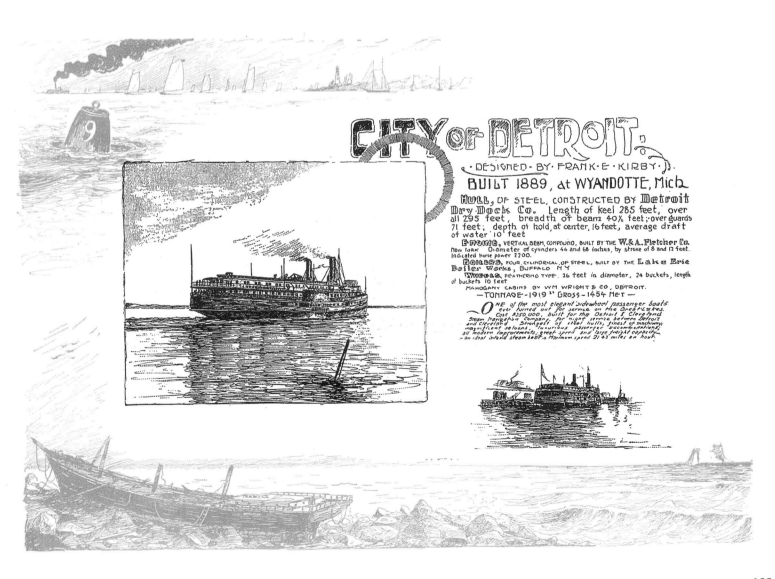

CITY OF DETROIT.

·DESIGNED·BY·FRANK·E·KIRBY·

BUILT 1889, at WYANDOTTE, Mich.

HULL, OF STEEL, CONSTRUCTED BY Detroit Dry Dock Co. Length of keel 285 feet, over all 295 feet, breadth of beam 40½ feet; over guards 71 feet; depth of hold, at center, 16 feet, average draft of water 10 feet

ENGINE, VERTICAL BEAM, COMPOUND, BUILT BY THE W.&A. Fletcher Co. New York. Diameter of cylinders 44 and 68 inches, by stroke of 8 and 12 feet. Indicated horse power 2700.

BOILERS, FOUR CYLINDRICAL, OF STEEL, BUILT BY THE Lake Erie Boiler Works, BUFFALO NY

WHEELS, FEATHERING TYPE. 26 feet in diameter, 24 buckets, length of buckets 10 feet.

MAHOGANY CABINS BY WM WRIGHT & CO, DETROIT.

— TONNAGE -1919 " GROSS -1454 NET —

ONE of the most elegant sidewheel passenger boats ever turned out for service on the Great Lakes. Cost $250,000, built for the Detroit & Cleveland Steam Navigation Company, for night service between Detroit and Cleveland. Strongest of steel hulls, finest of machinery, magnificent saloons, luxurious passenger accommodations, all modern improvements, great speed and large freight capacity; — an ideal inland steam boat. Maximum speed 21.43 miles an hour.

LONG ISLAND SOUND STEAMBOAT CONNECTICUT, 1889.

CONNECTICUT:

BUILT 1889, at NOANK, Conn.

HULL, OF WOOD, CONSTRUCTED BY ROBERT PALMER & SONS. Length on load line 345 feet; over all 358 feet; breadth of beam, 48 feet; over guards 87 feet; depth of hold 18 feet. Five water-tight bulkheads. Frames of white oak and hackmatack; floor timbers filled in solid for 180 feet of the length of the vessel; keelsons and ceiling of yellow pine; bottom planking of white oak.

ENGINE, DOUBLE-EXPANSION, COMPOUND, INCLINED, DIRECT-ACTING, SURFACE CONDENSING, OSCILLATING; CONSTRUCTED BY THE WM. CRAMP & SONS SHIP AND ENGINE BUILDING COMPANY, PHILADELPHIA. Diameter of cylinders 56 and 104 inches, by stroke of 11 feet.

BOILERS, SIX, OF STEEL; EACH 12½ feet in diameter; 20¾ feet long; set fore and aft in two nests of three each, having athwartship fire-rooms at extreme ends.

WHEELS, FEATHERING TYPE. Diameter, 28 feet from centre to centre of bucket trunnions; number of buckets each wheel 12; length of buckets 14 feet; width of buckets 4½ feet; average dip of wheel 6 feet.

JOINER WORK, BY WILLIAM ROWLAND, NEW YORK

TONNAGE: 3399 Gross; 1872 Net.

ONE OF THE most graceful and well proportioned of the great Long Island Sound floating palaces. The CONNECTICUT was built for the Providence & Stonington Steamship Company, for the route from New York to Providence, being used as a night boat, and accommodating from 700 to 800 people with berths. Mammoth saloons, broad galleries, grand stairways, elaborate furnishings, rich carving, electric lights, bells, etc., and all the characteristics that go to make up one of these wonderful specimens of marine architecture are to be found on this boat.

NEW YORK AND VENEZUELA STEAMSHIP CARACAS, 1889.

POTOMAC RIVER STEAMBOAT CHARLES MACALESTER, 1889.

CHARLES MACALESTER

BUILT 1889,
at WILMINGTON, Del.,
By the HARLAN & HOLLINGSWORTH COMPANY.

HULL, OF STEEL. Length 195 feet; breadth of beam 30 feet; depth of hold 10 feet 7 inches.

ENGINE, VERTICAL BEAM. Diameter of cylinder 44 inches, by 10 feet stroke.

BOILERS, TWO OF STEEL. Diameter 100 inches; length 23 feet 2 inches; working pressure 56 pounds.

WHEELS, diameter 23 feet, each with 12 "feathering" buckets, 8 feet 4 inches long by 33 inches wide; average dip of wheel 3 feet.

TONNAGE 624⁶⁸ Gross, 462⁵³ Net

A HANDSOME, modern, passenger steamer of the medium size, running on the Potomac River from Washington to Mount Vernon. Capacity for 1500 persons. Owned by the Mt. Vernon & Marshall Hall Steamboat Company. Speed 20 miles an hour.

GREAT LAKES STEAMSHIP LIVINGSTONE, 1889.

LIVINGSTONE.

DESIGNED BY FRANK E KIRBY

BUILT 1889,
at WYANDOTTE, MICH.

HULL, COMPOSITE, BUILT BY THE Detroit Dry Dock Comp'y.
Length, keel, 280 feet; over all 299 feet; extreme beam 42 feet; depth of hold 22 feet 6 inches

ENGINE, TRIPLE EXPANSION, CONSTRUCTED BY THE Frontier Iron Works, DETROIT Diameter of cylinders 20½, 33 and 55 inches by 42 inches stroke

BOILERS, TWO, OF STEEL, BUILT BY THE Lake Erie Boiler Works, BUFFALO Each 12 feet in diameter by 11 feet in length; working pressure 160 lbs steam to square inch.

WHEEL, FOUR BLADES, 12½ feet in diameter, 14 feet pitch

∴ TONNAGE 2134 3% Gross 1622 3% Net ∴

A LARGE and substantially built steamer of the Great Lakes. Owned by the "Percheron Steam Navigation Company," and used in the ore, coal, grain and package freight carrying trade. Capacity 3000 tons. —

INDIAN RIVER (FLORIDA) STEAMBOAT SANTA LUCIA.

SANTA LUCIA;

~ FORMERLY "NELLIE HUDSON, N.° 2." ~

BUILT 1889, at PITTSBURGH, PA

HULL, OF WOOD
Length 158 feet; breadth of beam, 28 feet
7 inches; depth of hold 3 feet.

ENGINES, TWO, POPPET-VALVE LEVER; CON-
STRUCTED BY James Rees & Sons, PITTS-
BURGH Diameter of cylinders 12 inches by
5 feet stroke of piston

BOILERS, TWO, CYLINDRICAL FLUE. Diameter of
each 36 inches, and 26 feet in length

TONNAGE   193 65 Gross
          170 93 Net

BUILT for the passenger route between
Pittsburgh and the Allegheny River.
A typical shoal water western river
steamer. Refitted 1892, for service on the Indian
River, in Florida, and called "SANTA LUCIA."

STEAM YACHT JATHNIEL, 1889.

JATHNIEL: DESIGNED BY
EDWARD BURGESS.

BUILT 1889, at EAST BOSTON.

HULL, OF IRON, BUILT BY The Atlantic Works.
Length on water line 110 feet; over all 134 feet; breadth of
beam 18 feet 8 inches; depth of hold 11 feet 3 inches;
average draft of water 8 feet 10 inches.

ENGINE, VERTICAL TRIPLE-EXPANSION, CONSTRUCTED BY
THE Fore River Engine Co., WEYMOUTH, MASS. Diameter of
cylinders 12½, 22- and 34 inches, by 18 inches stroke.

BOILERS, TORPEDO TYPE, BUILT BY H.S. Robinson
& Co., EAST BOSTON

TONNAGE   40 04 GROSS
           70 66 NET

A HANDSOME, well built
steam yacht, belong-
ing to the Eastern
Yacht Club, etc, and
owned by Daniel S.
Ford, of Boston, Mass.
Beautifully furnished and
of excellent speed.

ATLANTIC COAST LIGHTHOUSE SUPPLY STEAMER ARMERIA, 1890.

ARMERIA

ORIGINAL DESIGN BY CHARLES W. COPELAND

BUILT 1890, at CAMDEN, N.J.
By JOHN H DIALOGUE & SON.

HULL, OF STEEL. Length over all 208 feet, breadth of beam 34⅚ feet, depth of hold 17½ feet; draft of water, loaded, 12 feet.

ENGINES, TWO, COMPOUND. Diameter of cylinders 22 & 40 inches, by 36 inches stroke. Indicated horse power 1200

BOILERS, TWO, SCOTCH RETURN TUBULAR. Size of each 10½ feet by 14½ feet; total heating surface 4200 sq. feet, consumption of fuel per hour 1200 lbs

WHEELS, TWO, 4 BLADES ON EACH. Diameter 9 feet 8 inches; pitch 16 feet

TONNAGE (REGISTERED) 631.97

ONE of the finest vessels ever turned out for the United States Light House service. She is staunchly built and finely arranged, being used as a supply steamer along the entire Atlantic and Gulf coasts. Cost about $200,000, and has a speed of 13 knots. Could serve admirably as an auxiliary cruiser in case of war.

LAKE MICHIGAN STEAMBOAT CITY OF CHICAGO, 1890.

CITY OF CHICAGO

→BUILT 1890, at WEST BAY CITY, Mich ←

HULL, OF STEEL, CONSTRUCTED BY F. W. WHEELER & CO. Length 226 feet, breadth of beam 34 feet; depth of hold 13 feet. Lengthened 1891, 12 feet, making total length 238 feet

ENGINE, VERTICAL BEAM, COMPOUND, BUILT BY THE W. & A. FLETCHER CO., NEW YORK Diameter of cylinders 36 and 54 inches, by 6 ft. 8 ins. and 10 feet stroke

BOILERS, TWO, OF STEEL

WHEELS, FEATHERING, 22½ feet in diameter; 10 buckets each wheel

TONNAGE: 1,164 07 GROSS 735 45 NET

A BEAUTIFULLY FINISHED and luxuriously furnished steamboat, belonging to the Graham & Morton Transportation Company and plying between Chicago and Benton Harbor, on Lake Michigan. Sleeping accommodations for 300 people, all modern improvements and excellent speed go to make the City of Chicago a model inland steamboat. Cost $235,000.

191

NEW YORK AND SOUTH AMERICAN STEAMSHIP SEGURANCA, 1890.

SEGURANCA:

Designed by J. M. Lachlan
BUILT 1890, at CHESTER, PA.
By JOHN ROACH & SON

HULL, OF STEEL, WEB FRAMES. Length of keel 320 feet; over all 346 feet; breadth of beam 45 feet, depth of hold 26 feet 3 inches; average draft of water 20 feet

ENGINE, TRIPLE EXPANSION. Diameter of cylinders 28, 44 and 78 inches, by 48 inches stroke Indicated horse power 2600

BOILERS, SIX OF STEEL, "SCOTCH" TYPE Total grate surface 270 square feet, total heating surface 9,700 square feet

WHEEL, FOUR BLADES Diameter 15½ feet, Pitch, 20 feet entering, 22 feet mean, 24 feet leaving

TONNAGE 4033 24 Gross
2806 34 Net

BUILT for the United States and Brazil Mail Steamship Company, for the route between New York and Rio de Janeiro, and one of the largest and finest passenger steamships ever turned out in America. Handsomely furnished; accommodations for 100 first class and 42 steerage passengers, carrying capacity, 3430 tons Speed 14½ knots Transferred 1893 to the Ward Line of steamships to the Island of Cuba

LAKE MICHIGAN PROPELLER INDIANA, 1890.

INDIANA

BUILT 1890, at MANITOWOC, WIS.

Hull, of wood, constructed by Burger and Burger. Length 201 feet; Breadth 35 feet (overguards 40 feet); Depth of hold 14 feet, and to second deck 23 feet.

Engine, one Fore and Aft Compound, 28 and 50 inches diameter of cylinders, by 36 inches stroke; built by Charles F. Elmes, Chicago.

Two steel Boilers, by John Mohr & Sons, Chicago; each 16 feet in length and 108 inches in diameter, allowed 125 pounds of steam.

Gross tonnage 1,777.71   Net tonnage 961.96.

No stauncher or more elaborately furnished steamer was ever built in this country than the INDIANA. She was constructed for the Goodrich Transportation Company, to ply between Chicago and the ports north of there, on the west shore of Lake Michigan, in conjunction with numerous other steamers of the line.

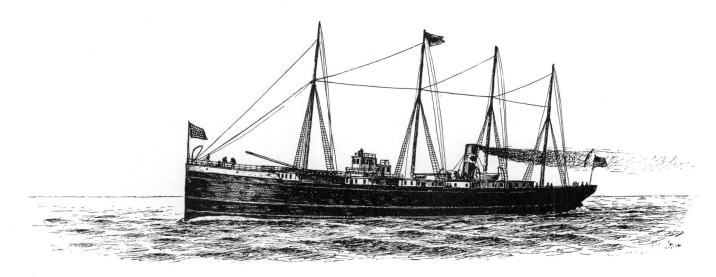

GREAT LAKES STEAMSHIP SARANAC, 1890.

SARANAC.

BUILT 1890, at CLEVELAND, OHIO.

STEEL HULL, WEB FRAMES Length of keel 290 feet, over all 307 feet, breadth of beam 40 feet; depth of hold 13 feet 6 inches — to main deck 25½ feet, draft of water 8 feet, light, 14 to 16 feet when loaded

ENGINE, TRIPLE EXPANSION. Diameter of cylinders 24, 38 and 61 inches, by 42 inches stroke.

THREE BOILERS, RETURN TUBULAR, of steel Total grate surface 162 square feet; total heating surface 5574 square feet; consumption of fuel per hour 3140 lbs

Diameter of propeller wheel, 14 feet; four blades, pitch 17½ feet Speed 14 miles per hour.

GROSS TONNAGE 2,669 47. NET TONNAGE 1,939 26.

THIS steamship was built by the Globe Iron Works Company being one of the fleet belonging to the Lehigh Valley Transportation Company and used in the line between Buffalo and Chicago, on the Great Lakes She cost $260,000.

GREAT LAKES STEAMSHIP MARYLAND, 1890.

MARYLAND.

BUILT 1890, at WYANDOTTE, MICH,
by the
DETROIT DRY DOCK COMP'Y

HULL, OF STEEL; Length of keel 316 feet, length over
all 334 feet 6 inches; width of hull 42 feet; depth
of hold 20 feet 4 inches

ENGINE, TRI-COMPOUND; Diameter of cylinders 22, 35 and 56
inches, by 44 inches stroke of piston Indicated horse
power 1,400

BOILERS, TWO, OF STEEL, "SCOTCH TYPE, each 14 feet 2
inches in diameter by 11 feet 6 inches in length
Grate surface 152 square feet ; steam pressure 160 lbs

WHEEL, SECTIONAL SCREW, 13 feet 2 inches in diameter;
pitch 16 feet

— GROSS TONNAGE 2,419 ^{94} —
— NET TONNAGE 1,892 ^{33} —

ONE of the large modern cargo carrying steamers of the
Great Lakes. Built for the Inter-Ocean Transportation Co.
During the 127 days she was in commission in 1890, she
carried 29 cargoes of iron ore between Escanaba and
South Chicago, aggregating 92,749 gross tons, or an average
of 3,198 gross tons per cargo. Her largest load that year
was 3,720 net tons of ore. Her load on a 16-foot draught was
3,475 net tons, including fuel. When loaded the MARYLAND'S
speed is 13¾ miles per hour.

NEW YORK DOUBLE SCREW FERRYBOAT JOHN G. McCULLOUGH, 1891.

JOHN G. McCULLOUGH:

BUILT 1890,
at PHILADELPHIA,
BY
NEAFIE & LEVY.

HULL, OF STEEL Length of keel 200 feet;
over all 215 feet; breadth of beam 38 feet;
over guards 62 feet; depth of hold 16½ feet.
ENGINE, COMPOUND, DOUBLE SCREW Diameter
of cylinders 26 and 50 inches, by 30 inches
stroke, Shaft is continuous, 200 feet in length and
8¾ inches in diameter, with screw on either end
BOILERS, TWO, SCOTCH TYPE Each 12 feet 3 inches
in diameter, by 11 feet in length, working pressure 100 lbs
WHEELS, Two, each 8 feet 6 inches in diameter.
~ TONNAGE ~ 1309 4/? GROSS ~
1007 ?/? NET

THE JOHN G. McCULLOUGH was the second
double-screw ferryboat constructed
for use in New York waters.
A well built serviceable craft.
Splendidly fitted up
Owned by the N.Y, L.E. & W. R.R Co
and used on their ferry route between
New York and Jersey City.

UNITED STATES CRUISER SAN FRANCISCO, 1890.

SAN FRANCISCO:
BUILT 1888-90 AT SAN FRANCISCO Cal.
⇒ By the UNION IRON WORKS ⇐

HULL, OF STEEL, 4088 tons displacement
Length 310 feet; breadth of beam 49¼ feet,
depth of hold 18 feet 9 inches

ENGINES, TWO TRIPLE EXPANSION Diameter
of cylinders 42, 60 and 94 inches, by 36
inches stroke

BOILERS, FIVE OF STEEL Four double ended
each 14 feet 8 inches in diameter, 19½ feet in length
with 24 furnaces, and one single ended 8 feet in
diameter, by 8 feet long, with one furnace Total grate
surface 567 square feet, Total heating surface 20134 square feet.

WHEELS, TWO, each 13½ feet in diameter, with 18¾ feet pitch.

ONE of the United States'
modern naval fleet
The SAN FRANCISCO is
a 'protected cruiser';
she cost $1,428,000,
and earned for her builders
a premium of $100,000 for
speed above that called for in the contract.

PUGET SOUND STEAMBOAT BAILEY GATZERT, 1890.

BAILEY GATZERT:

BUILT 1890 at BALLARD WASH

HULL, OF WOOD, BUILT BY J J HOLLAND. Length of keel 177 feet 4 inches, breadth of beam 32 feet 4 inches, depth of hold 8 feet

ENGINES, TWO LOW PRESSURE, BALANCE-LEVER POPPET VALVE, CONSTRUCTED BY JAMES REES & SONS, PITTSBURGH, PA. Diameter of cylinder of each 22 inches, by 6 feet stroke Indicated horse power 1300.

BOILER, OF STEEL, LOCOMOTIVE TYPE, BY JAMES REES & SONS Total grate surface 49 square feet, total heating surface 3800 square feet.

WHEEL, 17 BUCKETS, EACH 18 feet in length

TONNAGE 560 TS GROSS 444 TS NET

THE BAILEY GATZERT is a type of the fast sternwheel steamboat constructed for passenger service on the rivers of the Pacific coast She was built for John Leary. At first on the route between Seattle and Tacoma on Puget Sound. She was used in different lines on that sheet of water. And also ran on the Columbia River. Average speed 18 to 20 miles per hour. Made the run from Tacoma to Seattle in 1 hour, and 23 minutes, also in 1 hour 27½ minutes, and 1 hour and 28 minutes Also made over 30 runs in less than 1 hour and 36 minutes, a speed of over 20 miles an hour

NEW ENGLAND COAST STEAMBOAT PORTLAND, 1890.

PORTLAND;

BUILT 1890, at BATH, Me.

HULL, of wood, built by The New England Company. Length of keel 280½ feet; length over all 291 feet; width of hull 42 feet (over guards 68 feet); depth of hold 15½ feet; draft of water 10 feet.

ENGINE, vertical beam, constructed by The Portland Company, Portland Me. Diameter of cylinder 62 inches, by length of stroke 12 feet. Indicated horse power 1200.

BOILERS, two, of iron, return tubular, constructed by the Bath Iron Works, Bath, Me. Total grate surface 183 square feet; total heating surface 6126 square feet; consumption of fuel per hour 1¾ tons anthracite coal

WHEELS, 35 feet in diameter, 26 buckets to each wheel, 8 feet in length, 24 inches wide, dipping 4 feet.

GROSS TONNAGE 2283⁵⁶ NET TONNAGE 1517¹⁰

The PORTLAND was built for the Portland Steam Packet Company for the night line between Portland Me. and Boston Mass. She was designed by William P. Pattee and cost $250,000, and undoubtedly was one of the finest coastwise steamboats ever constructed, being of great strength, seaworthy and unusually roomy and comfortable. Decorations white and gold. Speed 12 nautical miles per hour, carrying capacity 400 tons freight; 156 staterooms and accommodations for 700 passengers.

GREAT LAKES FREIGHT STEAMSHIP MATOA, 1890.

Matoa:

BUILT 1890, at CLEVELAND, Ohio,
By the GLOBE IRON WORKS COMPANY.

HULL, OF STEEL   Length of keel 292 feet; over all
308 feet; breadth of beam 40 feet; depth of
hold 24 feet 6 inches;   draft of water, light
8 feet; loaded 14 to 16 feet,

ENGINE, TRIPLE EXPANSION.   Diameter of cylinders
24, 38 and 61 inches,   by 42 inches stroke,

BOILERS, TWO, OF STEEL, SCOTCH TYPE. Total grate surface
135 square feet; total heating surface 4710 square
feet.   Consumption of fuel per hour .2630 lbs, on
a speed of 14 miles per hour,

WHEEL, FOUR BLADES; 14 FEET IN DIAMETER, 17 FEET
6 inches pitch.

TONNAGE   2511 01 Gross
1836 95 Net

A LARGE, MODERN, STEEL-HULL
FREIGHT CARRIER OF THE
GREAT LAKES   OWNED BY THE
MINNESOTA STEAMSHIP COMPANY
AND USED IN THE ORE CARRYING TRADE
STRONGLY BUILT AND OF LARGE CAPACITY
COST $206,750.

MISSISSIPPI RIVER STEAMBOAT OUACHITA, 1890.

OUACHITA:

BUILT 1890 at JEFFERSONVILLE, IND

Hull: OF WOOD, BUILT BY ED. J. HOWARD. LENGTH OF KEEL 185 FEET; OVER ALL 189 FEET; BREADTH 38 FEET. OVER GUARDS 52 FEET; DEPTH OF HOLD 6 FEET 6 INCHES.

Engines: TWO HORIZONTAL HIGH PRESSURE, CONSTRUCTED BY AINSLIE, COCHRANE & CO., LOUISVILLE, KY. DIAMETER OF CYLINDERS 18 INCHES, BY 8 FEET STROKE OF PISTON.

Boilers: THREE HORIZONTAL FLUE, BY MITCHELL & BRO. LOUISVILLE EACH 28 FEET IN LENGTH BY 44 INCHES IN DIAMETER

Wheel: 28 FEET IN DIAMETER, WITH BUCKETS 26 FEET IN LENGTH, BY 14 INCHES WIDE.

— TONNAGE 457 45 —

THE OUACHITA is an excellent example of the medium sized Mississippi River passenger and cotton carrying steamer. Her capacity is 3800 bales of cotton. The main cabin, on second deck, is 24 by 130 feet, being well furnished and nicely furnished. There are 24 state rooms on this deck and 14 rooms in Texas. Draft of water light 3 feet 3 inches, and 10 feet loaded. Built for the New Orleans and Monroe, La, route.

WITH A LOAD OF COTTON.

ATLANTIC COAST STEAMSHIP ALGONQUIN, 1890.

ALGONQUIN:
BUILT 1890, at PHILADELPHIA, PA.
BY THE
William Cramp & Sons Ship & Engine Building Co

HULL, OF STEEL. Length 281 feet, breadth of beam 43 feet; depth of hold 20 feet 6 inches; to spar deck 28 feet 6 inches.

ENGINE, VERTICAL TRIPLE-EXPANSION. Diameter of cylinders 21, 34 and 56 inches, by 36 inches stroke. Indicated horse power 1350.

BOILERS, FOUR, OF STEEL, CYLINDRICAL INTERNALLY FIRED, RETURN TUBULAR; Steam pressure allowed 160 lbs to sq. inch; total grate surface 179.8 square feet; total heating surface 4800 square feet

WHEEL, FOUR BLADES; Diameter 13 feet, pitch 15 feet.

→ TONNAGE 2832 66/100 gross ←
2257 88/100 net

ONE OF A fleet of passenger and freight steamships owned by Wm P Clyde & Co, built for the route between New York, Charleston, S.C. and Jacksonville, Florida. On account of limited depth of water on bar at entrance to Charleston and the St Johns River, the Algonquin was built without a keel, but furnished with bilge keelsons

Finely and comfortably furnished, and a popular boat, carrying large numbers of tourists between the North and the South. Cargo capacity 134,758 cubic feet, speed 11¼ knots.

GREAT LAKES EXCURSION STEAMBOAT FRANK E. KIRBY, 1890.

ATLANTIC COAST STEAMSHIP COTTAGE CITY, 1890.

PUGET SOUND PASSENGER STEAMBOAT GREYHOUND, 1890.

GREYHOUND:
BUILT 1890 at PORTLAND, Oregon
— Designed by James W. Troup. —

WOODEN HULL, built by Claude Troup, Length of keel 140 feet; over all 165 feet; breadth of beam 18 feet; over guards 22 feet; depth of hold 6 feet 4 inches; draught of water (including wheel) 4 feet 8 inches.
TWO ENGINES, Poppet valve variety, constructed by the Iowa IRON WORKS, Dubuque, Iowa. Diameter of cylinder of each 14½ inches, by 6 feet stroke. Indicated horse power 400.
ONE BOILER, fire box, of steel, by WILLAMETTE IRON WORKS, Portland, Ore. Total grate surface 12 square feet; total heating surface 3200 square feet; consumption of fuel per hour, ¾ of a cord of fir wood.
STERN WHEEL, 21 feet in diameter; 16 buckets, 10 feet 6 inches in length, 20 inches wide; 22 inches dip.
JOINER WORK, by P. CARSTENS, Portland, Ore.
GROSS TONNAGE 180.67. NET TONNAGE 166.96
— Cost $15,000. Maximum speed 20 miles. —

THE GREYHOUND or as she is familiarly called along the water front the Pup, was taken down the Columbia river and also Cape Flattery immediately after being finished, and placed on the Seattle and Tacoma route, under lease to the Union Pacific Railway Company. After the expiration of the lease she was operated by her owners on the Seattle and Tacoma route for a short time. She was then placed on the Seattle and Everett run, making three round trips each day, the distance between points being 35 miles. It is claimed by her owners that she is the fastest stern-wheel boat ever built. She has beaten the propellers City of Seattle, City of Kingston, Premier and Fleetwood, and the sternwheelers built or leased State of Washington and Multnomah, and passes the other Puget Sound steamer with ease, under half her allowance of steam. Considering her size and and cost she is a phenomenally successful and fast boat.

GREAT LAKES STEAMSHIP W. H. GILCHER, 1892.

W·H·GILCHER·

BUILT 1891, at CLEVELAND, O.
By the CLEVELAND SHIPBUILDING CO.

HULL, OF STEEL. length of keel 301½ feet;
over all 320 feet; breadth of beam
41 feet; depth of hold 24 feet 4 inches.

ENGINE, TRIPLE EXPANSION. Diameter of cylinders
20, 33 and 54 inches, by 40 inches stroke.

~TONNAGE 2414⁶⁴ GROSS. 1986⁷⁰ NET~

The W H GILCHER was a large cargo
carrying steamer of the Great
Lakes, owned by J.C Gilchrist.
She held the record for some time
of having carried the largest cargo of wheat
—113,885 bushels— that had ever been
transported by a single vessel between
Chicago and Buffalo.

She foundered during a gale on Lake
Michigan on the night of Oct 28, 1892,
all on board perishing. Valued
when lost, at $200,000.

ERIE CANAL STEAM CANAL BOAT ACME, 1891.

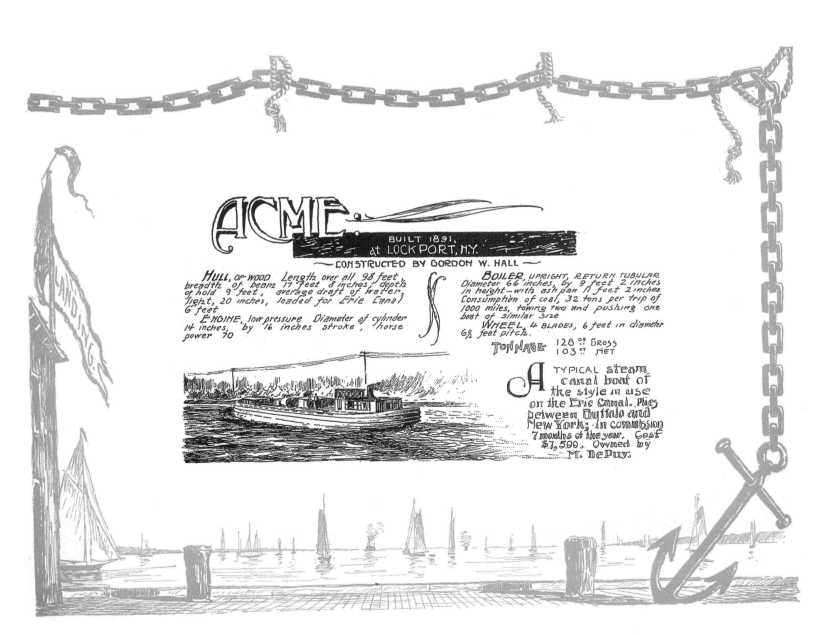

ACME.

BUILT 1891,
at LOCKPORT, N.Y.
— CONSTRUCTED BY GORDON W. HALL —

HULL, OF WOOD Length over all 98 feet, breadth of beam 17 feet 8 inches, depth of hold 9 feet, average draft of water, light, 20 inches, loaded for Erie Canal 6 feet

ENGINE low pressure Diameter of cylinder 14 inches, by 16 inches stroke, horse power 70

BOILER UPRIGHT, RETURN TUBULAR Diameter 66 inches, by 9 feet 2 inches in height—with ash pan 11 feet 2 inches. Consumption of coal, 32 tons per trip of 1000 miles, towing two and pushing one boat of similar size

WHEEL 4 BLADES, 6 feet in diameter 6½ feet pitch.

TONNAGE 128 °⁄₁₀₀ GROSS
103 °⁄₁₀₀ NET

A TYPICAL steam canal boat of the style in use on the Erie Canal. Plies between Buffalo and New York; in commission 7 months of the year. Cost $7,500. Owned by M. DePuy.

207

NEW YORK AND ROCKAWAY BEACH EXCURSION STEAMBOAT GENERAL SLOCUM, 1891.

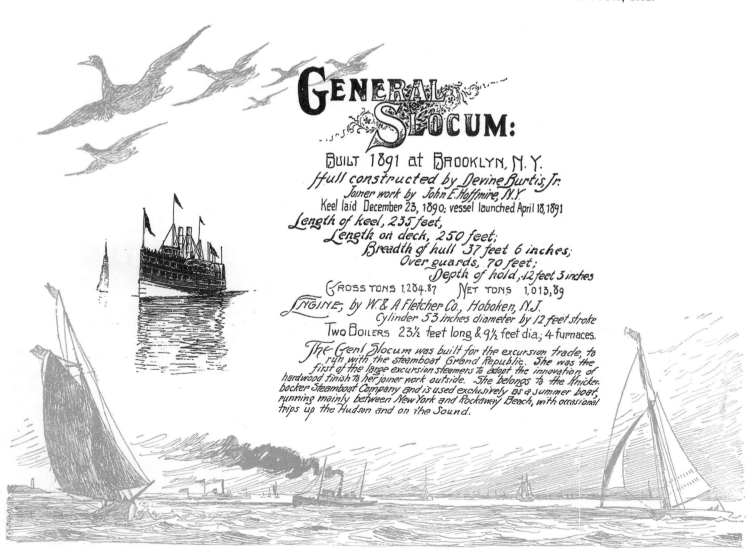

GENERAL SLOCUM:

Built 1891 at Brooklyn, N.Y.
Hull constructed by Devine Burtis, Jr.
Joiner work by John E. Hoffmire, N.Y.
Keel laid December 23, 1890; vessel launched April 18, 1891
Length of keel, 235 feet,
Length on deck, 250 feet;
Breadth of hull 37 feet 6 inches;
Over guards, 70 feet;
Depth of hold, 12 feet 3 inches
Gross tons 1,284.87   Net tons 1,013.89
Engine, by W. & A. Fletcher Co., Hoboken, N.J.
Cylinder 53 inches diameter by 12 feet stroke
Two Boilers 23½ feet long & 9½ feet dia.; 4 furnaces.

The Gen'l Slocum was built for the excursion trade, to run with the steamboat Grand Republic. She was the first of the large excursion steamers to adopt the innovation of hardwood finish to her joiner work outside. She belongs to the Knickerbocker Steamboat Company and is used exclusively as a summer boat, running mainly between New York and Rockaway Beach, with occasional trips up the Hudson and on the Sound.

NEW YORK HARBOR TUGBOAT DOROTHY, 1891.

DOROTHY,

Designed by Horace See
BUILT 1891 at NEWPORT NEWS, Va.

HULL, OF IRON. Length over all 90 feet, beam,
moulded, 19 feet, depth of hold 10 feet 9 inches

ENGINE, VERTICAL SURFACE-CONDENSING
QUADRUPLE EXPANSION, DESIGNED BY
HORACE SEE. Diameter of cylinders
9¾, 13¼, 18¾ and 26 inches, by 22 inches
stroke of piston

BOILER, OF STEEL, CYLINDRICAL RETURN TUBU-
LAR Diameter 9½ feet, by 10½ feet in length.

WHEEL, SOLID, 7 FEET IN DIAMETER.

~ 130⁰⁰ Gross, 65⁰⁰ Net Tons ~

The DOROTHY is a fine example of
the class of handy tugboats for
which New York Harbor has become
renowned. She was built by the
Newport News Shipbuilding & Dry Dock
Company, for the N.Y. and Northern Railway
Co. To be used for towing heavy car floats.
This was the first tug built with quadruple
expansion engines. Coal consumption 30%
less than that of ordinary boats of her class.
Filled with all modern improvements, iron deck
houses, etc. The Dorothy was transferred
in 1894 to the New York Central Lighterage
Co's fleet.

209

STEAM YACHT VAMOOSE, 1891.

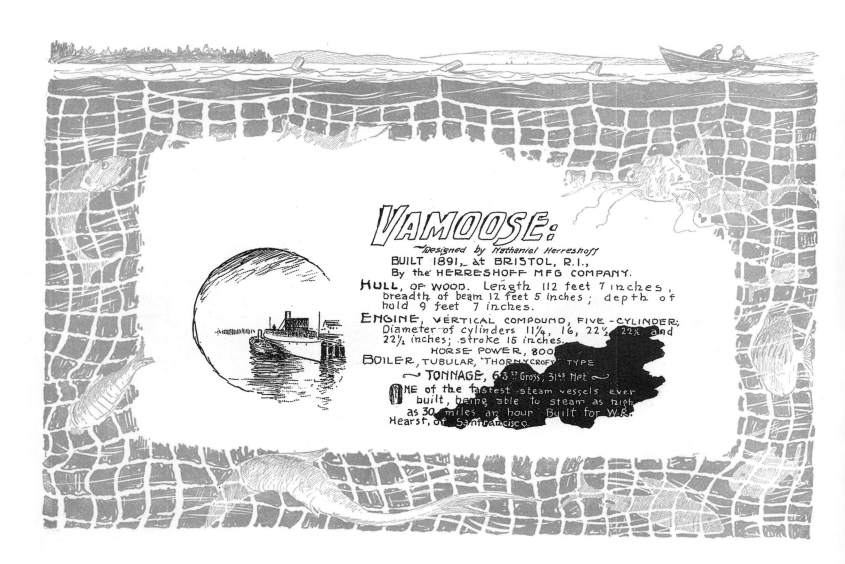

VAMOOSE:
Designed by Nathaniel Herreshoff
BUILT 1891, at BRISTOL, R.I.,
By the HERRESHOFF MFG COMPANY.

HULL, OF WOOD. Length 112 feet 7 inches,
breadth of beam 12 feet 5 inches; depth of
hold 9 feet 7 inches.

ENGINE, VERTICAL COMPOUND, FIVE-CYLINDER;
Diameter of cylinders 11¼, 16, 22½ 22½ and
22½ inches; stroke 15 inches.
HORSE POWER, 800
BOILER, TUBULAR, "THORNYCROFT" TYPE

TONNAGE, 63°° Gross; 31⁴⁸ Net

ONE of the fastest steam vessels ever
built, being able to steam as high
as 30 miles an hour. Built for W.R.
Hearst, of Sanfrancisco.

NEW YORK DOUBLE-SCREW FERRYBOAT BREMEN, 1891.

BREMEN:

BUILT 1891, at NEWBURGH, N.Y.

HULL, OF STEEL, CONSTRUCTED BY T. S. MARVEL & Co. Length between perpendiculars 217 feet; over all 222 feet; moulded breadth 40 feet; over guards 62 feet; depth of hold at center, 17 feet; at ends 15 feet 6 inches. Two longitudinal and 3 athwartship bulkheads

ENGINE, DOUBLE-COMPOUND, 4 CYLINDERS, BUILT BY THE W & A. FLETCHER CO., HOBOKEN, N.J. Diameter of cylinders, two of 20 inches, and 2 of 36 inches, with a piston stroke of 28 inches

BOILERS, TWO, CYLINDRICAL TUBULAR, BY THE W. & A. FLETCHER CO. Each 21 feet in length by 9 feet in diameter; working pressure 125 lbs steam

WHEELS, SCREW ON EITHER END, ONE CONNECTION WITH ENGINE Number of blades of each, 4; diameter 8½ feet, pitch 11 feet

TONNAGE 1252.95 GROSS.
822.91 NET.

A FIRST-CLASS modern ferryboat, built for the Hoboken Ferry Company, for the route between New York and Hoboken. Splendidly adapted to the business, being a large carrier with excellent speed, and artistically fitted up.

ETHEL.

BUILT 1891, at SAVANNAH, Ga.

HULL, OF WOOD, BUILT BY JOHN WESTERMAN Length 130 feet; breadth of beam 26 feet; depth of hold 5 feet (8 feet at bow and 6½ ft. depth at stern). Flat bottom, straight sides, "model" bow and square stern.

BOILERS, TWO, BUILT BY M. SWEENEY & BRO. Length of each 16 feet; diameter 40 inches, steam 150 lbs. Taken from old steamboat ETHEL.

ENGINES, TWO, HIGH PRESSURE, CONSTRUCTED BY M SWEENEY & BRO, JEFFERSONVILLE, IND. Diameter of cylinders 14 inches, by 5 feet stroke of piston.

WHEEL, AT STERN, 16 feet in diameter, with buckets 19 feet long.

JOINER WORK, from steamboat ETHEL, built 1873, by JOHN WESTERMAN.

TONNAGE 425 89/100 GROSS 218 41/100 NET.

THE ETHEL is a type of light-draft passenger and freight steamboat used in shallow rivers of the West and South. She was built for the route between Savannah, Ga., and Stony Bluff, S.C. Her carrying capacity is about 300 tons, dead weight, on a draft of 4 feet; when light she draws only 18 inches of water. Her saloon, a commodious apartment on the second deck, contains 27 staterooms.

ALPHA.

BUILT 1890, at MATHEWS BLUFF, Ga.

HULL, OF IRON, BUILT BY JOHN WESTERMAN. Length 123 feet 9 inches; breadth of beam 36 feet 9 inches, depth of hold 6 feet 9 inches.

ENGINES, TWO, INCLINED LOW PRESSURE, CONSTRUCTED BY JOHN RUCKE, at Savannah, Ga. Cylinders 16 inches in diameter by 5 feet stroke of piston.

BOILER, BUILT BY G. W. WILLIAMS, CHARLESTON, S.C. Length 17 feet; diameter 66 inches, working steam pressure 145 lbs. to square inch.

WHEELS, 16 feet in diameter, with buckets 7 feet in length.

TONNAGE, 354 88/100 gross and 241 74/100 net.

BUILT for the Savannah, Ga., and Port Royal, S.C., route. An excellent day boat, comfortably furnished, and having good speed.

GREAT LAKES EXCURSION STEAMBOAT CITY OF TOLEDO, 1891.

CITY OF TOLEDO:

BUILT 1891, at TOLEDO, Ohio

HULL, OF STEEL, BUILT BY THE CRAIG SHIPBUILDING
COMPANY. Length over all 221 feet; breadth of beam
31½ feet; over guards 58 feet; depth of hold 12½ feet.

ENGINE, INCLINED TRIPLE EXPANSION, CONSTRUCTED BY THE
CLEVELAND SHIPBUILDING COMPANY. Diameter
of cylinders 26, 42 and 66 inches, by 6 feet stroke.

BOILERS, TWO, each 21 feet 7 inches in length, by 11 feet in
width.

WHEELS, FEATHERING BUCKETS

TONNAGE, 1003⁵⁰ Gross; 654⁵⁰ Net

An excellent type of a modern
passenger and excursion
steamer is the CITY OF
TOLEDO, built for the Toledo
and Put-in Bay route, Lake Erie.
Used during summer season of 1893
in transporting passengers from Chicago
to the World's Fair. The inclined engines
put into this boat were the first of
the kind ever built for a lake boat. She
cost $140,000.

ATLANTIC COAST TUGBOAT EDGAR F. LUCKENBACH, 1891.

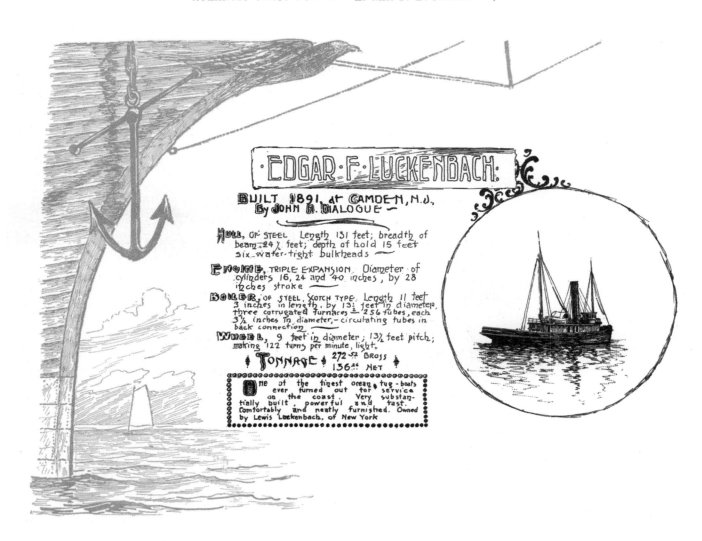

EDGAR·F·LUCKENBACH·

BUILT 1891, at CAMDEN, N.J.
By JOHN H. DIALOGUE —

HULL, OF STEEL   Length 151 feet; breadth of
beam 24½ feet; depth of hold 15 feet
six water-tight bulkheads —

ENGINE, TRIPLE EXPANSION. Diameter of
cylinders 16, 24 and 40 inches, by 28
inches stroke

BOILER, OF STEEL, SCOTCH TYPE. Length 11 feet
3 inches in length, by 13½ feet in diameter,
three corrugated furnaces — 256 tubes, each
3½ inches in diameter, - circulating tubes in
back connection —

WHEEL, 9 feet in diameter; 13½ feet pitch;
making 122 turns per minute, light.

TONNAGE   272 57/100 BROSS
136 25/100 NET

One of the finest ocean tug-boats
ever turned out for service
on the coast. Very substantially built, powerful and fast.
Comfortably and neatly furnished. Owned
by Lewis Luckenbach, of New York

LAKE MICHIGAN PASSENGER STEAMSHIP VIRGINIA, 1891.

VIRGINIA.

BUILT 1891, at CLEVELAND, Ohio, By the GLOBE IRON WORKS COMPANY.

HULL, OF STEEL. Length of keel 264 feet; over all 277 feet; breadth of beam 38 feet; depth of hold 15¼ feet; depth from spar deck 25 feet.

ENGINES, TWO, TRIPLE EXPANSION. Diameter of cylinders 20, 32 and 52 inches, by 36 inches stroke.

BOILERS, FOUR, OF STEEL, SCOTCH TYPE. Each 22 feet in length, and 13 feet in diameter; working pressure 160 lbs.; total grate surface 240 sq feet; total heating surface 7308 sq feet.

WHEELS, FOUR BLADED, each 11 feet in diameter; pitch 15 feet.

~ TONNAGE · 1606 65 Gross · 976 68 Net ~

A NOTABLE Great Lakes steamer, one of the finest in America. Built for the Goodrich Transportation Company for the route between Chicago and Milwaukee, on Lake Michigan. Magnificently fitted up, with mahogany cabins, richest of furnishings and all modern conveniences. Sleeping accommodations for 300 passengers. Cost $251,550; speed 18 miles an hour.

CHESAPEAKE BAY TUGBOAT JOHN I. BRADY, 1891.

JOHN I. BRADY:

BUILT 1891, at BALTIMORE, MD.

STEEL HULL. Length of keel 96 feet 9 inches; over all 100 feet; width of hull 20 feet; depth of hold 9 feet 9 inches; draft of water 8 feet 6 inches

ENGINE, fore and aft compound; diameter of high pressure cylinder 15 inches, low pressure 30 inches, by 22 inches stroke. Indicated horse power 200.

BOILER, one, of steel, Scotch return tubular; 9 feet 9 inches in diameter by 11 feet in length; total grate surface 49 square feet; total heating surface 1330 square feet.

GROSS TONNAGE 118^{64} NET TONNAGE 59^{32}

THE JOHN I BRADY was constructed entirely by the James Clark Company, for P. Dougherty & Co. of Baltimore. She is a representative American sea coast towing steamer and was built for use on Chesapeake Bay and adjacent waters, and for sea towing. She cost $31,000.

BOSTON HARBOR EXCURSION STEAMBOAT MAYFLOWER, 1891.

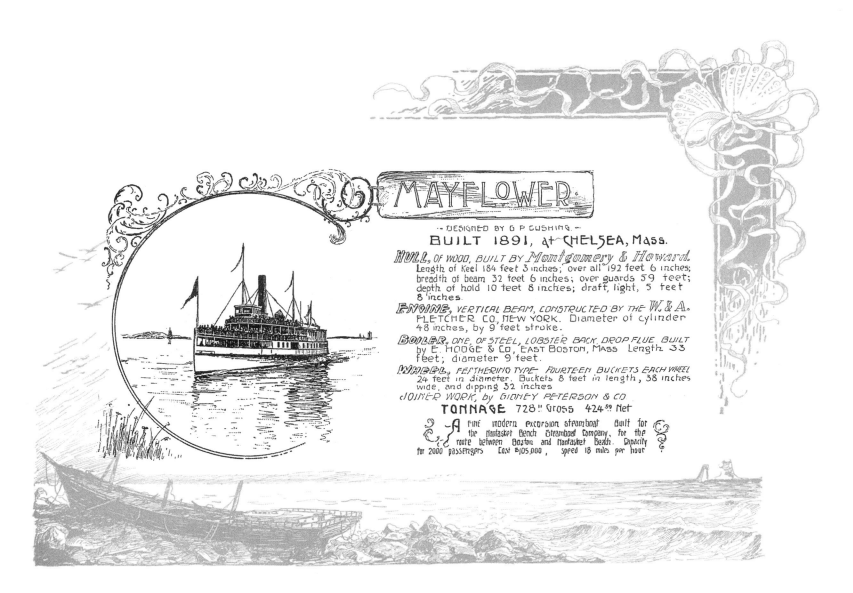

MAYFLOWER

- DESIGNED BY G P CUSHING -

BUILT 1891, at CHELSEA, Mass.

HULL, OF WOOD, BUILT BY Montgomery & Howard. Length of Keel 184 feet 3 inches; over all 192 feet 6 inches; breadth of beam 32 feet 6 inches; over guards 59 feet; depth of hold 10 feet 8 inches; draft, light, 5 feet 8 inches.

ENGINE, VERTICAL BEAM, CONSTRUCTED BY THE W.&A. FLETCHER CO, NEW YORK. Diameter of cylinder 48 inches, by 9 feet stroke.

BOILER, ONE, OF STEEL, LOBSTER BACK DROP FLUE BUILT by E. HODGE & Co, EAST BOSTON, Mass. Length 33 feet; diameter 9 feet.

WHEEL, FEATHERING TYPE FOURTEEN BUCKETS EACH WHEEL 24 feet in diameter. Buckets 8 feet in length, 38 inches wide, and dipping 32 inches

JOINER WORK, by GIDNEY PETERSON & CO

TONNAGE 728 $\frac{11}{100}$ Gross 424 $\frac{59}{100}$ Net

A fine modern excursion steamboat Built for the Nantasket Beach Steamboat Company, for the route between Boston and Nantasket Beach. Capacity for 2000 passengers Cost $105,000, speed 18 miles per hour

NEW YORK DOUBLE-SCREW FERRYBOAT CINCINNATI, 1891.

CINCINNATI

BUILT 1891, at ELIZABETHPORT, N. J.

HULL, OF STEEL, BUILT BY SAMUEL L. MOORE & SONS. Length between perpendiculars 180 feet; over all 206 feet; breadth of beam 46 feet; over guards 65 feet; depth of hold, in center 17 feet, at ends 16 feet; average draft of water 10 feet 10 inches. Constructed on the transverse system of framing.

ENGINES, TWO, STEEPLE-COMPOUND, DESIGNED BY H.S. HAYWARD, AND CONSTRUCTED BY THE PENNSYLVANIA RAILROAD COMPANY AT HOBOKEN, N.J. Cylinders of each 18 and 36 inches in diameter, by 26 inches stroke. The shafts are coupled between the two engines so that they can be disconnected and used independently.

BOILERS, TWO, OF STEEL, TUBULAR; Each 10 feet long and 10 feet in diameter; 49 square feet of grate surface, and 1750 square feet of heating surface; working pressure 120 lbs. of steam to square inch.

WHEELS, SECTIONAL, ONE ON EITHER END; Each 8 feet 9 inches in diameter, 13 feet 6 inches pitch, working together in either direction.

JOINER WORK by JOHN E. HOFFMIRE & SON, New York.

INTERIOR DECORATIONS AND OUTSIDE EMBELLISHMENTS, DESIGNED BY FURNESS, EVANS & CO., PHILADELPHIA.

TONNAGE: Gross 1255 63 Net 927 01

When the CINCINNATI appeared she created a sensation among the steamboat fraternity as well as the traveling public. Nothing so fine in the ferry line had ever before been attempted. With double decks, rich and artistic decorations, mosaic floors, grand stairways, observation windows, drawing room furnishings, electric lights, etc., she marked an epoch in ferryboats, a style which has since gained in popularity on other lines. The CINCINNATI was the first double-screw ferryboat built for use in New York waters, but she far outstripped her rivals in point of elegance and accommodation. Good speed and a success in every way.

COASTING STEAMSHIP KEWEENAW, 1891.

Foundered in gale on Pacific Coast in December, 1894; all on board perished.

KEWEENAW.

BUILT 1891, at WEST BAY CITY, Mich.

HULL, OF STEEL, BUILT BY F. W. WHEELER & CO. Length of keel 270 feet; breadth of beam 41 feet; depth of hold 26½ feet.

ENGINE, TRIPLE EXPANSION, CONSTRUCTED BY THE FRONTIER IRON WORKS, DETROIT, Mich. Diameter of cylinders 21, 34 and 56 inches, by 42 inches stroke.

BOILERS, TWO, OF STEEL; BY WICKES BROS. EAST SAGINAW, MICH. Diameter of each 112 inches; length 12 feet.

~ TONNAGE 2511⁴⁰ Gross 2004¹⁵ Net ~

BUILT for the Saginaw Steamship Co. for ocean service. The KEWEENAW was launched in two parts, to allow her to pass through the canal locks on her way from the Great Lakes to the Atlantic, via the St. Lawrence River. Soon after arriving at New York she left for the Pacific coast. A splendidly built and well arranged steamer, running very economically, having large carrying capacity and good speed.

DOUGLAS H. THOMAS:
BUILT 1891, at SPARROWS Pt, Md.
TONNAGE: GROSS 212 — NET 106 —

HULL, OF STEEL. Length of keel 116 feet; over all 122 feet 9 inches; breadth of beam, moulded, 21 feet; depth of hold 11 feet

ENGINE, TRIPLE EXPANSION. Diameter of cylinders 12½, 20½ & 34 inches, by 24 inches stroke of piston

BOILER, OF STEEL, SCOTCH TYPE. Length inside 10 feet 8 inches; diameter 11 feet Grate surface 42 square feet; working pressure 160 pounds of steam to square inch Coal bunkers 80 gross tons capacity

WHEEL, 8 feet 6 inches in diameter, pitch 10 feet

A FINE, modern sea-going tug. Built for P. Dougherty & Co., of Baltimore, by the Maryland Steel Co., for towing purposes. Used for awhile soon after built in towing ice barges on the Hudson river

Sold in 1893, To the Boston Towboat Company for use on the New England coast.

MADELEINE:
BUILT 1893, at CAPE ELIZABETH, Me.

HULL, OF WOOD, BUILT BY THE Portland Shipbuilding Co. Length of keel 86 feet: over all 90 feet, breadth of beam 18½ feet, depth of hold 6½ feet

ENGINE, COMPOUND, CONSTRUCTED BY L. B. Paine. Diameter of cylinders 11 and 22 inches, by 15 inches stroke

BOILER, built by the Almy Water Tube Boiler Co., Providence, R I Grate surface 3289 square feet

WHEEL, four blades, diameter 5 feet 3 inches , pitch 9 feet 3 inches

~ TONNAGE 74 4/10 Gross, 37 4/10 net ~

TYPE: of small American passenger propeller. The MADELEINE was built for use on Casco Bay, Maine, plying between Portland and Falmouth. Cost $12,500. Speed 11 miles

OHIO RIVER STEAMBOAT IRON QUEEN, 1892.

Burned to water's edge near Antiquity, Ohio, April 3. 1895.

IRON QUEEN.

~BUILT 1892, at MARIETTA, Ohio.~

HULL, OF WOOD, BUILT BY Knox & Son. Length 237½ feet; breadth of beam 37 feet 8 inches; depth of hold 6 feet

ENGINES, TWO, HIGH PRESSURE, CONSTRUCTED BY the Marietta Mfg. Co., MARIETTA, Ohio. Diameter of cylinders 18¼ inches; 7 feet stroke

BOILERS, ON DECK, each 42 inches in diameter, and 28 feet long, built by Geo. Stricker & Son, of MARIETTA, O.

~TONNAGE 642 ³⁰∕₁₀₀~

This boat, when completed, was pronounced to be the most beautifully finished steamer on the Ohio River. Of great strength, with elegant and commodious saloon and staterooms, large carrying capacity, and fitted with all modern improvements.

Carrying capacity 1000 tons; draught, when in trim, 30 inches; speed, up stream, 11 miles per hour — with current, going down stream 16 to 18 miles per hour

ATLANTIC COAST STEAMSHIP EL RIO, 1892.

EL RIO:
BUILT 1892,
at NEWPORT NEWS, Va.,
By the NEWPORT NEWS SHIP-BUILDING & DRY DOCK COMPANY

HULL, OF STEEL, 380½ feet in length on water line;
406 feet in length over all, breadth of beam 48 feet,
depth of hold 23 feet 10 inches. Five water-tight bulkheads

ENGINE, TRIPLE EXPANSION Diameter of cylinders
32, 52 and 84 inches, by 54 inches stroke of piston

BOILERS, THREE OF STEEL, SCOTCH TYPE, DOUBLE ENDED
Length 20½ feet, diameter 13 feet 10 inches, steam, 165 pounds

WHEEL, 4 BLADES, 18 feet in diameter

— TONNAGE 4664 80 GROSS, 2905 44 NET —

ONE of the finest steamships ever built in America
Launched October 26, 1892, and sailed from
New York for New Orleans on her first trip on
February 18, 1893. Built for freight service exclusively,
fitted with all the latest improvements, steered by steam
and lighted by electricity. For beauty of model, fine
workmanship and economy in running, this steamer has
never been excelled. Owned by Southern Pacific Co (Morgan Line).

COAST OF MAINE STEAMBOAT FRANK JONES, 1892.

GREAT LAKES PASSENGER PROPELLER CHICORA, 1892.

Foundered in Gale on Lake Michigan, January 21, 1895 ; all on board perished.

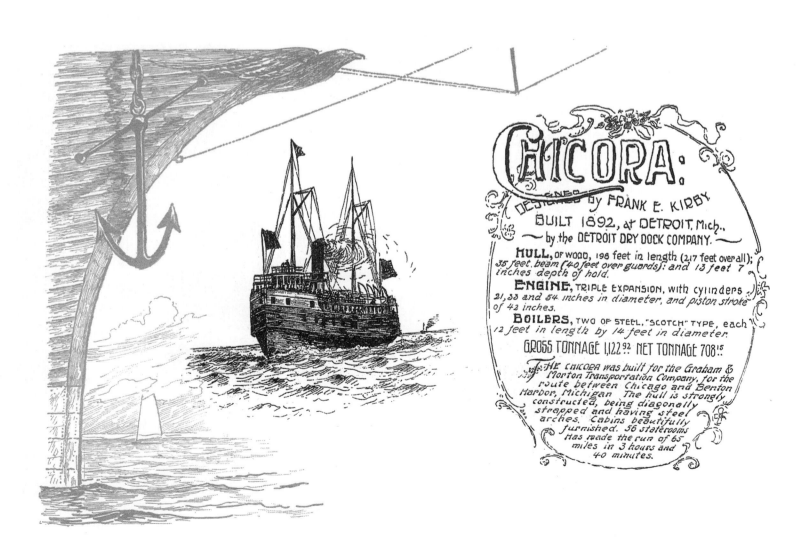

CHICORA.

DESIGNED by FRANK E. KIRBY

BUILT 1892, at DETROIT, Mich.,
— by the DETROIT DRY DOCK COMPANY. —

HULL, OF WOOD, 198 feet in length (217 feet overall);
35 feet, beam (40 feet over guards); and 13 feet 7
inches depth of hold.

ENGINE, TRIPLE EXPANSION, with cylinders
21, 33 and 54 inches in diameter, and piston stroke
of 42 inches.

BOILERS, TWO OF STEEL, "SCOTCH" TYPE, each
12 feet in length by 14 feet in diameter.

GROSS TONNAGE 1,122.92 NET TONNAGE 708.15

THE CHICORA was built for the Graham &
Morton Transportation Company, for the
route between Chicago and Benton
Harbor, Michigan The hull is strongly
constructed, being diagonally
strapped and having steel
arches. Cabins beautifully
furnished. 56 staterooms
Has made the run of 65
miles in 3 hours and
40 minutes.

WINFIELD S. CAHILL.
BUILT 1892 at BALTIMORE, MD.

HULL, OF WOOD. Length 71 feet on water line, 75 feet over all; breadth of beam 18 feet 6 inches; depth of hold 8 feet.

ENGINE, STEEPLE COMPOUND. Diameter of cylinders 10 and 20 inches, by 20 inches stroke of piston.

BOILER, OF STEEL, SINGLE FURNACE, "SCOTCH" TYPE. Diameter 7 feet 6 inches; length 10 feet 6 inches; working pressure 140 pounds of steam to square inch. Grate surface 20 square feet; heating surface 735 square feet.

WHEEL, 4 BLADES. Diameter 6 feet; pitch 8½ feet.

TONNAGE ~ 54 98/100 GROSS ~ 28 29/100 NET

AN EXCELLENT EXAMPLE OF the type of tug-boat in use in Baltimore Harbor and on Chesapeake Bay.

SAUSALITO:
BUILT 1877, at GREENPOINT, L.I., N.Y.

HULL, OF WOOD, CONSTRUCTED BY John Englis & Son. Length of keel 205 feet 6 inches; over all 220 feet; breadth of beam 32 feet; depth of hold 9 feet 9 inches.

ENGINE, VERTICAL BEAM, BUILT BY Fletcher & Harrison, NEW YORK. Diameter of cylinder 50 inches, by 11 feet stroke of piston.

TONNAGE 692 55/100 Gross, 401 11/100 Net

The SAUSALITO and her mate, the SAN RAFAEL, were built on Long Island, N.Y., and their hull timbers sent to the Pacific coast in a sailing vessel, and put together in California. Built for the San Francisco and Sausalito Ferry line. Handsome boats of their class, well fitted and very speedy, each costing $150,000. The SAUSALITO was burned on February 26, 1884, while lying at the wharf at Pt. St. Quentin. Total loss. Valued at $100,000.

NEW YORK OCEAN-GOING FISHING STEAMER AL. FOSTER, 1892.

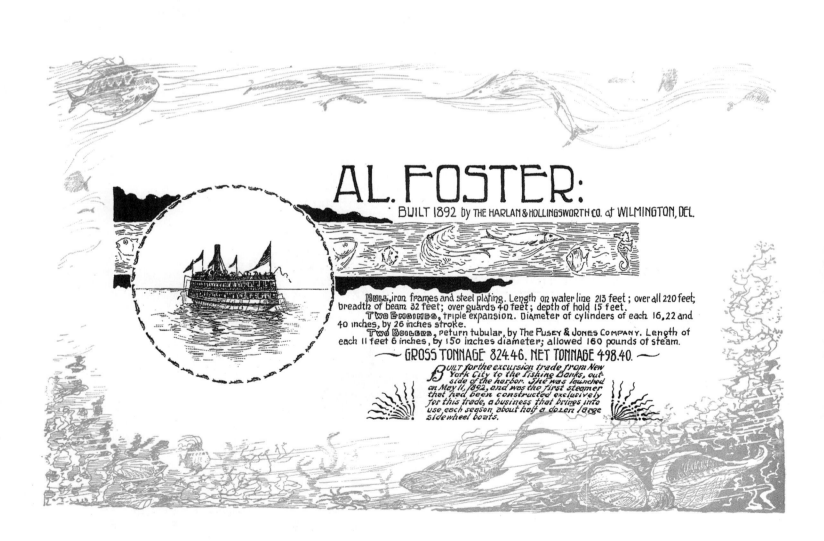

AL. FOSTER:

BUILT 1892 by THE HARLAN & HOLLINGSWORTH CO. at WILMINGTON, DEL.

HULL, iron frames and steel plating. Length on water line 213 feet ; over all 220 feet ; breadth of beam 32 feet ; over guards 40 feet ; depth of hold 15 feet.

TWO ENGINES, triple expansion. Diameter of cylinders of each 16, 22 and 40 inches, by 26 inches stroke.

TWO BOILERS, return tubular, by The PUSEY & JONES COMPANY. Length of each 11 feet 6 inches, by 150 inches diameter ; allowed 160 pounds of steam.

~ GROSS TONNAGE 824.46. NET TONNAGE 498.40. ~

BUILT for the excursion trade from New York City to the fishing Banks, outside of the harbor. She was launched on May 11, 1892, and was the first steamer that had been constructed exclusively for this trade, a business that brings into use each season about half a dozen large sidewheel boats.

ATLANTIC COAST TUGBOAT HONEY BROOK, 1892.

HONEY BROOK

BUILT 1892,
at PHILADELPHIA, Pa.,
By the NEAFIE & LEVY SHIP & ENGINE BUILDING CO.

HULL, OF IRON Length between perpendiculars 126 feet, over all 135 feet, breadth of beam 26 feet. depth of hold 16 feet

ENGINE, TRIPLE-EXPANSION Diameter of cylinders 16, 24 and 41 inches, by 30 inches length of stroke Indicated horse power 700

BOILER, OF STEEL Scotch Type Diameter 13½ feet, length 12 feet, steam pressure 155 lbs.

TONNAGE:
Gross 373 26 — Net 186 63

A MODERN sea-going tug of the most approved type, staunchly built and of excellent towing power Owned by the "Central Railroad of New Jersey Company" and used as a towboat on the upper Atlantic Coast

STEAM YACHT CLERMONT, 1892.

CLERMONT.

BUILT 1892,
at GREENPOINT, L.I.

HULL, OF WOOD, BUILT BY
Herbert Lawrence.
Frame of chestnut and oak. Length on
water line 150½ feet; over all 160¾ feet;
breadth of beam 25 feet; over guards
43 feet; depth of hold 10 feet 8 inches;
draft of water 5 feet 3 inches.
ENGINE, VERTICAL BEAM, CONSTRUCTED
by the W. & A. Fletcher Co.,
HOBOKEN, N.J. Diameter of cylinder 40 inches, by 6 feet stroke of
piston. Indicated horse power 800.
BOILER, OF STEEL, RETURN FLUE; BUILT BY THE W.& A. FLETCHER CO.
Shell 8 feet 1 inch in diameter, 9½ feet wide in front and 26 feet long.
Working pressure 60 lbs. to the square inch.
WHEELS, FEATHERING, 17 feet in diameter; steel buckets 6½
feet long.
JOINER WORK, by JOHN E. HOFFMIRE & SON, NEW YORK.

* TONNAGE * 259¹⁰ GROSS *
142⁵⁵ NET *

A HANDSOME side-wheel
steam yacht Built for
Commodore A Van Santvoord,
for use around New York Harbor,
on the Hudson River, and in adjacent waters
Very roomy and an excellent boat for cruising
purposes Interior fittings very elaborate and tasty,
the rich furnishings of the saloons and staterooms
not being excelled by any pleasure craft ever constructed. Speed 18 miles an hour.

LONG ISLAND SOUND PASSENGER PROPELLER MAINE, 1892.

MAINE.

BUILT 1892, at WILMINGTON, Del.,

Constructed by the HARLAN & HOLLINGSWORTH COMPANY.

HULL, OF STEEL. Length, on water line 302 feet 7 inches; over all 310 feet; breadth of beam 44 feet 10 inches; over guards 60 feet; depth of hold 17 feet 4 inches; average draft 12½ feet. 7 water-tight bulkheads.

ENGINE, INVERTED, DIRECT ACTING, SURFACE CONDENSING, TRIPLE EXPANSION, WITH FOUR CYLINDERS. Diameter of cylinders 28, 45, 51 and 81 inches, by 42 inches stroke.

BOILERS, FOUR, OF STEEL, SCOTCH TYPE. Each 13½ feet in diameter by 11½ feet in length.

WHEEL, 4 BLADES, LEFT HANDED. Diameter 13½ feet; pitch 18½ feet.

TONNAGE 2395 ^{07} GROSS 1505 ^{37} NET

THE MAINE, and her mate, the NEW HAMPSHIRE, coming out in 1892, were the first large passenger propellers of the modern class used on any of the great Long Island Sound lines. They were built for the Providence & Stonington Steamship Company for the route between New York and Stonington, and may be classed among the finest inland passenger steamers ever turned out in America. The saloons are handsome apartments, finished in artistic style, and fitted with all the comforts of the great sidewheelers. They have a speed of 20 miles an hour.

229

WESTERN RIVER STEAMBOAT JOHN K. SPEED, 1892.

JOHN K. SPEED.

Designed by R.W. Wise

BUILT 1892. at MADISON, IND.

HULL, OF WOOD, CONSTRUCTED AT MADISON MARINE WAYS.
Length .... 261 feet.
Breadth .... 42 "
Depth .... 8 "

ENGINES, TWO (Frisbie Patent), BUILT BY THE FRISBIE
ENGINE & MACHINE CO., AT CINCINNATI, OHIO.
Diameter of cylinders .... 22 inches
Stroke of piston .... 8 feet

BOILERS, FIVE, BUILT BY MILVAIN & SPEIGEL, CINCINNATI.
Length .... 28 feet
Diameter .... 44 inches.

Tonnage 1,090 27

THE JOHN K. SPEED was built for the Cincinnati and Memphis trade, to ply in connection with numerous other steamboats of the Memphis & Cincinnati Packet Company. In 1893 her regular trips were extended to New Orleans. She is one of the best of modern western river steamers being equipped with all the latest improvements. Has iron cylinder timbers, iron pen tails, iron boiler and deck beams, etc. Capacity 1600 tons of freight and 200 cabin passengers. One of the fastest steamers in the West. With 1000 tons of freight aboard her speed against stream is 18 miles per hour.

GREAT LAKES STRAIGHT BACK STEAMSHIP CODORUS, 1892.

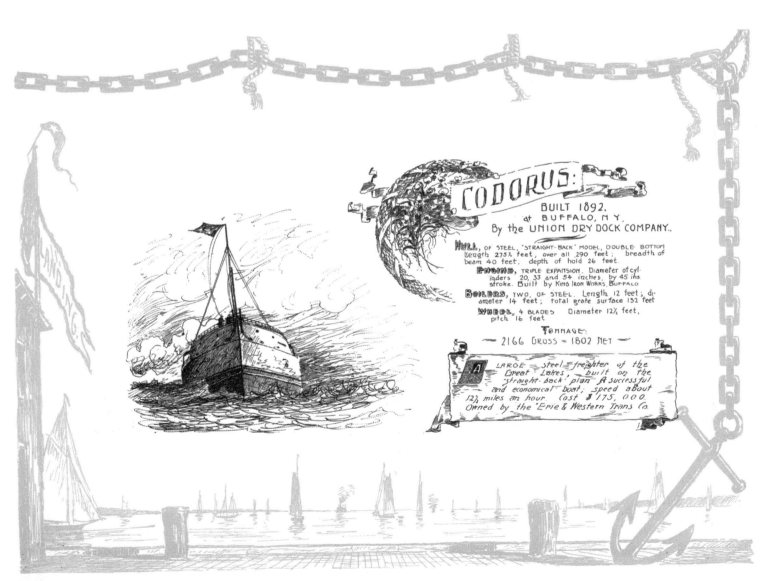

CODORUS:

BUILT 1892.
at BUFFALO, N.Y,
By the UNION DRY DOCK COMPANY.

HULL, OF STEEL, "STRAIGHT-BACK" MODEL, DOUBLE BOTTOM Length 275¼ feet, over all 290 feet; breadth of beam 40 feet, depth of hold 26 feet.

ENGINE, TRIPLE EXPANSION. Diameter of cylinders 20, 33 and 54 inches, by 45 ins. stroke. Built by King Iron Works, Buffalo

BOILERS, TWO, OF STEEL, Length 12 feet; diameter 14 feet; total grate surface 152 feet

WHEEL, 4 BLADES   Diameter 12½ feet, pitch 16 feet

TONNAGE:
2166 GROSS = 1802 NET

A LARGE steel freighter of the Great Lakes, built on the 'straight-back' plan. A successful and economical boat; speed about 12½ miles an hour. Cost $175,000. Owned by the 'Erie & Western Trans Co.

UNITED STATES CRUISER OLYMPIA, 1893.

OLYMPIA:

BUILT 1890-93,
at SAN FRANCISCO, CAL.,
By the UNION IRON WORKS.

HULL, OF STEEL, 5570 tons displacement Length 340 feet; breadth of beam 53 feet; depth of hold 20 feet 8½ inches.

ENGINES, TWO TRIPLE EXPANSION. Cylinders 42, 59 and 92 inches in diameter by 42 inches stroke.

BOILERS, SIX, OF STEEL. FOUR, double ended, each 15 feet 3 inches in diameter and 21 feet 3 inches in length, with a total of 32 furnaces; two, single ended, each 15 feet 3 inches in diameter and 10 feet 11½ inches in length, with a total of 8 furnaces. Total grate surface 824 square feet, total heating surface 28,299 square feet.

PROPELLER WHEELS, Two, each 14 feet 9 inches in diameter, with 19 feet pitch

THE cruiser OLYMPIA is one of the finest of the new Navy of the United States. She cost $1,796,000, and on her trial trip, December 15, 1893, won for her builders a bonus of $300,000 for speed.

CHESAPEAKE BAY PASSENGER PROPELLER ALABAMA, 1892.

ALABAMA:

BUILT 1892, at SPARROWS PT., MD.
By the MARYLAND STEEL COMPANY.

HULL, OF STEEL WEB FRAMES Length of keel 293 feet, over all 305 feet, breadth of beam 43 feet; over guards 55 feet, depth of hold 18 feet

ENGINE, FOUR-CYLINDER TRIPLE EXPANSION. Diameter of cylinders 24½, 40, 47 and 47 inches, by 42 inches stroke. Indicated horse power 2100.

BOILERS, FOUR OF STEEL, RETURN TUBULAR Each 12 feet 9 inches in diameter by 10 feet 8 inches long, with 3 furnaces in each Total grate surface 264 square feet

WHEEL, SECTIONAL Diameter 12 feet 9 inches; pitch 19 feet

~ TONNAGE 1938 81 Gross, 1370 97 Net ~

THE FINEST passenger boat ever turned out for service on Chesa-peake Bay Owned by the Baltimore Steam Packet Company and built for the night route between Baltimore and Norfolk A beautifully finished, staunch and speedy vessel—one of the handsomest passenger propellers yet built Speed 20 miles an hour

NEW YORK HARBOR TUGBOAT ANDREW J. WHITE, 1892.

ANDREW J. WHITE

BUILT 1892, at PERTH AMBOY, N.J

HULL, OF WOOD, CONSTRUCTED BY HUGH RAMSAY.
Length 67 feet 7 inches; breadth
of beam 19½ feet; depth of hold
8 feet 10 inches.

ENGINE, FROM TUG THREE BROTHERS; BUILT
by HEIPERSHAUSEN BROS., NEW YORK.
Diameter of cylinder 18 inches, by 24
inches stroke

BOILER, OF STEEL, BY HEIPERSHAUSEN BROS.
Length 14 feet; diameter 90 inches

— TONNAGE —
— 70²¹ GROSS :: 35¹² NET —

TYPICAL harbor tug
of the Port of New
York.

LONG ISLAND SOUND PASSENGER PROPELLER RICHARD PECK, 1892.

RICHARD PECK:

Designed by A. CARY SMITH

BUILT 1892, at WILMINGTON, Del.,
By the HARLAN & HOLLINGSWORTH CO.

HULL, IRON FRAMES, STEEL PLATING. Length on water line 300 feet; over all 316 feet; breadth of beam 48 feet; over guards 62 feet, depth of hold 18½ feet, draft, loaded, 10½ feet.

ENGINES, TWO, TRIPLE EXPANSION Diameter of cylinders 24, 36 and 60 inches, by 30 inches stroke.

BOILERS, SIX, OF STEEL, SCOTCH TYPE Each 13 feet in diameter by 12 feet in length; grate surface 400 square feet.

WHEELS, TWO, FOUR BLADED, Diameter 10½ feet; pitch 15½ feet.

TONNAGE 2906 GROSS
         1819 NET

THE RICHARD PECK was built for the NewHaven Steamboat Company's line between New York and New Haven, and has proven to be one of the speediest passenger vessels afloat. Beautiful cabins, large and well furnished staterooms, excellent freight space and all modern improvements and conveniences make this boat an ideal vessel for the business engaged in. Speed over 20 miles an hour.

INDIA:
BUILT 1871 at BUFFALO, N.Y.

HULL, OF IRON, BUILT BY J. Craig. Length 210 feet; breadth of beam 32 feet 7 inches; depth of hold 14 feet.
ENGINE, ONE PAIR, CONSTRUCTED BY THE Shepard Iron Works, BUFFALO, N.Y. Diameter of cylinder of each 36 inches by 36 inches stroke
BOILER, ONE, OF IRON, BUILT BY THE Shepard Iron Works. Length 18 feet; diameter 11½ feet; steam pressure 50 lbs. to square inch.
→ TONNAGE, 1239⁴⁴ Gross, 932⁹² Net ~

A LARGE and first-class passenger propeller of the Great Lakes, of the old type, and strong and serviceable. Has been employed on various passenger and freight routes.

MERIDA:
BUILT 1893, at WEST BAY CITY, Mich.

HULL, OF STEEL, BUILT BY F.W. WHEELER & Company. Length of keel 360 feet; over all 378 feet, extreme beam 45 feet; depth of hold 25 feet.
ENGINE, TRIPLE EXPANSION, CONSTRUCTED BY THE FRONTIER IRON WORKS, DETROIT. Diameter of cylinders 23, 37 and 62 inches, by 44 inches stroke.
BOILERS, THREE, RETURN TUBULAR, BUILT BY WICKES BROS., SAGINAW, MICH. Length of each 12 feet; diameter 12½ feet.
WHEEL, 4 BLADES. Diameter 14 feet; pitch 17½ feet.
→ TONNAGE 3261 Gross 2610 Net ~
A MAGNIFICENT modern cargo carrying steamship of the Great Lakes. Owned by D. C. Whitney.

SAXON:
BUILT 1890, at CLEVELAND, Ohio., By the GLOBE IRON WORKS CO.

HULL, OF STEEL. Length 296 feet; breadth of beam 40 feet 5 inches; depth of hold 21 feet.
ENGINE, TRIPLE EXPANSION. Diameter of cylinders 24, 38 and 61 inches, by 42 inches stroke.
BOILERS, TWO, OF STEEL. "SCOTCH" TYPE. Length 12½ feet, diameter 14 feet.
WHEEL, FOUR BLADES. Diameter 14 feet, pitch 17½ feet
~ TONNAGE 2348⁴³ Gross 1875²³ Net ~

OWNED by the Menominee Transit Company, and built for the ore carrying trade on the Great Lakes. Speed, loaded, 12½ miles per hour, light, 14 miles.

Thomas Cranage:
BUILT 1893, at WEST BAY CITY, Mich.

HULL, OF WOOD, BUILT BY JAMES DAVIDSON. Length between perpendiculars 305 feet; over all 330 feet; breadth of beam 43 feet; depth of hold 21 feet 6 inches.
ENGINE, TRIPLE EXPANSION, CONSTRUCTED BY THE DRY DOCK ENGINE WORKS, DETROIT. Diameter of cylinders 20, 33 and 54 inches, by 42 inches stroke.
BOILERS, TWO, OF STEEL. SCOTCH TYPE, BY DRY DOCK ENGINE WORKS. Each 12 feet in length, by 14 feet in diameter; steam pressure 160 pounds.
WHEEL, FOUR BLADES; 12½ feet in diameter, pitch 15 feet
→ TONNAGE 2220 Gross 1856 Net ~
A LARGE wooden cargo carrier of the first class, used on the Great Lakes, and owned by Thomas Cranage and others. Supplied with all the latest improved appliances, and strongly built, having double steel keelsons, steel arches and diagonally strapped. Capacity 110,000 bushels of wheat, or 3000 gross tons, on a mean draft of 16 feet.

MISSISSIPPI RIVER FERRYBOAT THOMAS PICKLES, 1892.

THOMAS PICKLES.

DESIGNED BY THOMAS DUNBAR

BUILT 1892, at JEFFERSONVILLE, Indiana

TWIN HULLS, OF STEEL, CONSTRUCTED BY ED. J. HOWARD.
Length of keels 125 feet, over all 130 feet, width (from outside of one hull to outside of other) 65 feet; over guards 77 feet; depth of hold 7 feet; draft of water 3 feet

ENGINES, TWO HIGH PRESSURE LEVER, BUILT BY THURMAN & POWELL. Diameter of cylinders 17 inches Stroke of piston 6 feet

BOILERS, TWO, EACH 25 FEET IN LENGTH 42 inches in diameter.

WHEEL, IN CENTER, BETWEEN THE HULLS, 14 Buckets, each 17 feet long and 26 inches wide

~ TONNAGE 237³² ~

A TYPICAL Western River ferry boat Built for use on the Mississippi River at New Orleans. One of the best of the modern boats, having all late improvements, such as steam steering gear, electric lights, etc Draft of water light 30 inches forward and 3 feet aft

ATLANTIC COAST TUGBOAT SCRANTON, 1892.

SCRANTON:

BUILT 1892, at CAMDEN, N.J.,
By JOHN H. DIALOGUE & SON.

HULL, OF STEEL, Length 125 feet; breadth of beam 26 feet; depth of hold 14 feet 5 inches

ENGINE, TRIPLE EXPANSION, Diameter of cylinders 16, 24 and 40 inches, by 24 inches stroke

BOILER, OF STEEL, Diameter 162 inches, length 13¾ feet.

WHEEL, 4 BLADES, diameter 9 feet, pitch 13 feet

TONNAGE 300⁷⁰ GROSS 150⁰⁵ NET

A POWERFUL sea-going tugboat, one of the finest on the Atlantic Coast. Owned by the Delaware, Lackawanna & Western Railroad Company, and used in towing coal barges between New York and New England ports

GREAT LAKES PASSENGER STEAMSHIP MANITOU, 1893.

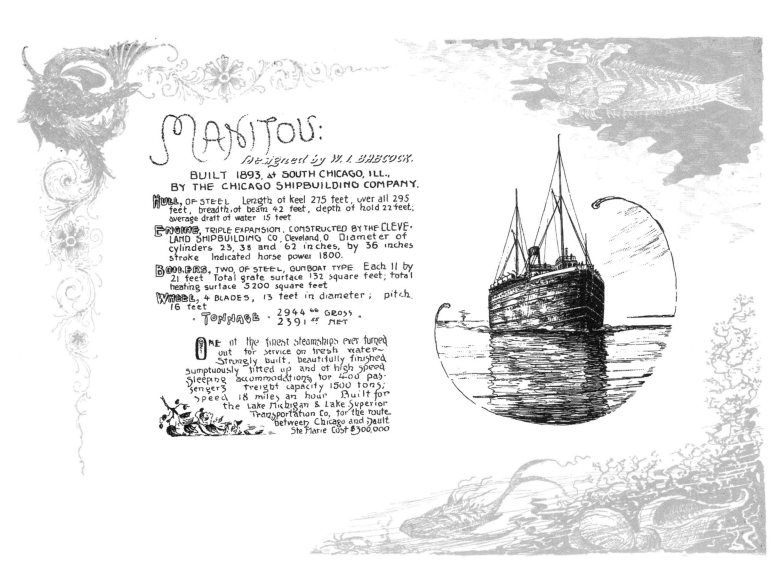

MANITOU:

Designed by W. I. BABCOCK.

BUILT 1893, at SOUTH CHICAGO, ILL.,
BY THE CHICAGO SHIPBUILDING COMPANY.

HULL, OF STEEL. Length of keel 275 feet, over all 295 feet, breadth of beam 42 feet, depth of hold 22 feet; average draft of water 15 feet

ENGINE, TRIPLE EXPANSION, CONSTRUCTED BY THE CLEVELAND SHIPBUILDING CO, Cleveland, O. Diameter of cylinders 23, 38 and 62 inches, by 36 inches stroke. Indicated horse power 1800.

BOILERS, TWO, OF STEEL, GUNBOAT TYPE. Each 11 by 21 feet. Total grate surface 132 square feet; total heating surface 5200 square feet

WHEEL, 4 BLADES, 13 feet in diameter; pitch, 16 feet

TONNAGE · 2944 66/100 GROSS · 2391 55/100 NET ·

ONE of the finest steamships ever turned out for service on fresh water— Strongly built, beautifully finished sumptuously fitted up and of high speed. Sleeping accommodations for 400 passengers freight capacity 1500 tons; speed 18 miles an hour. Built for the Lake Michigan & Lake Superior Transportation Co, for the route between Chicago and Sault Ste Marie. Cost $300,000

PHILADELPHIA AND BALTIMORE (CANAL LINE) PROPELLER ANTHONY GROVES, JR., 1893.

"ANTHONY GROVES JR."

BUILT 1893, at PHILADELPHIA, PA
BY
The Charles Hillman Ship & Engine Building Co.

HULL, OF IRON Length of keel 199 feet,
over all 209 feet; beam 23 feet; depth
of hold 8 feet.

ENGINE, COMPOUND. Diameter of cylinders
20 and 40 inches, by 28 inches stroke.

BOILER, ONE OF STEEL, BUILT BY THE WILLIAM
CRAMP & SONS SHIP & ENGINE BUILDING
CO. Diameter 150 inches; length 11½ feet

TONNAGE: 605 ³³ GROSS
482 ⁰⁰ Net

A LARGE and comfortable passenger
propeller, running between Baltimore and Philadelphia; built
to pass through the locks in the
Delaware & Chesapeake canal
Owned by the Baltimore & Philadelphia
Steamboat Company (Ericsson Line).

240

GREAT LAKES PASSENGER WHALEBACK STEAMSHIP CHRISTOPHER COLUMBUS, 1893.

Christopher Columbus.

BUILT 1892, at WEST SUPERIOR, Wis.

HULL, OF STEEL, "WHALEBACK" MODEL. Length over all 362 feet; breadth of beam 42 feet; depth of hold 24 feet. Nine bulkheads.

ENGINE, TRIPLE EXPANSION, CONSTRUCTED BY SAMUEL RHODGE & CO, DETROIT. Diameter of cylinders 26, 42 and 70 inches, by 42 inches stroke

BOILERS, SIX, OF STEEL, BUILT BY THE CLEVELAND SHIPBUILDING COMPY. Each 11 feet in diameter and 12 feet in length. Return tubular

WHEEL, 4 BLADES, diameter 14 feet; pitch 19 feet.

TONNAGE 1511.05 GROSS
945.95 NET

THE most novel passenger steamer turned out in America during late years. Designed by Alexander McDougall, and constructed by the "American Steel Barge Co" for use as an excursion boat at Chicago during the World's Fair, 1893. This vessel, differing so in appearance from the regulation passenger propeller, combines great strength, fine speed, and a roominess quite unknown among the majority of boats. The model of the McDougall "whaleback" type is unpainly in appearance but it possesses advantages which the other style of hull does not; with an excellent model below the water line, a clean run, and with powerful machinery, great speed is attained. Cabin luxuriously fitted up

NEW YORK BAY TUGBOAT COMMANDER, 1893.

COMMANDER:
BUILT 1893 at WILMINGTON, DEL

HULL, OF WOOD, BUILT BY JACKSON AND SHARP COMPANY Length 87½ feet; breadth of beam 22 feet; depth of hold 7½ feet

ENGINE, COMPOUND, CONSTRUCTED BY FRED'K A. VERDON, HOBOKEN, N.J. Diameter of cylinders 14 and 29 inches, by 24 inches stroke

BOILER, WATER-TUBE, WATSON-DIXON PATENT, CONstructed BY HEIPERSHAUSEN BROS.

THE COMMANDER was constructed for A. Mackenzie and Eli B. Conine for use around the port of New York, and is a good example of a first-class American harbor tugboat.

DETROIT RIVER FERRYBOAT PLEASURE, 1893.

Pleasure.

BUILT 1893, at WEST BAY CITY, MICH,

BY

~ F. W. WHEELER & CO. ~

HULL, OF WOOD Length 140 feet;
breadth of beam, on water line, 35 feet,
top sides 40 feet, on deck 52 feet;
depth of hold 15 feet, average draft
of water 12 feet.
ENGINE, THREE CYLINDER COMPOUND.
Diameter 34, 24 and 34 inches, by stroke
of 24 inches
BOILERS, Scotch each 10 foot shell
and 12½ feet long.
WHEEL, 4 BLADES Diameter 10
feet; pitch 13 feet.

THE PLEASURE was
built for the
Detroit, Belle Isle &
Windsor Ferry Company,"
and is a typical Detroit River
ferry, the finest ever turned
out up to 1894 Speed
16 miles an hour; capacity
for a large number of
passengers

NEW YORK PROPELLER FAVORITE.

FAVORITE.

FIRST TRIPLE SCREW AMERICAN MERCHANT STEAMER

BUILT 1894, at TOMPKINS COVE, NY

HULL, OF WOOD, BUILT BY H J RODERMOND Length of keel 129 feet, length over all 144 feet, breadth of beam 30 feet, over guards 36 feet, depth of hold 9 feet

ENGINES, THREE, FORE-AND AFT COMPOUND, CONSTRUCTED by FRED A VERDON, HOBOKEN, N J Middle engine 13 and 26 inches diameter of cylinders, by 18 inches stroke; side engines each 11 and 23 inches diameter of cylinders by 14 inches stroke

BOILERS, OF STEEL, BUILT BY HEIPERSHAUSEN BROTHERS, NEW YORK. Two IN NUMBER, each 6½ feet in diameter, by 14 feet in length; steam pressure allowed 130 pounds.

WHEELS, THREE, SECTIONAL, 4 BLADED MIDDLE WHEEL 6½ feet in diameter, OTHER TWO 5½ feet in diameter

THE FIRST triple-screw merchant steamer built for service in American waters Capacity for 1100 passengers Engaged in the excursion business in New York Harbor in summer of 1894 Burned at Newark July 23, 1894; rebuilt by H J Rodermond 1895

— The Favorite of 1894 —

ATLANTIC COAST TUGBOAT NOTTINGHAM, 1894.

NOTTINGHAM:
DESIGNED BY H.C. WINTRINGHAM.
BUILT 1894, at CAMDEN, N.J.,
By JOHN H. DIALOGUE & SON

HULL, OF STEEL. Length over all 138 feet 9 inches, breadth of beam 27 feet; depth of hold 17' feet.

ENGINE, TRIPLE EXPANSION, with cylinders 16½, 24 and 41 inches in diameter by 30 inches stroke.

BOILERS, TWO, OF STEEL, each 10 feet in length, and 134 inches in diameter.

TONNAGE 409 GROSS 204 NET

A LARGE, powerful, North Atlantic coast tugboat of the first class. Built for the Central Railroad of New Jersey Co. for towing coal barges between New York and New England points.

ATLANTIC COAST STEAMSHIP JAMESTOWN, 1894.

JAMESTOWN:

BUILT 1894, at CHESTER, PA.,

By the DELAWARE RIVER IRON SHIPBUILDING & ENGINE WORKS.

HULL, OF STEEL. Length moulded 300 feet; over all 342 feet; breadth of beam 40 feet; depth of hold 26 feet 9 inches.

ENGINE, TRIPLE EXPANSION Diameter of cylinders 28, 44 and 73 inches, by 54 inches stroke

BOILERS, FOUR, OF STEEL. Diameter 13 feet 9 inches; length 12½ feet Steam pressure 180 lbs

TONNAGE 2898 GROSS 2126 NET

A MODERN coasting passenger and freight carrying steamer, one of the finest ever built. Has a mate in the YORKTOWN. Used in the Old Dominion Steamship Company's line between New York and Norfolk, Va.

UNITED STATES TORPEDO BOAT ERICSSON, 1894.

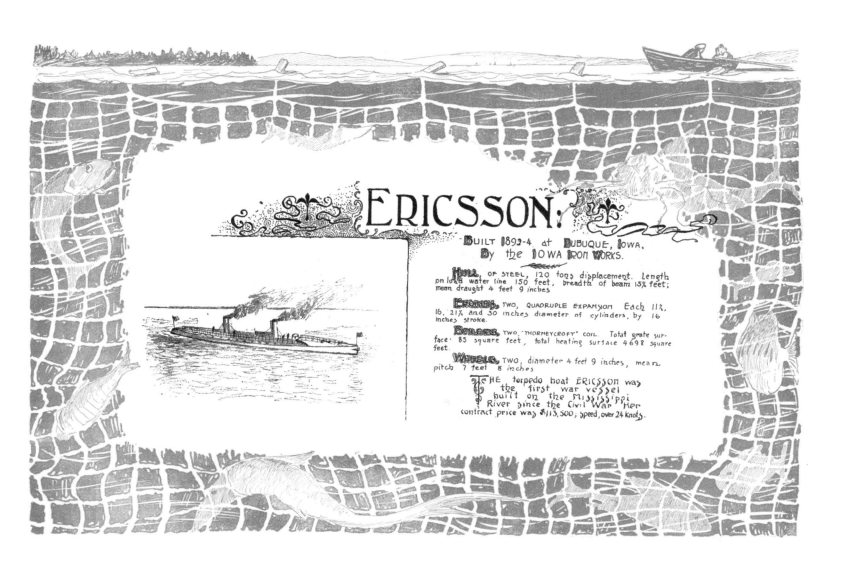

ERICSSON.

Built 1893-4 at Dubuque, Iowa,
By the Iowa Iron Works.

Hull, of steel, 120 tons displacement. Length on load water line 150 feet, breadth of beam 15¾ feet; mean draught 4 feet 9 inches

Engines, two, quadruple expansion. Each 11¾, 16, 21¾ and 30 inches diameter of cylinders, by 16 inches stroke.

Boilers, two, "Thornycroft" coil. Total grate surface 85 square feet, total heating surface 4698 square feet.

Wheels, two, diameter 4 feet 9 inches, mean pitch 7 feet 8 inches

The torpedo boat ERICSSON was the first war vessel built on the Mississippi River since the Civil War. Her contract price was $113,500; speed, over 24 knots.

LONG ISLAND SOUND PASSENGER PROPELLER CITY OF LOWELL, 1894.

CITY OF LOWELL.

Designed by A. CARY SMITH

BUILT 1894, at BATH, Me.,
By the BATH IRON WORKS

HULL, of steel, six bulkheads. Length
on water line 319 feet; over all 336 feet;
breadth of beam 49; feet over
guards 66 feet; depth of hold 17 feet
7 inches.

ENGINES, TWO, TRIPLE EXPANSION.
Diameter of cylinders 26, 40 &
64 inches, by 36 inches stroke.

BOILERS, SIX, FLUE & RETURN TUBULAR.
Each 12½ feet in length by 162
inches in diameter, working pressure 165 lbs.

Tonnage
2975 ½ Gross
1877 ¼ Net.

A LARGE and elegantly furnished
Long Island Sound passenger
propeller, one of the finest
of the modern class to be found
on any waters, strongly
built, beautifully equipped
and of superior speed.

UNITED STATES ARMORED CRUISER MINNEAPOLIS, 1894.

MINNEAPOLIS.

BUILT 1892-4, at PHILADELPHIA,
By the WILLIAM CRAMP & SONS SHIP & ENGINE BUILDING CO.

HULL, OF STEEL, 7350 tons displacement.
Length 412 feet, breadth 58 feet, depth of
hold 22 feet 6½ inches.

ENGINES, THREE, TRIPLE EXPANSION Diameter
of cylinders 42, 59 and 92 inches, by 42
inches stroke

BOILERS, TEN, OF STEEL, EIGHT OF THEM BEING
15 feet 9 inches in diameter by 20 feet in length,
with a total of 64 furnaces; TWO (AUXILIARY) BOILERS
10 feet in diameter by 8½ feet in length, 4 furnaces;
total grate surface 1520 square feet; total heating
surface 50,147 square feet.

PROPELLER WHEELS, THREE; 2 OUTSIDE 15
feet in diameter; middle wheel 14 feet in diameter,
20½ feet mean pitch.

THE MINNEAPOLIS IS a protected
steel cruiser, the finest of
her class ever constructed
Her unparalleled speed, on
her trial trip, 23,073 knots an hour,
won for her builders a bonus of $414,600
and placed her in the position of being
the fastest war vessel of large size in the
World Her cost was $2,690,000.

249

GREAT LAKES PASSENGER STEAMSHIP NORTH WEST, 1894.

NORTH WEST:

BUILT 1894 at CLEVELAND, O., By the GLOBE IRON WORKS COMPY.

HULL, OF STEEL.. Length between perpendiculars 360 feet; over all 383 feet; breadth of beam moulded 44 feet; depth of hold 26 feet; from spar deck 34 feet 5 inches.

ENGINES, TWO, VERTICAL QUADRUPLE EXPANSION. Diameter of cylinders 25, 36, 51½ and 74 inches, by 42 inches stroke.

BOILERS, 28, OF IRON AND STEEL, "BELLEVILLE" TYPE

WHEELS, TWO, FOUR BLADED, SECTIONAL, EACH 13 feet in diameter; 18½ feet pitch.

TONNAGE: 4244.°° GROSS
2339.°° NET

WHEN THE NORTH WEST appeared, in 1894, she was, without doubt the finest steam vessel ever turned out for service on the Great Lakes, and was one of the finest ever constructed in America. Built for the "Northern Steamship Company," for the route between Buffalo and Duluth, and cost $650,000. Completely and sumptuously furnished, being designed for carrying passengers only, accommodations on board for 350 first-class and 300 second class passengers.

250

U. S. HARBOR DEFENSE RAM KATAHDIN, 1895.

KATAHDIN.

BUILT 1891-94, at BATH, Maine,
BY THE
BATH IRON WORKS.

HULL, OF STEEL, 2183 tons displacement,
250 feet 9 inches length on water line, 43 feet
5 inches breadth of beam, and 15 feet mean draft

ENGINES, TWO TRIPLE-EXPANSION. Diameter
of cylinders 25, 36 and 56 inches, by 36 inches stroke

BOILERS, TWO MAIN & ONE AUXILIARY, OF STEEL
Main Boilers, double ended, 13 feet 8¾ inches in diameter
by 22½ feet in length, total number of furnaces 12.
Auxiliary boiler, single ended, 13 feet 8¾ inches in di-
ameter, by 11 feet 7¼ inches in length, with 3 furnaces
Total grate surface 354 sq. feet, total heating surface 12,150 sq. feet

WHEELS, TWIN PROPELLERS, 10½ feet in
diameter and 15 feet 3¾ inches mean pitch

A FORMIDABLE war vessel, designed for
use as a harbor defense ram,
being of powerful build and excellent speed. Designed by Admiral
Daniel Ammen. Contract price $930,000.

251

STEAM YACHT ELEANOR, 1894.

Eleanor:

Designed by CHARLES RIDDLEY HANSCOM.
BUILT 1894, at BATH, ME.,
~By the BATH IRON WORKS~

HULL OF STEEL, length of keel 185 feet, on water line 202 feet, over all 232 feet, breadth of beam 32 feet, depth of hold 17 feet 5 inches, mean draft 13 feet 4 inches, displacement 1,136 tons.

ENGINES, VERTICAL, INVERTED, DIRECT-ACTING, TRIPLE-EXPANSION. Diameter of cylinders 18, 28 and 45 inches, by 30 inches stroke.

BOILERS, TWO OF STEEL, Scotch type. Length 12½ feet, by 11 feet 5 inches in diameter. Total heating surface 4016 square feet, total grate surface 120 square feet; working pressure 165 pounds.

WHEEL, 4 BLADES. Diameter 10 feet 4½ inches; pitch 17 feet.

TONNAGE
~803 Gross = 401 Net~

The ELEANOR is unquestionably one of the finest products of the American shipyards in the line of steam yachts. She was built for W. A. Slater, of Norwich, Conn., and was designed especially for lengthy cruises, her rig being that of a bark, with a total sail area of 13,215 square feet. Beautifully fitted up

UNITED STATES BATTLE SHIP INDIANA, 1895.

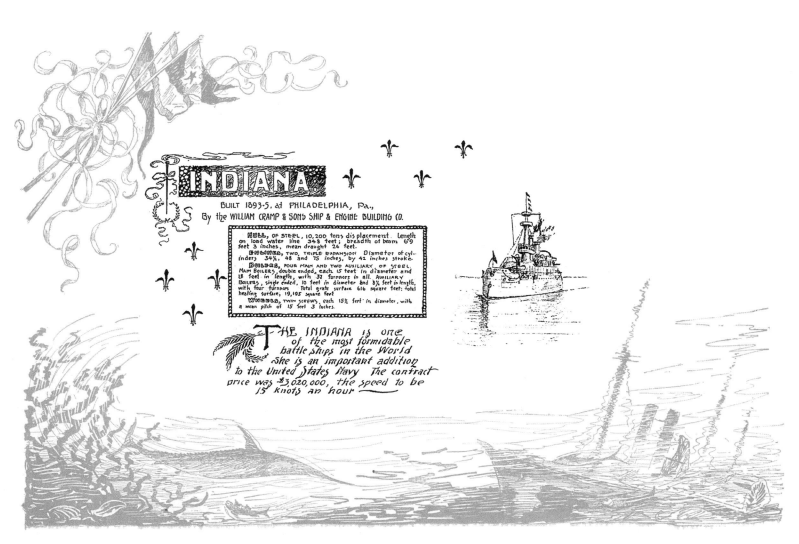

INDIANA

BUILT 1893-5 at PHILADELPHIA, Pa.,
By the WILLIAM CRAMP & SONS SHIP & ENGINE BUILDING CO.

HULL, OF STEEL, 10,200 tons displacement. Length on load water line 348 feet; breadth of beam 69 feet 3 inches, mean draught 24 feet.
ENGINES, TWO, TRIPLE EXPANSION Diameter of cylinders 34½, 48 and 75 inches, by 42 inches stroke.
BOILERS, FOUR MAIN AND TWO AUXILIARY OF STEEL. MAIN BOILERS, double ended, each 15 feet in diameter and 18 feet in length, with 32 furnaces in all. AUXILIARY BOILERS, single ended, 10 feet in diameter and 8¾ feet in length, with four furnaces. Total grate surface 616 square feet; total heating surface, 19,195 square feet.
WHEELS, TWIN SCREWS, each 15½ feet in diameter, with a mean pitch of 15 feet 3 inches.

THE INDIANA is one of the most formidable battle ships in the World. She is an important addition to the United States Navy. The contract price was $3,020,000, the speed to be 15 knots an hour

LONG ISLAND SOUND STEAMBOAT PRISCILLA, 1894.

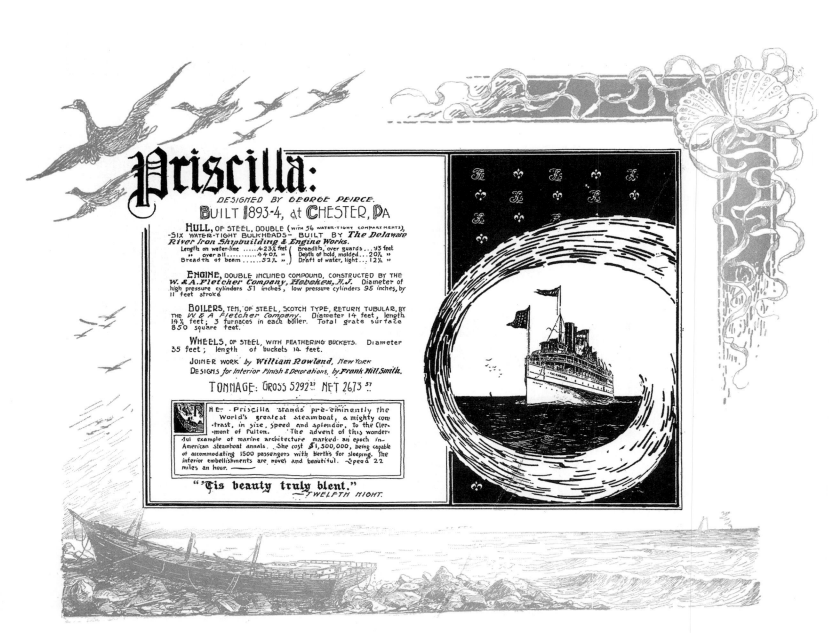

Priscilla:

DESIGNED BY GEORGE PEIRCE.
BUILT 1893-4, at CHESTER, PA

HULL, OF STEEL, DOUBLE (WITH 56 WATER-TIGHT COMPARTMENTS),
SIX WATER-TIGHT BULKHEADS— BUILT BY *The Delaware River Iron Shipbuilding & Engine Works.*

Length on water-line ......423½ feet   Breadth, over guards ...93 feet
  "   over all ....440½ "   Depth of hold, molded...20½ "
Breadth of beam ......52½ "   Draft of water, light...12½ "

ENGINE, DOUBLE INCLINED COMPOUND, CONSTRUCTED BY THE
W. & A. Fletcher Company, Hoboken, N.J. Diameter of
high pressure cylinders 51 inches, low pressure cylinders 95 inches, by
11 feet stroke

BOILERS, TEN, OF STEEL, SCOTCH TYPE, RETURN TUBULAR, BY
THE *W. & A. Fletcher Company.* Diameter 14 feet, length
14½ feet; 3 furnaces in each boiler. Total grate surface
850 square feet.

WHEELS, OF STEEL, WITH FEATHERING BUCKETS. Diameter
35 feet; length of buckets 14 feet.

JOINER WORK by *William Rowland,* NEW YORK
DESIGNS for *Interior Finish & Decorations,* by *Frank Hill Smith.*

TONNAGE: GROSS 5292²⁷ NET 2673³⁷

THE Priscilla stands pre-eminently the
World's greatest steamboat, a mighty con-
trast, in size, speed and splendor, to the Clermont of Fulton. The advent of this wonderful example of marine architecture marked an epoch in
American steamboat annals. She cost $1,500,000, being capable
of accommodating 1500 passengers with berths for sleeping. The
interior embellishments are novel and beautiful. Speed 22
miles an hour.

"'Tis beauty truly blent."
—TWELFTH NIGHT.

TRANSATLANTIC PASSENGER STEAMSHIP ST. LOUIS, 1895.

St. Louis:

BUILT 1894-5, at PHILADELPHIA, By the WILLIAM CRAMP & SONS SHIP & ENGINE BUILDING COMPANY.

HULL, OF STEEL. Length over all 554 feet 2 inches; length between perpendiculars 535 feet 8 inches; breadth of beam, extreme, 63 feet; depth of hold, moulded, 42 feet. Load displacement 15,600 tons.

ENGINES, TWO, QUADRUPLE EXPANSION.

BOILERS, SIX, OF STEEL, DOUBLE-ENDED, each 20 feet in length, by 15 feet 7½ inches in diameter; 39 furnaces; total grate surface 830 square feet, total heating surface 30,000 square feet.

WHEELS, THREE-BLADED, TWIN SCREWS.

~ TONNAGE 10,700 GROSS ~

The St. Louis, and her mate the St. Paul, are the finest examples of naval architecture ever produced in the United States for the merchant marine. Built for the "American Line" of steamships between New York and Southampton, England, they constitute the highest attainment in the mechanical arts, being complete in every detail and possessing features and improvements not found in the vessels of any other part of the World. Their advent marked an epoch in the annals of American shipbuilding.